BOY1

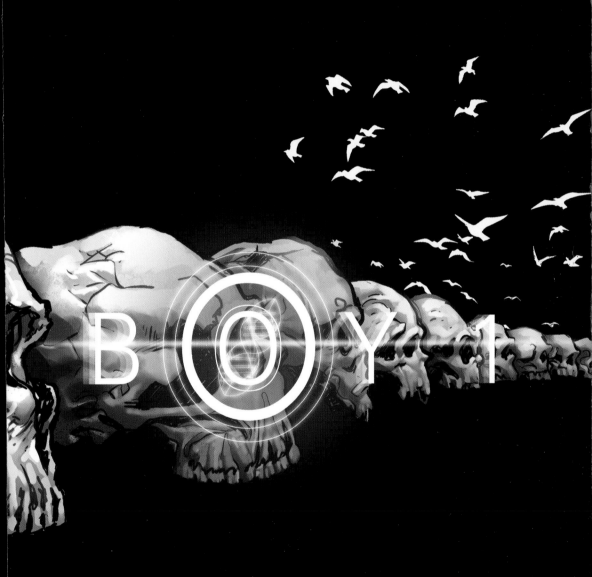

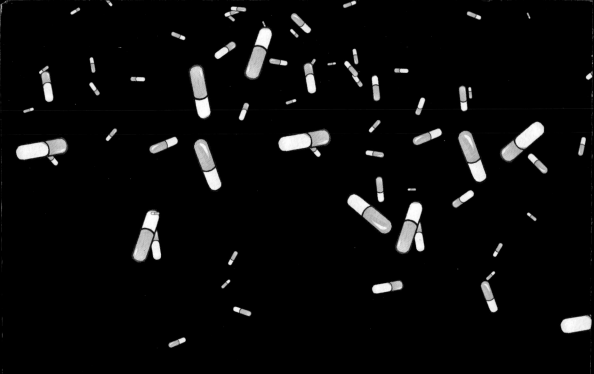

Written and Created by **H.S. Tak**
Art by **Amancay Nahuelpan**
Colors by **Sebastian Cheng**
Letters by **Dezi Sienty**
Series Edits by **Denton J. Tipton**
Producer: **Jeremy Entin**

Cover by **Leila del Duca**
Cover Colors by **Sebastian Cheng**
Collection Edits by **Justin Eisinger** and **Alonzo Simon**
Published by **Ted Adams**
Collection Design by **Shawn Lee**

For international rights, contact **licensing@idwpublishing.com**

ISBN: 978-1-63140-529-7

19 18 17 16   1 2 3 4

www.IDWPUBLISHING.com

Ted Adams, CEO & Publisher
Greg Goldstein, President & COO
Robbie Robbins, EVP/Sr. Graphic Artist
Chris Ryall, Chief Creative Officer/Editor-in-Chief
Matthew Ruzicka, CPA, Chief Financial Officer
Dirk Wood, VP of Marketing
Lorelei Bunjes, VP of Digital Services
Jeff Webber, VP of Licensing, Digital and Subsidiary Rights
Jerry Bennington, VP of New Product Development

Facebook: **facebook.com/idwpublishing**
Twitter: **@idwpublishing**
YouTube: **youtube.com/idwpublishing**
Tumblr: **tumblr.idwpublishing.com**
Instagram: **instagram.com/idwpublishing**

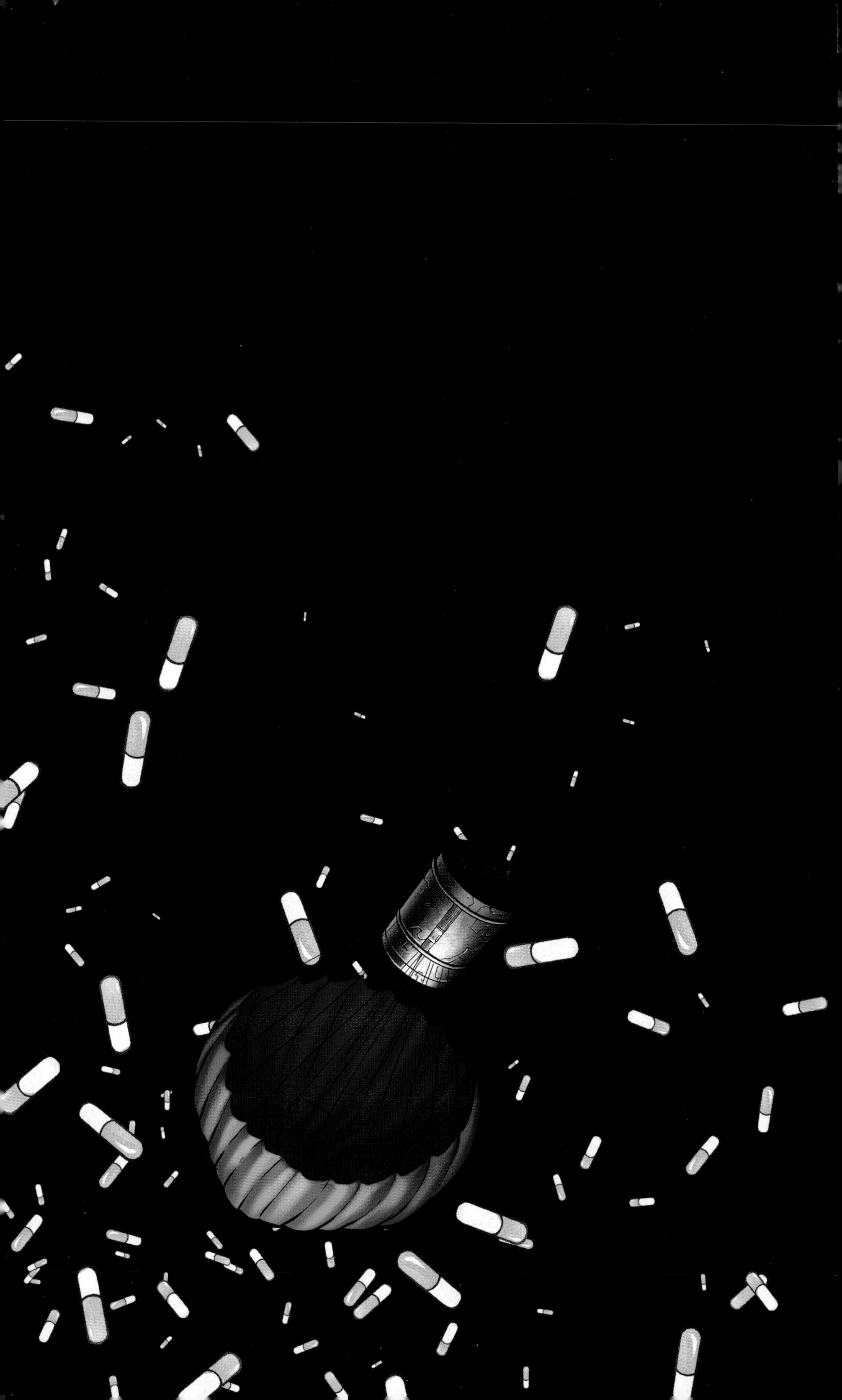

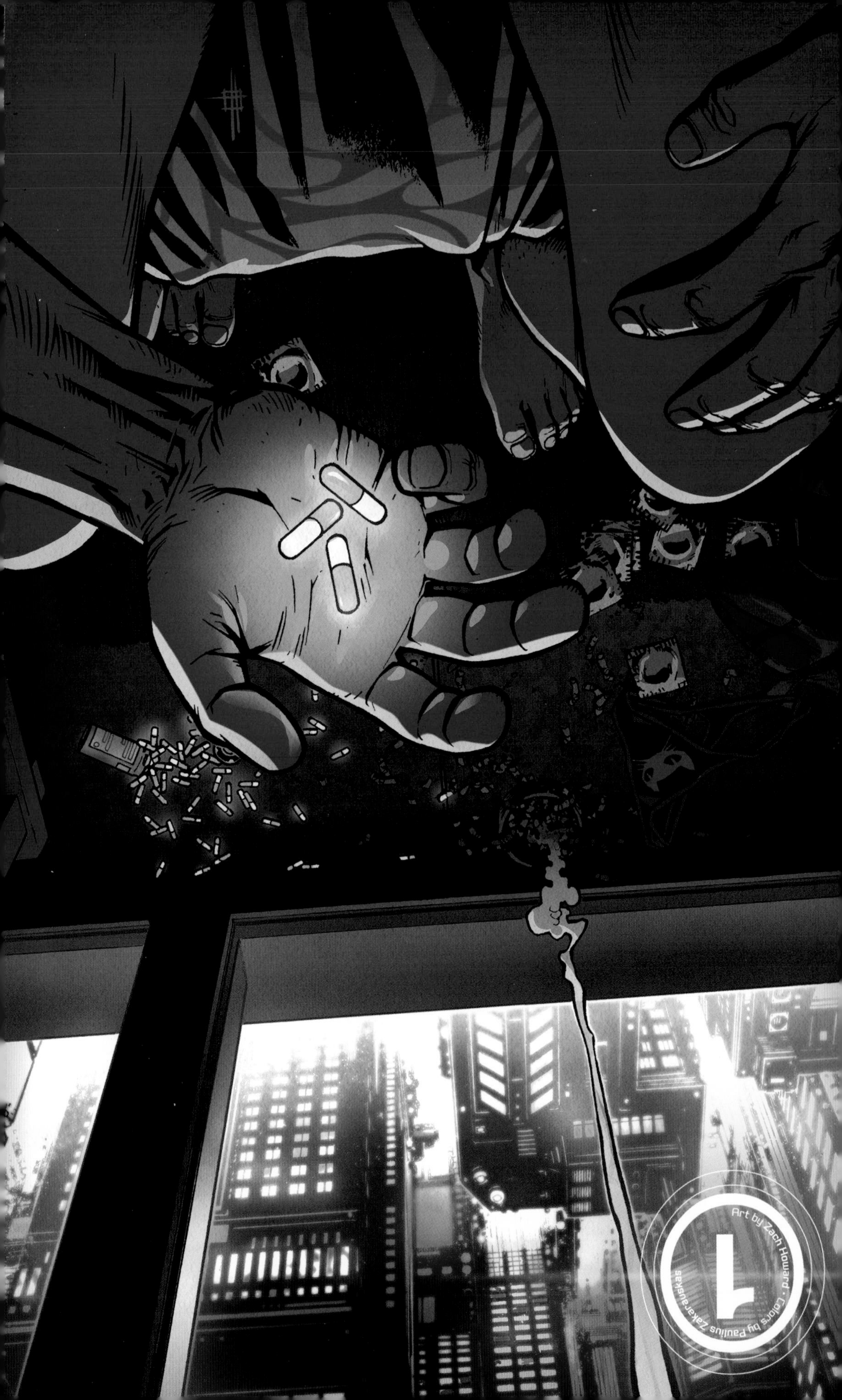
Art by Zach Howard • Colors by Paulius Zakarauskas

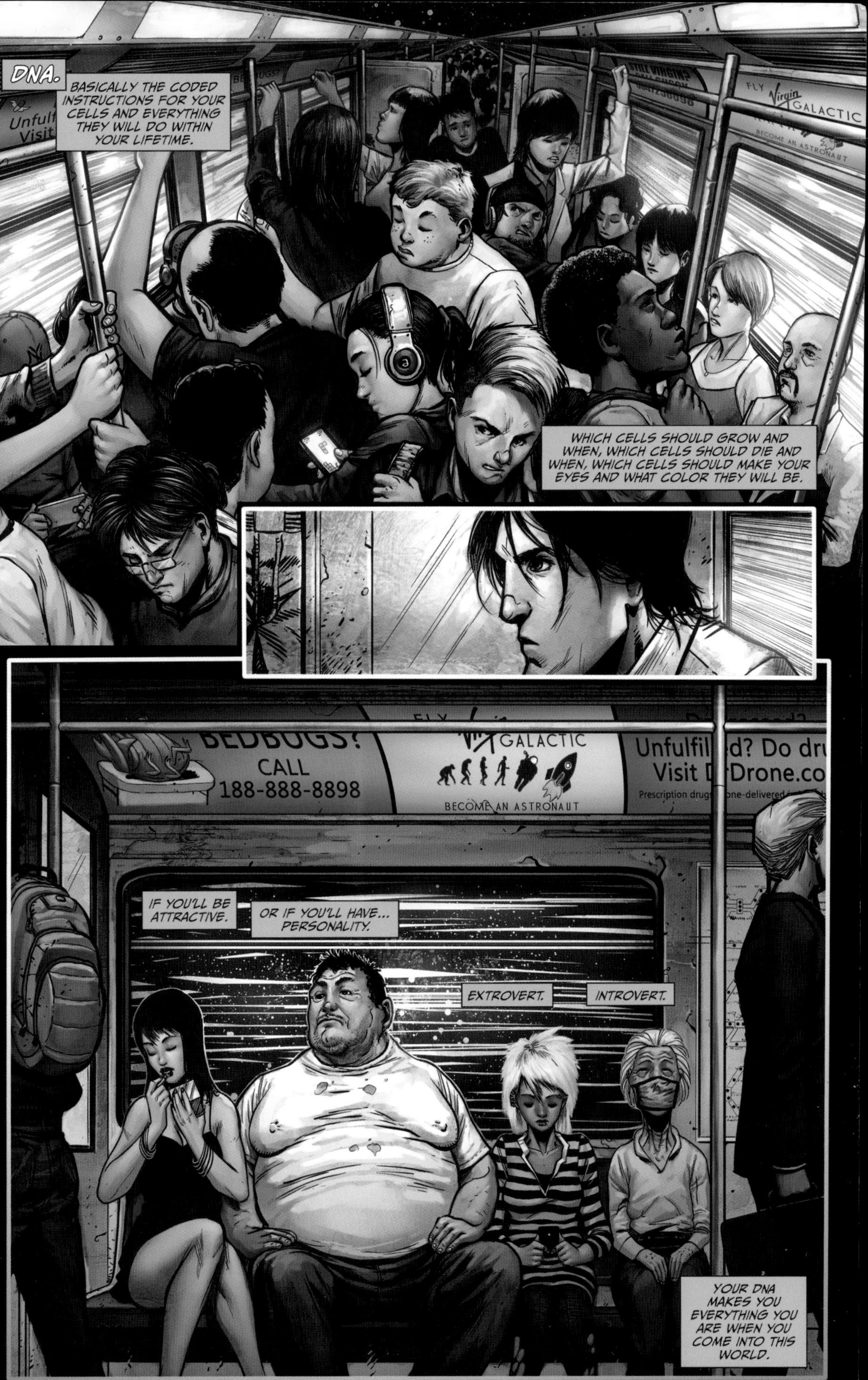
DNA.
BASICALLY THE CODED INSTRUCTIONS FOR YOUR CELLS AND EVERYTHING THEY WILL DO WITHIN YOUR LIFETIME.
FLY Virgin GALACTIC
BECOME AN ASTRONAUT
WHICH CELLS SHOULD GROW AND WHEN, WHICH CELLS SHOULD DIE AND WHEN, WHICH CELLS SHOULD MAKE YOUR EYES AND WHAT COLOR THEY WILL BE.
CALL 188-888-8898
GALACTIC
BECOME AN ASTRONAUT
IF YOU'LL BE ATTRACTIVE.
OR IF YOU'LL HAVE... PERSONALITY.
EXTROVERT.
INTROVERT.
YOUR DNA MAKES YOU EVERYTHING YOU ARE WHEN YOU COME INTO THIS WORLD.

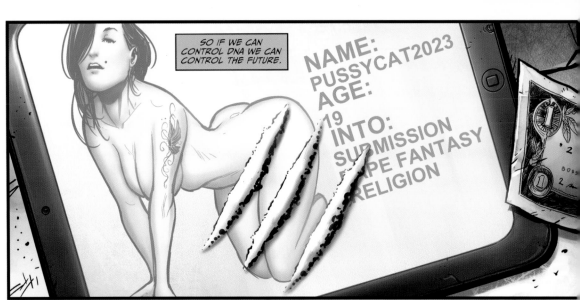

SO IF WE CAN CONTROL DNA WE CAN CONTROL THE FUTURE.

NAME: PUSSYCAT2023
AGE: 19
INTO: SUBMISSION RAPE FANTASY RELIGION

WE CAN FINALLY HAVE SOME SAY IN WHO WE BECOME.

SNRT

MMMM. BREAKFAST OF CHAMPIONS, JADAS?

YOU KNOW IT'S MY MEDICATION, WENDELL. I JUST CUSTOMIZED ITS APPLICATION A BIT.

I'M TALKING ABOUT PUSSYCAT2023.

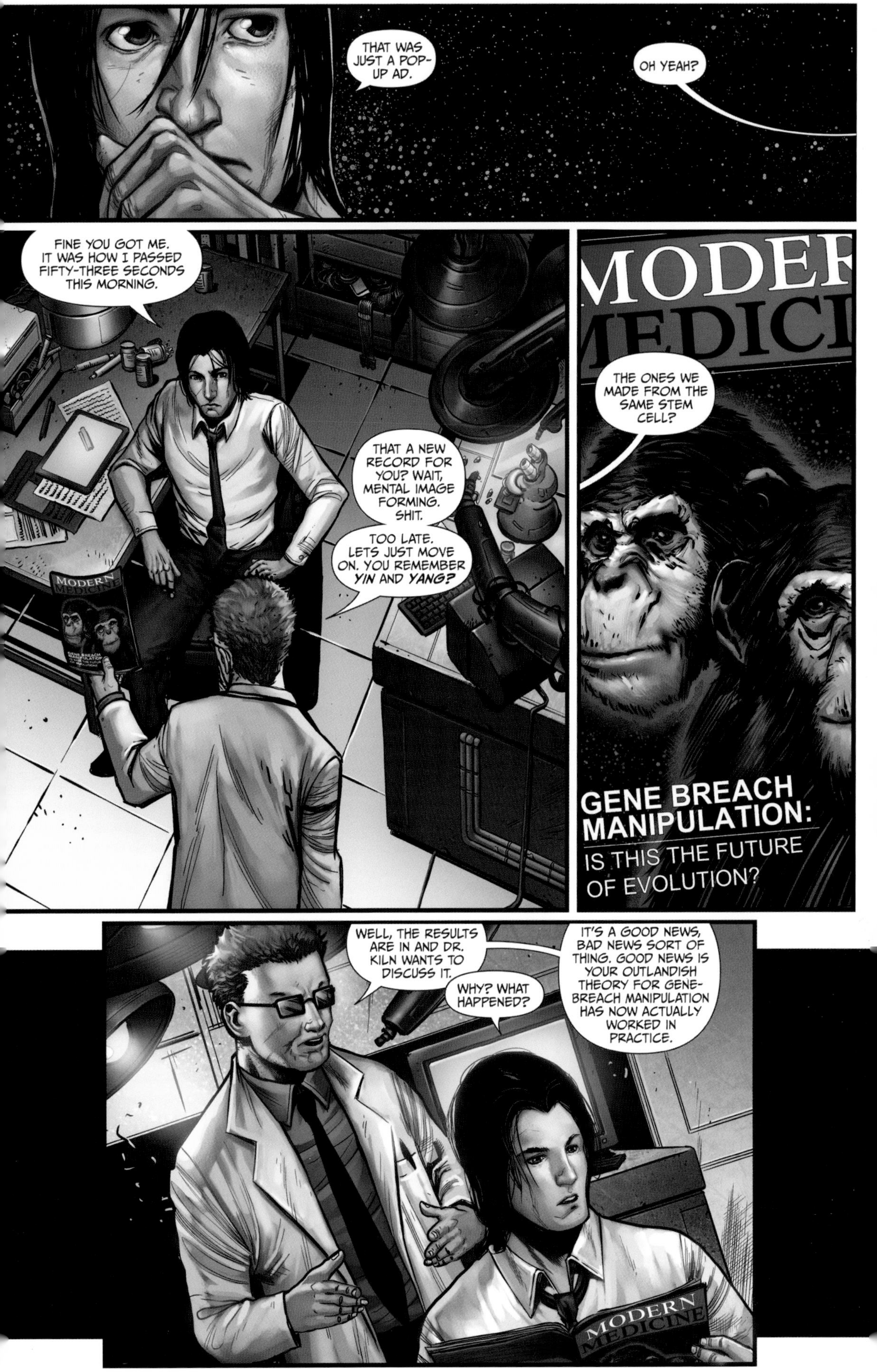
THAT WAS JUST A POP-UP AD.
OH YEAH?
FINE YOU GOT ME. IT WAS HOW I PASSED FIFTY-THREE SECONDS THIS MORNING.
MODERN MEDICINE
THAT A NEW RECORD FOR YOU? WAIT, MENTAL IMAGE FORMING. SHIT.
TOO LATE. LETS JUST MOVE ON. YOU REMEMBER *YIN* AND *YANG?*
THE ONES WE MADE FROM THE SAME STEM CELL?
GENE BREACH MANIPULATION:
IS THIS THE FUTURE OF EVOLUTION?
WELL, THE RESULTS ARE IN AND DR. KILN WANTS TO DISCUSS IT.
WHY? WHAT HAPPENED?
IT'S A GOOD NEWS, BAD NEWS SORT OF THING. GOOD NEWS IS YOUR OUTLANDISH THEORY FOR GENE-BREACH MANIPULATION HAS NOW ACTUALLY WORKED IN PRACTICE.
MODERN MEDICINE

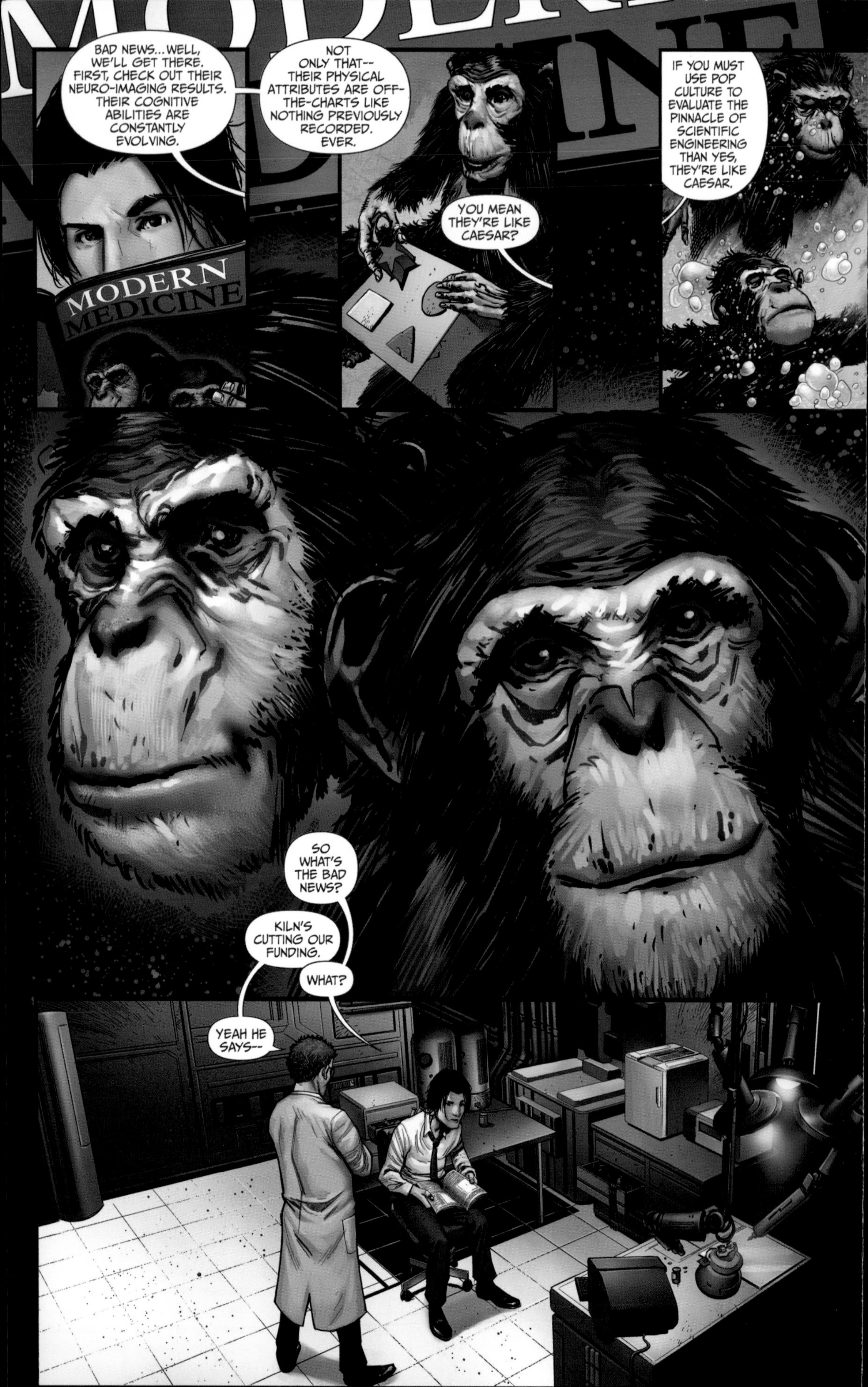
BAD NEWS...WELL, WE'LL GET THERE. FIRST, CHECK OUT THEIR NEURO-IMAGING RESULTS. THEIR COGNITIVE ABILITIES ARE CONSTANTLY EVOLVING.
NOT ONLY THAT-- THEIR PHYSICAL ATTRIBUTES ARE OFF-THE-CHARTS LIKE NOTHING PREVIOUSLY RECORDED. EVER.
YOU MEAN THEY'RE LIKE CAESAR?
IF YOU MUST USE POP CULTURE TO EVALUATE THE PINNACLE OF SCIENTIFIC ENGINEERING THAN YES, THEY'RE LIKE CAESAR.
MODERN MEDICINE
SO WHAT'S THE BAD NEWS?
KILN'S CUTTING OUR FUNDING.
WHAT?
YEAH HE SAYS--

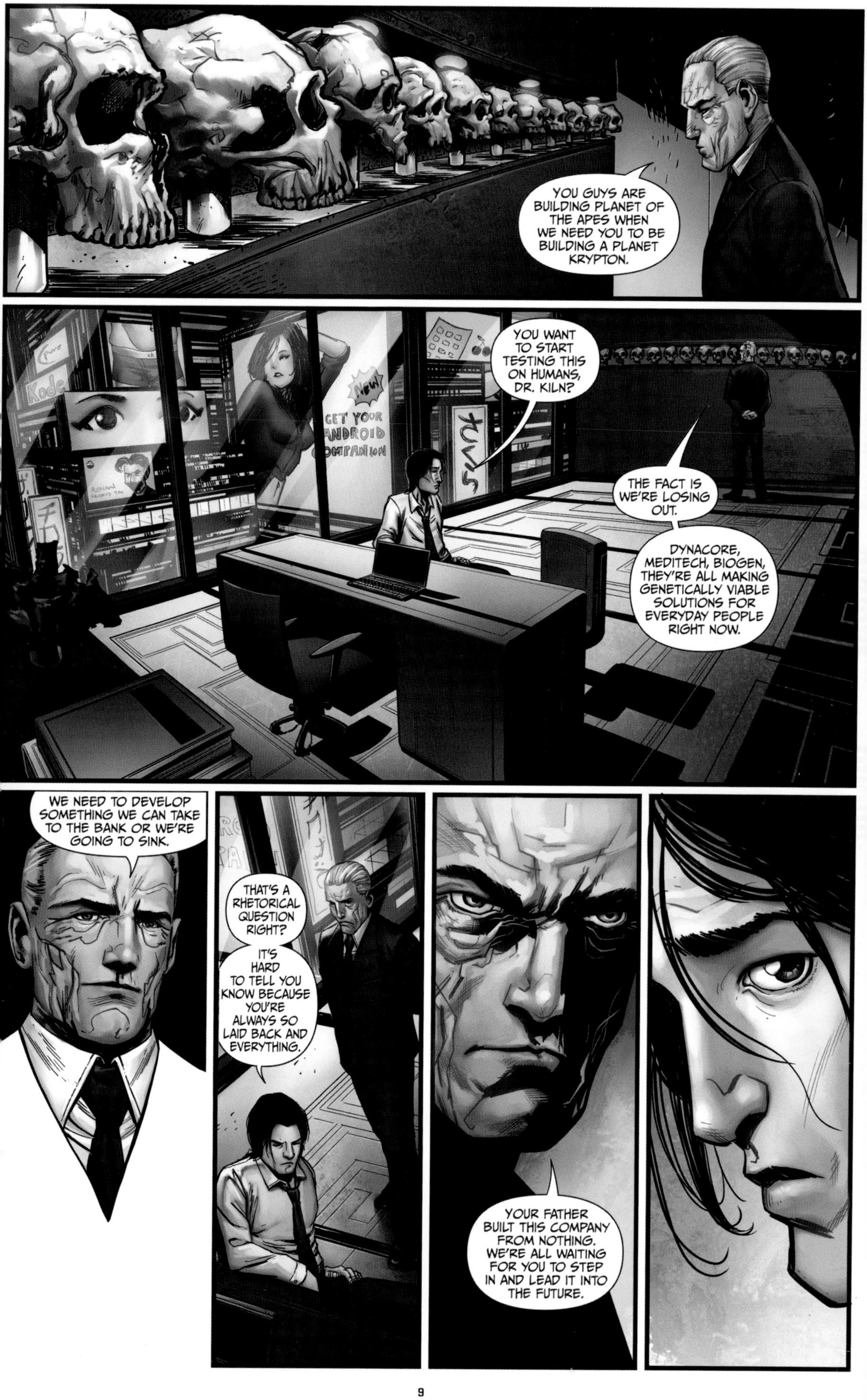
YOU GUYS ARE BUILDING PLANET OF THE APES WHEN WE NEED YOU TO BE BUILDING A PLANET KRYPTON.
Kode
NEW!
GET YOUR ANDROID COMPANION
YOU WANT TO START TESTING THIS ON HUMANS, DR. KILN?
THE FACT IS WE'RE LOSING OUT.
DYNACORE, MEDITECH, BIOGEN, THEY'RE ALL MAKING GENETICALLY VIABLE SOLUTIONS FOR EVERYDAY PEOPLE RIGHT NOW.
WE NEED TO DEVELOP SOMETHING WE CAN TAKE TO THE BANK OR WE'RE GOING TO SINK.
THAT'S A RHETORICAL QUESTION RIGHT?
IT'S HARD TO TELL YOU KNOW BECAUSE YOU'RE ALWAYS SO LAID BACK AND EVERYTHING.
YOUR FATHER BUILT THIS COMPANY FROM NOTHING. WE'RE ALL WAITING FOR YOU TO STEP IN AND LEAD IT INTO THE FUTURE.

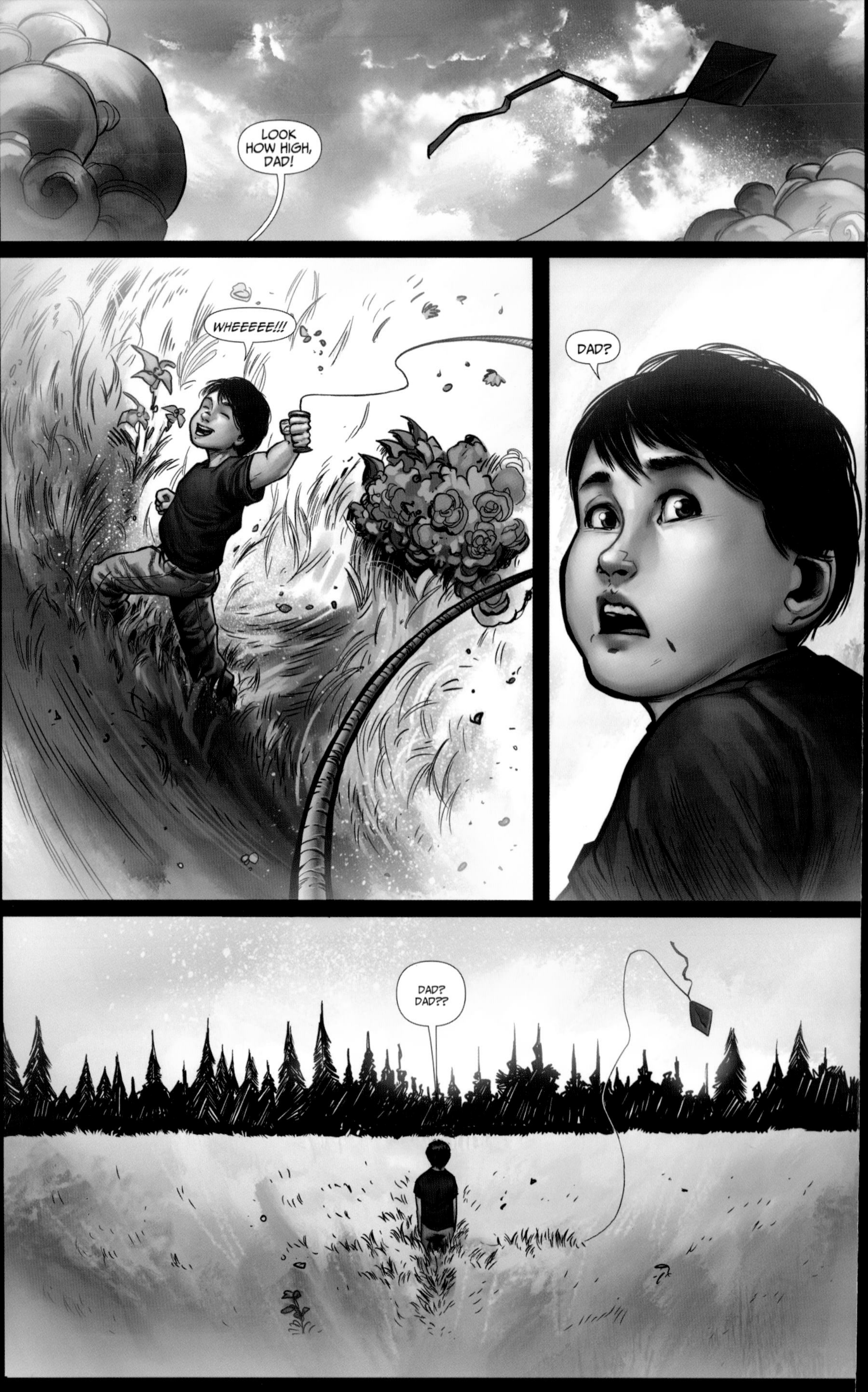
LOOK HOW HIGH, DAD!
WHEEEEE!!!
DAD?
DAD? DAD??

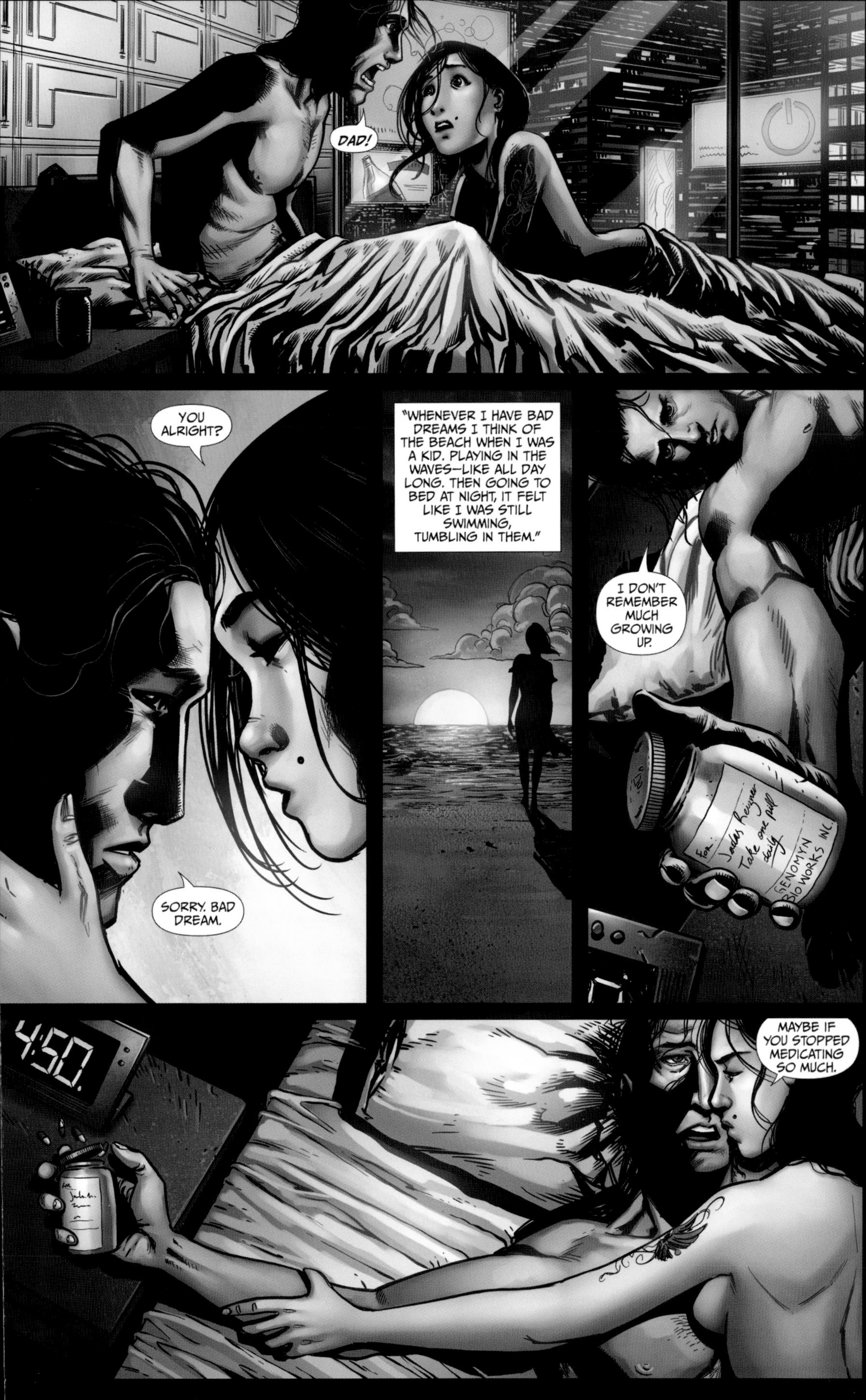
DAD!
YOU ALRIGHT?
SORRY. BAD DREAM.
"WHENEVER I HAVE BAD DREAMS I THINK OF THE BEACH WHEN I WAS A KID. PLAYING IN THE WAVES—LIKE ALL DAY LONG. THEN GOING TO BED AT NIGHT, IT FELT LIKE I WAS STILL SWIMMING, TUMBLING IN THEM."
I DON'T REMEMBER MUCH GROWING UP.
For: Jadas Reizner
Take one pill daily
GENOMYN BIOWORKS INC.
4:50
MAYBE IF YOU STOPPED MEDICATING SO MUCH.

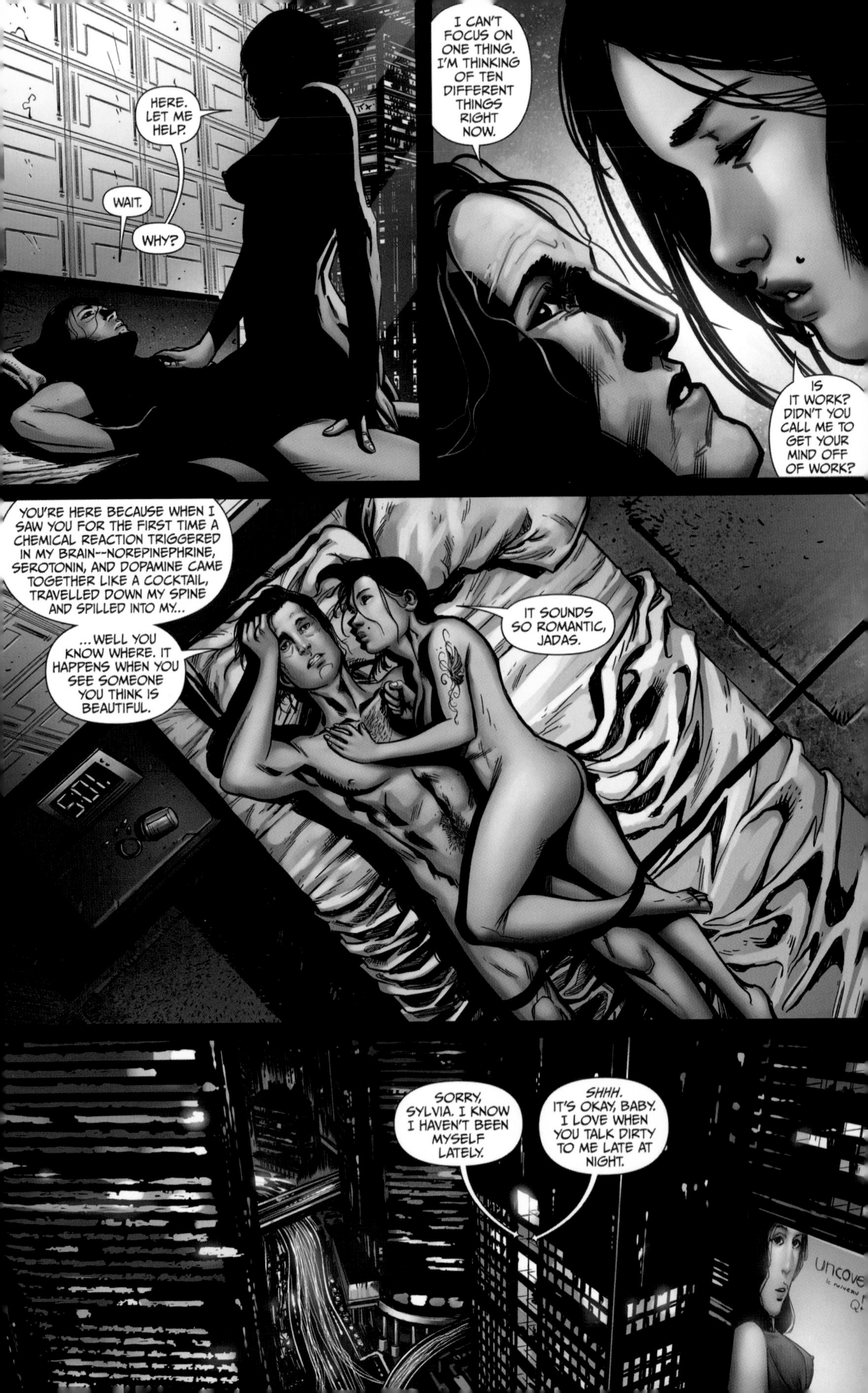
HERE. LET ME HELP.
WAIT.
WHY?
I CAN'T FOCUS ON ONE THING. I'M THINKING OF TEN DIFFERENT THINGS RIGHT NOW.
IS IT WORK? DIDN'T YOU CALL ME TO GET YOUR MIND OFF OF WORK?
YOU'RE HERE BECAUSE WHEN I SAW YOU FOR THE FIRST TIME A CHEMICAL REACTION TRIGGERED IN MY BRAIN--NOREPINEPHRINE, SEROTONIN, AND DOPAMINE CAME TOGETHER LIKE A COCKTAIL, TRAVELLED DOWN MY SPINE AND SPILLED INTO MY...
...WELL YOU KNOW WHERE. IT HAPPENS WHEN YOU SEE SOMEONE YOU THINK IS BEAUTIFUL.
IT SOUNDS SO ROMANTIC, JADAS.
SORRY, SYLVIA. I KNOW I HAVEN'T BEEN MYSELF LATELY.
SHHH. IT'S OKAY, BABY. I LOVE WHEN YOU TALK DIRTY TO ME LATE AT NIGHT.

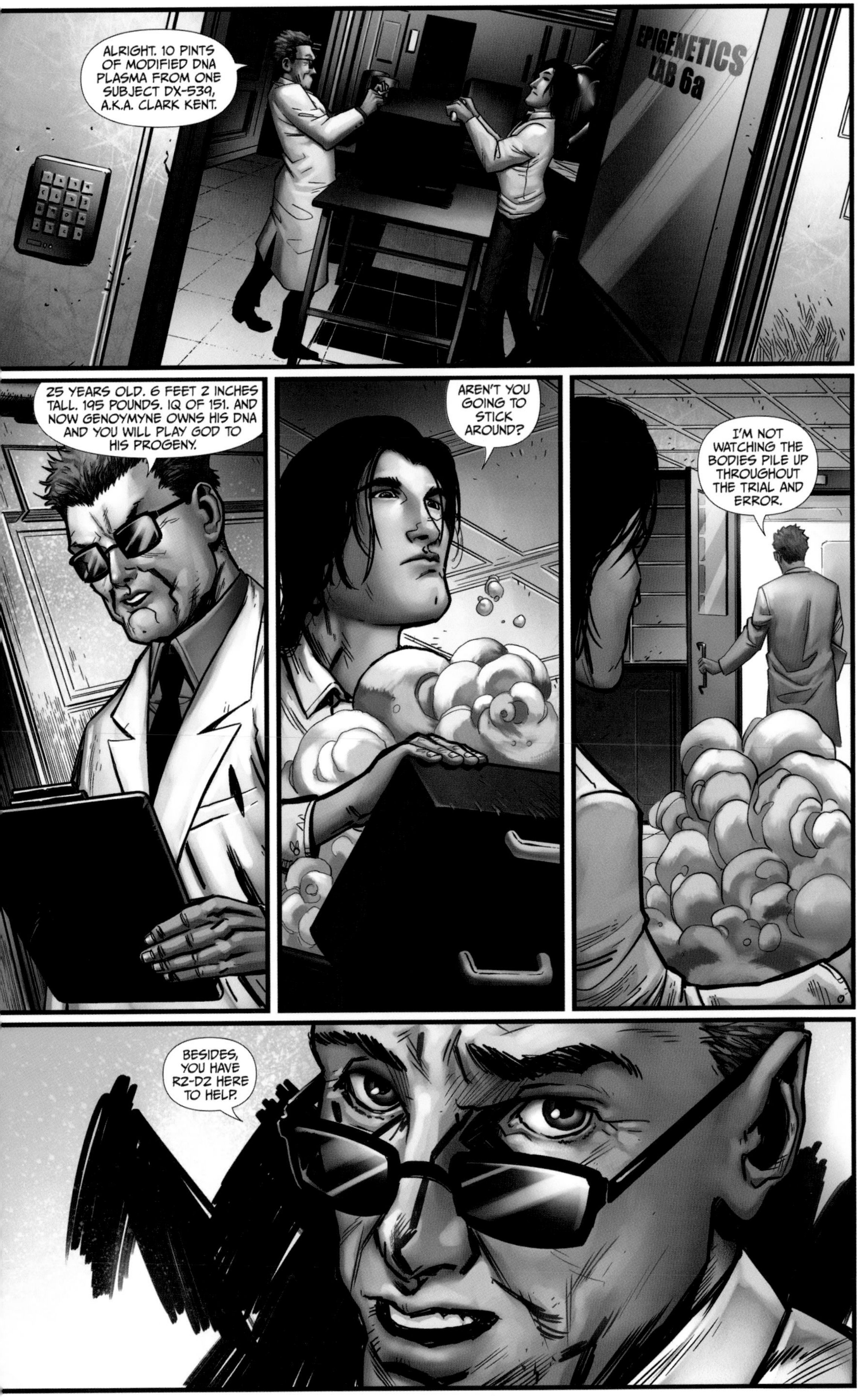
ALRIGHT. 10 PINTS OF MODIFIED DNA PLASMA FROM ONE SUBJECT DX-539, A.K.A. CLARK KENT.
EPIGENETICS LAB 6a
25 YEARS OLD. 6 FEET 2 INCHES TALL. 195 POUNDS. IQ OF 151. AND NOW GENOYMYNE OWNS HIS DNA AND YOU WILL PLAY GOD TO HIS PROGENY.
AREN'T YOU GOING TO STICK AROUND?
I'M NOT WATCHING THE BODIES PILE UP THROUGHOUT THE TRIAL AND ERROR.
BESIDES, YOU HAVE R2-D2 HERE TO HELP.

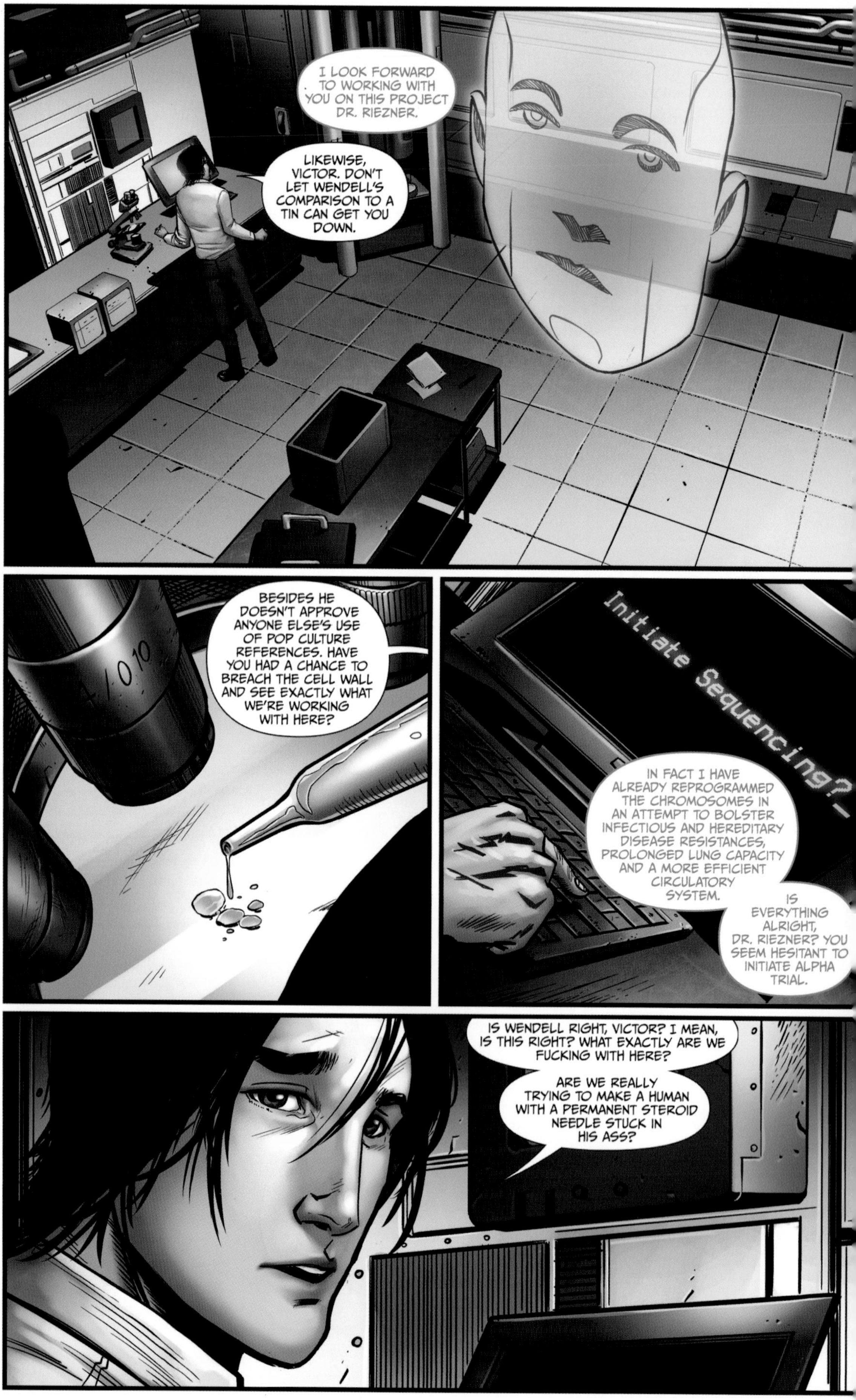

I LOOK FORWARD TO WORKING WITH YOU ON THIS PROJECT DR. RIEZNER.
LIKEWISE, VICTOR. DON'T LET WENDELL'S COMPARISON TO A TIN CAN GET YOU DOWN.
BESIDES HE DOESN'T APPROVE ANYONE ELSE'S USE OF POP CULTURE REFERENCES. HAVE YOU HAD A CHANCE TO BREACH THE CELL WALL AND SEE EXACTLY WHAT WE'RE WORKING WITH HERE?
Initiate Sequencing?_
IN FACT I HAVE ALREADY REPROGRAMMED THE CHROMOSOMES IN AN ATTEMPT TO BOLSTER INFECTIOUS AND HEREDITARY DISEASE RESISTANCES, PROLONGED LUNG CAPACITY AND A MORE EFFICIENT CIRCULATORY SYSTEM.
IS EVERYTHING ALRIGHT, DR. RIEZNER? YOU SEEM HESITANT TO INITIATE ALPHA TRIAL.
IS WENDELL RIGHT, VICTOR? I MEAN, IS THIS RIGHT? WHAT EXACTLY ARE WE FUCKING WITH HERE?
ARE WE REALLY TRYING TO MAKE A HUMAN WITH A PERMANENT STEROID NEEDLE STUCK IN HIS ASS?

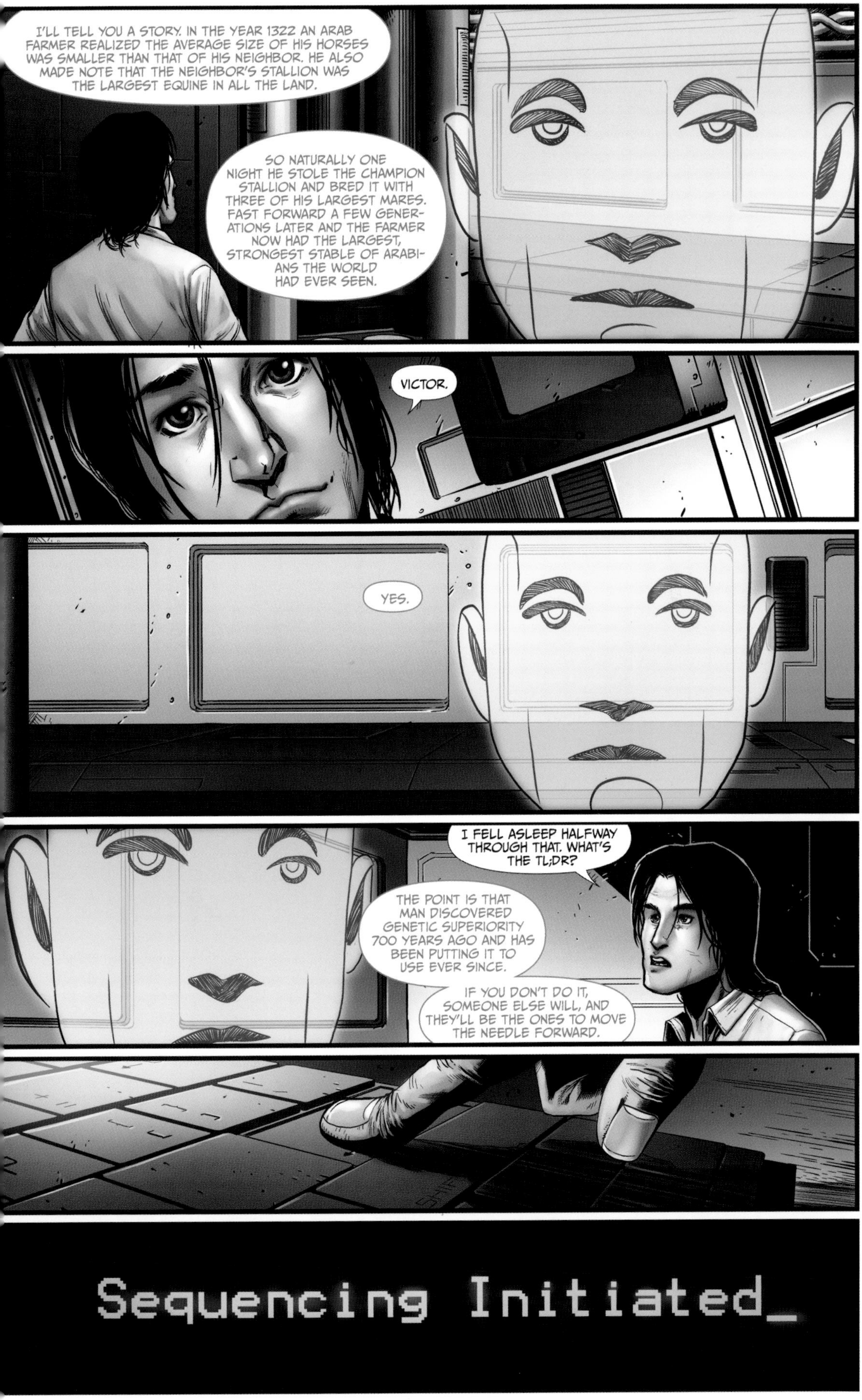

I'LL TELL YOU A STORY. IN THE YEAR 1322 AN ARAB FARMER REALIZED THE AVERAGE SIZE OF HIS HORSES WAS SMALLER THAN THAT OF HIS NEIGHBOR. HE ALSO MADE NOTE THAT THE NEIGHBOR'S STALLION WAS THE LARGEST EQUINE IN ALL THE LAND.
SO NATURALLY ONE NIGHT HE STOLE THE CHAMPION STALLION AND BRED IT WITH THREE OF HIS LARGEST MARES. FAST FORWARD A FEW GENERATIONS LATER AND THE FARMER NOW HAD THE LARGEST, STRONGEST STABLE OF ARABIANS THE WORLD HAD EVER SEEN.
VICTOR.
YES.
I FELL ASLEEP HALFWAY THROUGH THAT. WHAT'S THE TL;DR?
THE POINT IS THAT MAN DISCOVERED GENETIC SUPERIORITY 700 YEARS AGO AND HAS BEEN PUTTING IT TO USE EVER SINCE.
IF YOU DON'T DO IT, SOMEONE ELSE WILL, AND THEY'LL BE THE ONES TO MOVE THE NEEDLE FORWARD.
Sequencing Initiated_

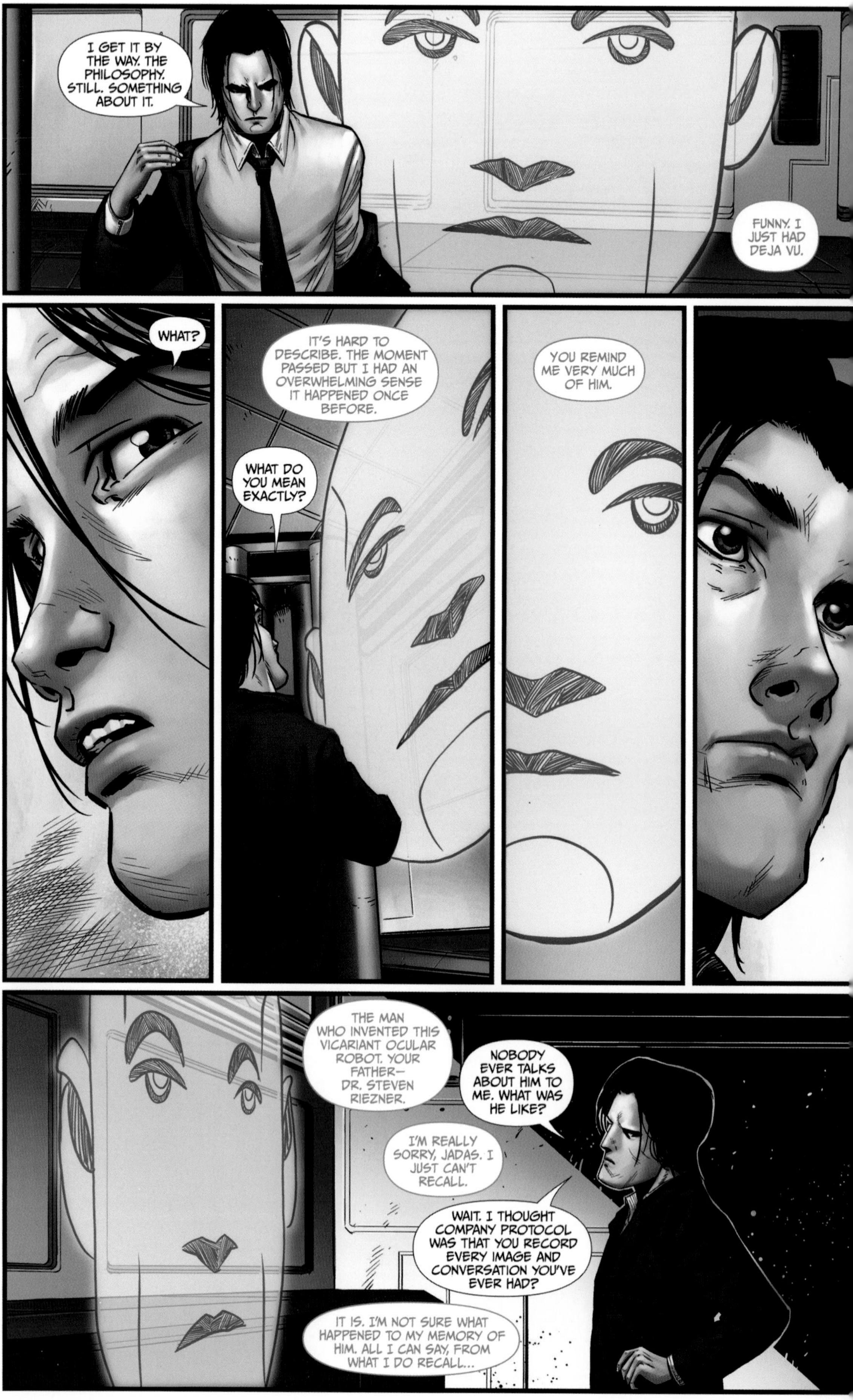

I GET IT BY THE WAY. THE PHILOSOPHY. STILL. SOMETHING ABOUT IT.
FUNNY. I JUST HAD DEJA VU.
WHAT?
IT'S HARD TO DESCRIBE. THE MOMENT PASSED BUT I HAD AN OVERWHELMING SENSE IT HAPPENED ONCE BEFORE.
WHAT DO YOU MEAN EXACTLY?
YOU REMIND ME VERY MUCH OF HIM.
THE MAN WHO INVENTED THIS VICARIANT OCULAR ROBOT. YOUR FATHER— DR. STEVEN RIEZNER.
NOBODY EVER TALKS ABOUT HIM TO ME. WHAT WAS HE LIKE?
I'M REALLY SORRY, JADAS. I JUST CAN'T RECALL.
WAIT. I THOUGHT COMPANY PROTOCOL WAS THAT YOU RECORD EVERY IMAGE AND CONVERSATION YOU'VE EVER HAD?
IT IS. I'M NOT SURE WHAT HAPPENED TO MY MEMORY OF HIM. ALL I CAN SAY, FROM WHAT I DO RECALL...

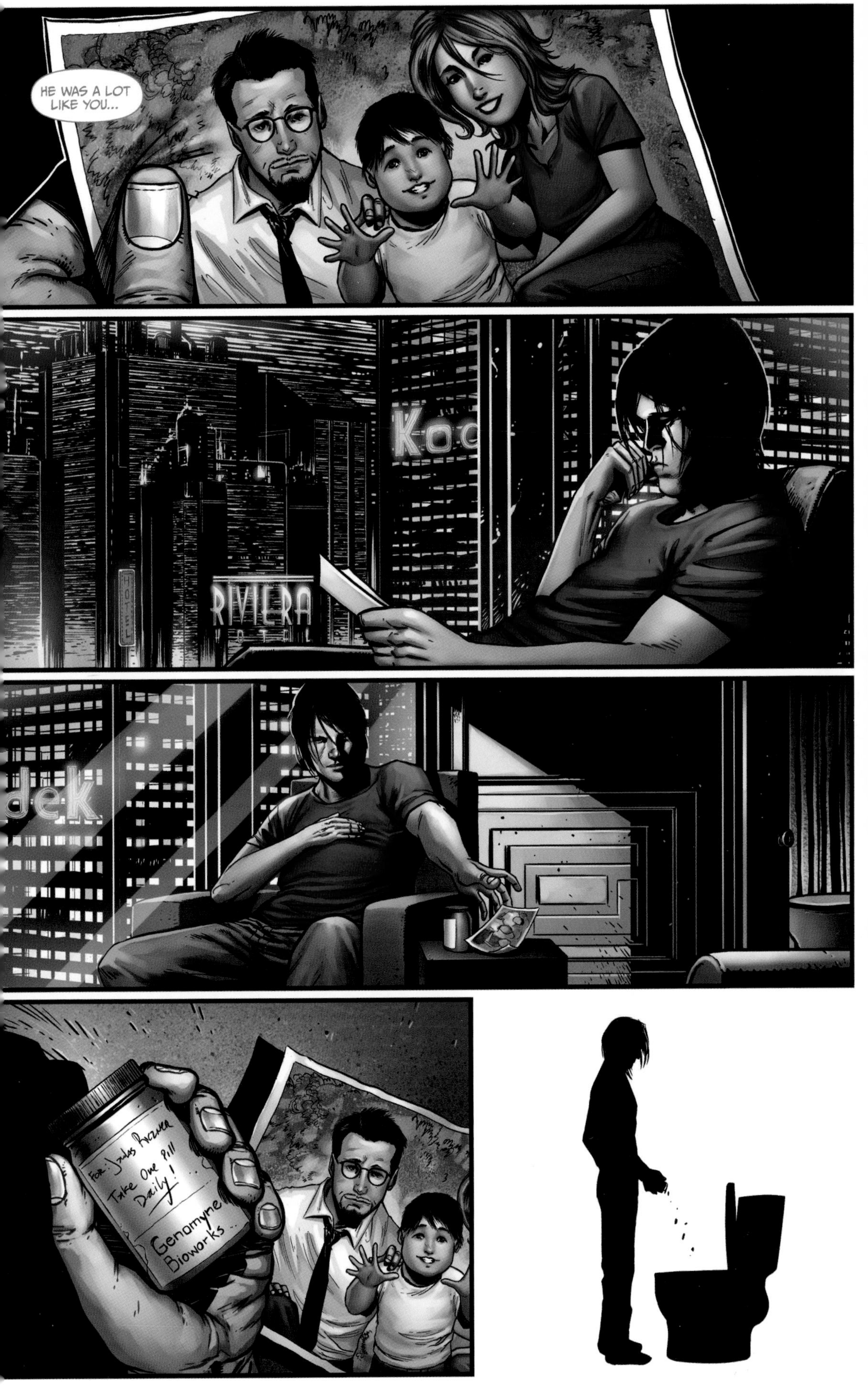
HE WAS A LOT LIKE YOU...
HOTEL
RIVIERA
Take One Pill Daily!
Genomyne Bioworks

KNOCK KNOCK.

THOMAS RINGER
INVESTIGATIONS
AND SECURITY

YOU GUYS OPEN?

WE ARE NOW. LEMME GUESS. YOUR GIRLFRIEND IS CHEATING AND YOU NEED SOME CONFIRMATION?

I'M LOOKING FOR SOMEONE WHO DISAPPEARED A LONG TIME AGO.

99% OF THE TIME IT'S THE CHEATING. OTHER 1% IT'S MISCELLANEOUS, LIKE DAUGHTER'S BOYFRIEND BACKGROUND CHECKS, OR COLLEAGUE IS BLACKMAILING ME WITH THE DICK PICS I SENT THEM, OR THE MOST BORING OF ALL--

--DEBUG MY DAMN COMPUTER AFTER I CLICKED ON SOME TEENAGE TRANSGENDER ANIMAL PORN. ANYWAY, WHO YOU NEED TO LOCATE--FRIEND OR FAMILY?

FAMILY.

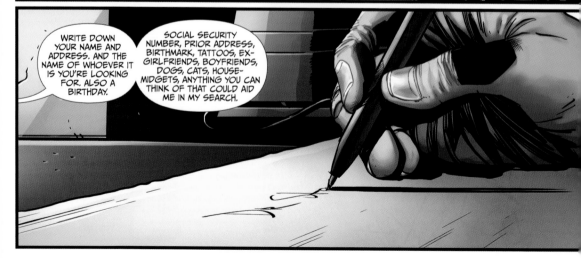

WRITE DOWN YOUR NAME AND ADDRESS. AND THE NAME OF WHOEVER IT IS YOU'RE LOOKING FOR. ALSO A BIRTHDAY.

SOCIAL SECURITY NUMBER, PRIOR ADDRESS, BIRTHMARK, TATTOOS, EX-GIRLFRIENDS, BOYFRIENDS, DOGS, CATS, HOUSE-MIDGETS, ANYTHING YOU CAN THINK OF THAT COULD AID ME IN MY SEARCH.

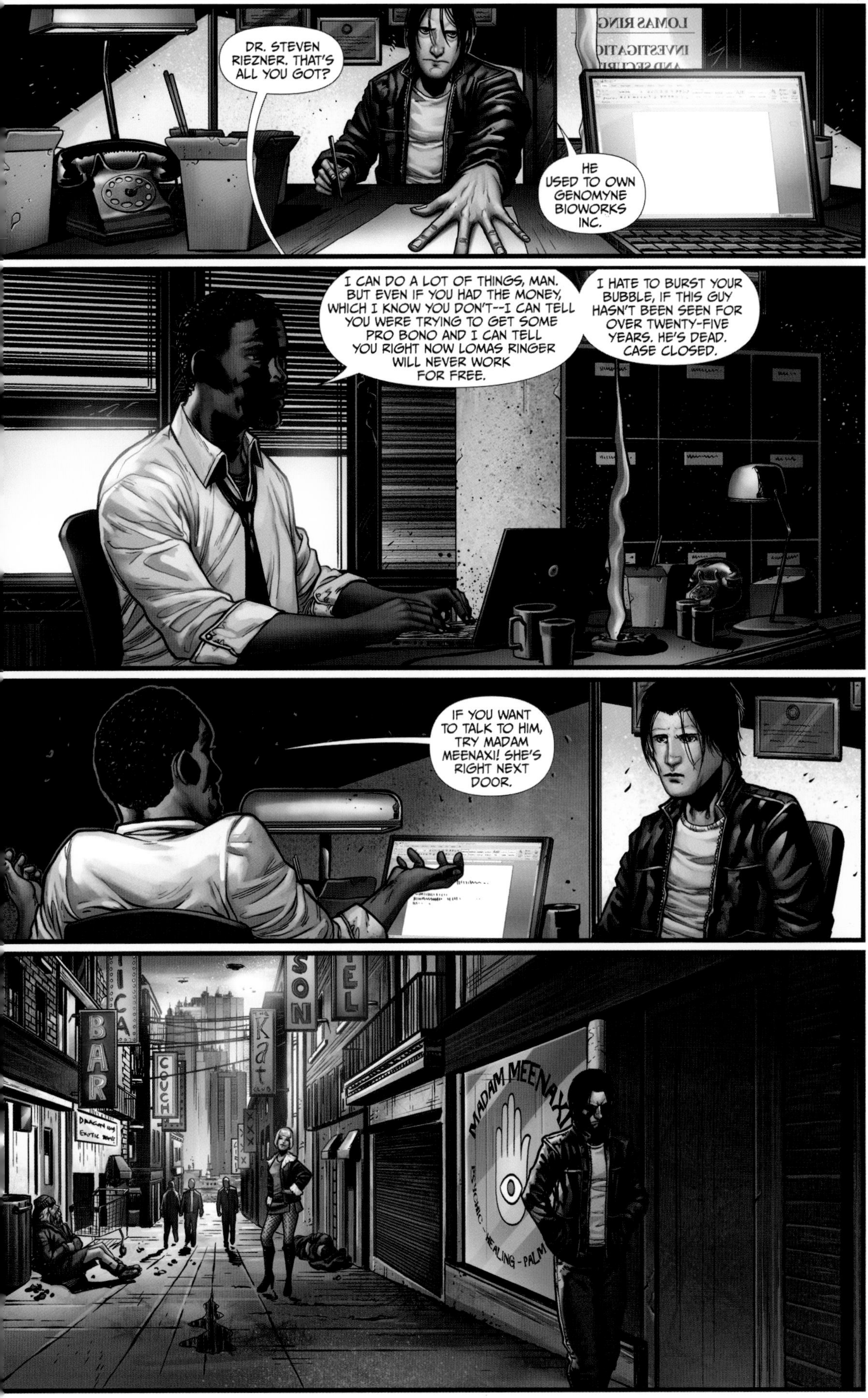

DR. STEVEN RIEZNER. THAT'S ALL YOU GOT?
HE USED TO OWN GENOMYNE BIOWORKS INC.
I CAN DO A LOT OF THINGS, MAN. BUT EVEN IF YOU HAD THE MONEY, WHICH I KNOW YOU DON'T--I CAN TELL YOU WERE TRYING TO GET SOME PRO BONO AND I CAN TELL YOU RIGHT NOW LOMAS RINGER WILL NEVER WORK FOR FREE.
I HATE TO BURST YOUR BUBBLE, IF THIS GUY HASN'T BEEN SEEN FOR OVER TWENTY-FIVE YEARS. HE'S DEAD. CASE CLOSED.
IF YOU WANT TO TALK TO HIM, TRY MADAM MEENAXI! SHE'S RIGHT NEXT DOOR.
BAR
COUCH
Kat
SON
MADAM MEENAXI
PSYCHIC - HEALING - PALM

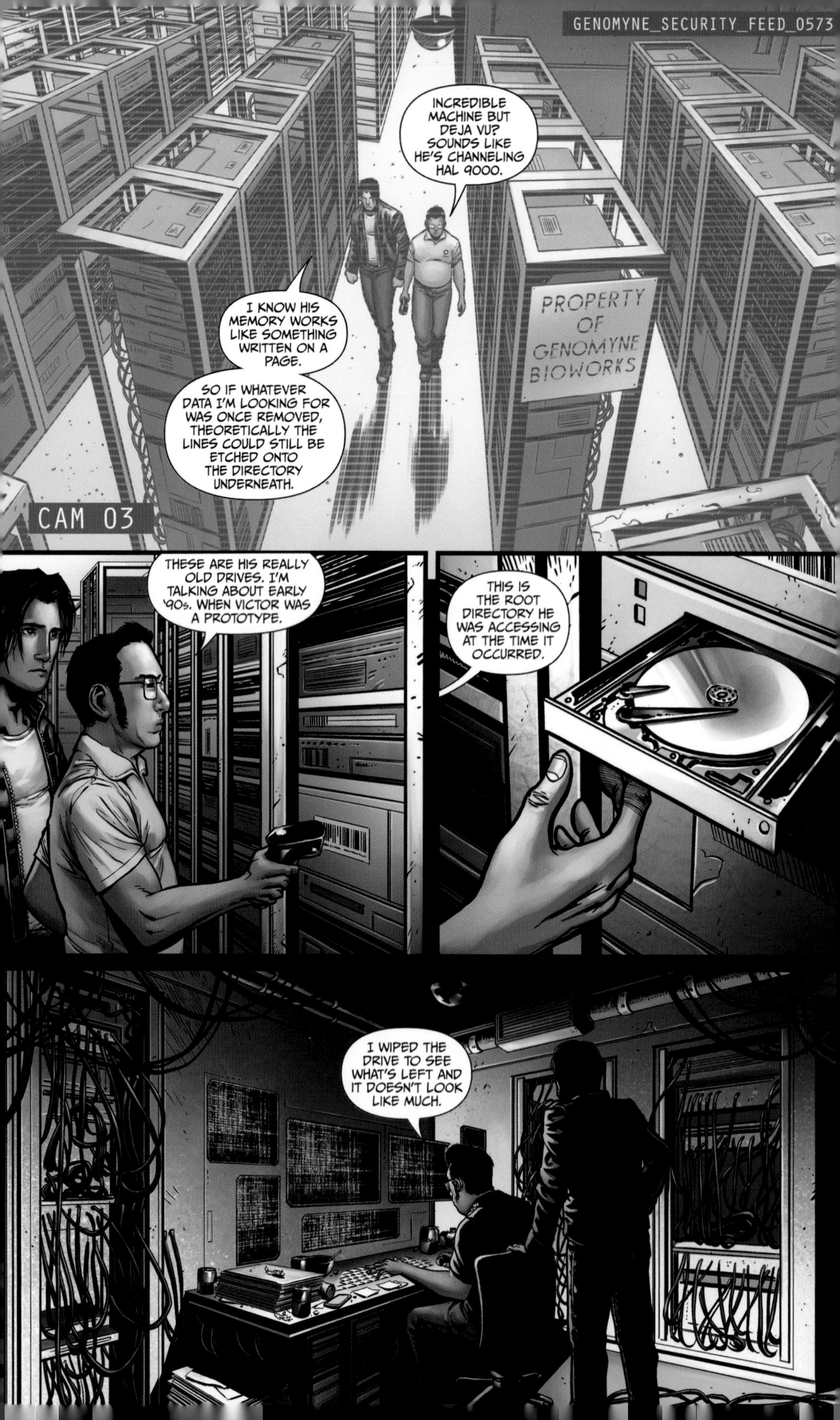
GENOMYNE_SECURITY_FEED_0573
INCREDIBLE MACHINE BUT DEJA VU? SOUNDS LIKE HE'S CHANNELING HAL 9000.
I KNOW HIS MEMORY WORKS LIKE SOMETHING WRITTEN ON A PAGE.
SO IF WHATEVER DATA I'M LOOKING FOR WAS ONCE REMOVED, THEORETICALLY THE LINES COULD STILL BE ETCHED ONTO THE DIRECTORY UNDERNEATH.
PROPERTY OF GENOMYNE BIOWORKS
CAM 03
THESE ARE HIS REALLY OLD DRIVES. I'M TALKING ABOUT EARLY '90s. WHEN VICTOR WAS A PROTOTYPE.
THIS IS THE ROOT DIRECTORY HE WAS ACCESSING AT THE TIME IT OCCURRED.
I WIPED THE DRIVE TO SEE WHAT'S LEFT AND IT DOESN'T LOOK LIKE MUCH.

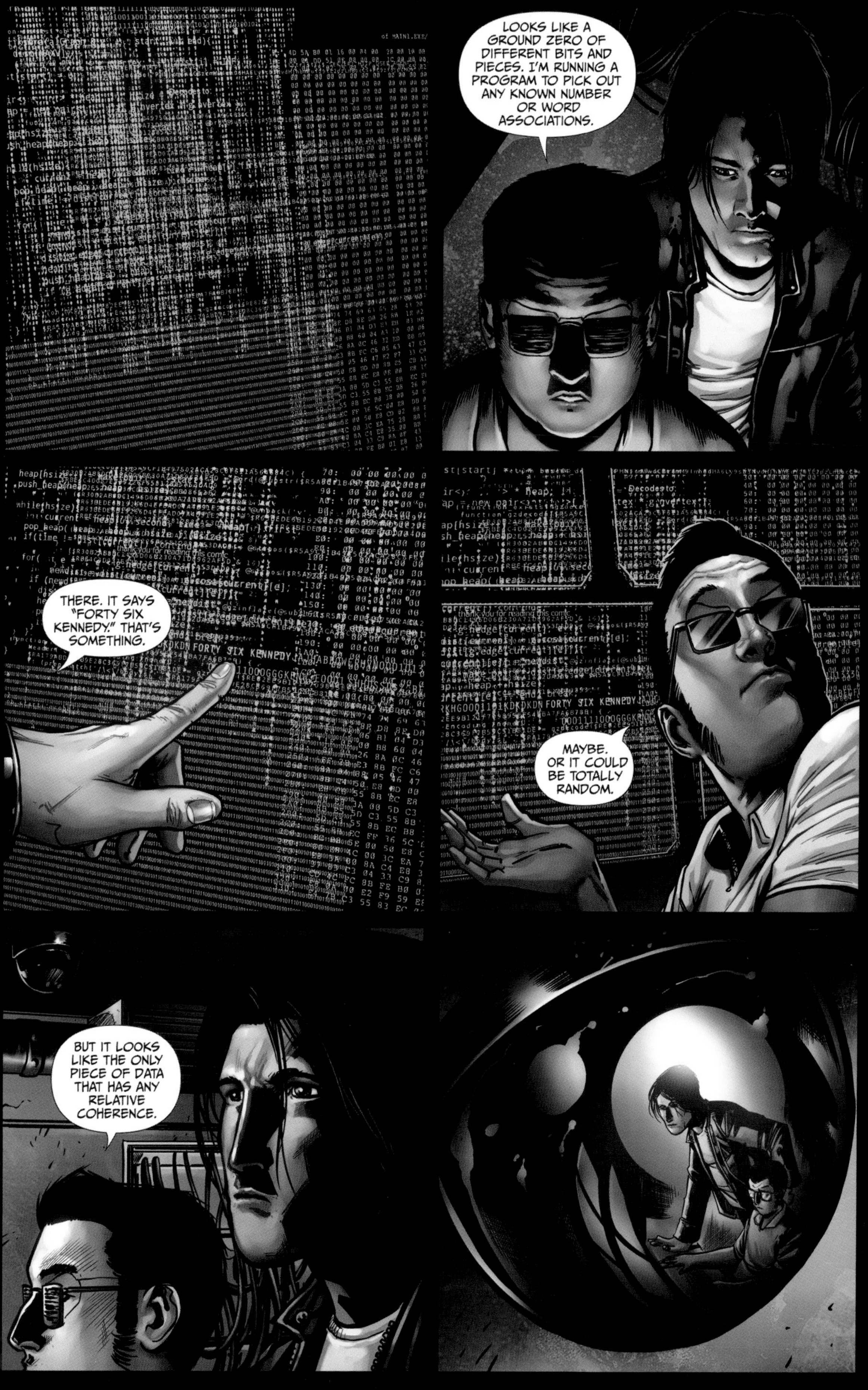

LOOKS LIKE A GROUND ZERO OF DIFFERENT BITS AND PIECES. I'M RUNNING A PROGRAM TO PICK OUT ANY KNOWN NUMBER OR WORD ASSOCIATIONS.
THERE. IT SAYS "FORTY SIX KENNEDY." THAT'S SOMETHING.
FORTY SIX KENNEDY
MAYBE. OR IT COULD BE TOTALLY RANDOM.
BUT IT LOOKS LIKE THE ONLY PIECE OF DATA THAT HAS ANY RELATIVE COHERENCE.

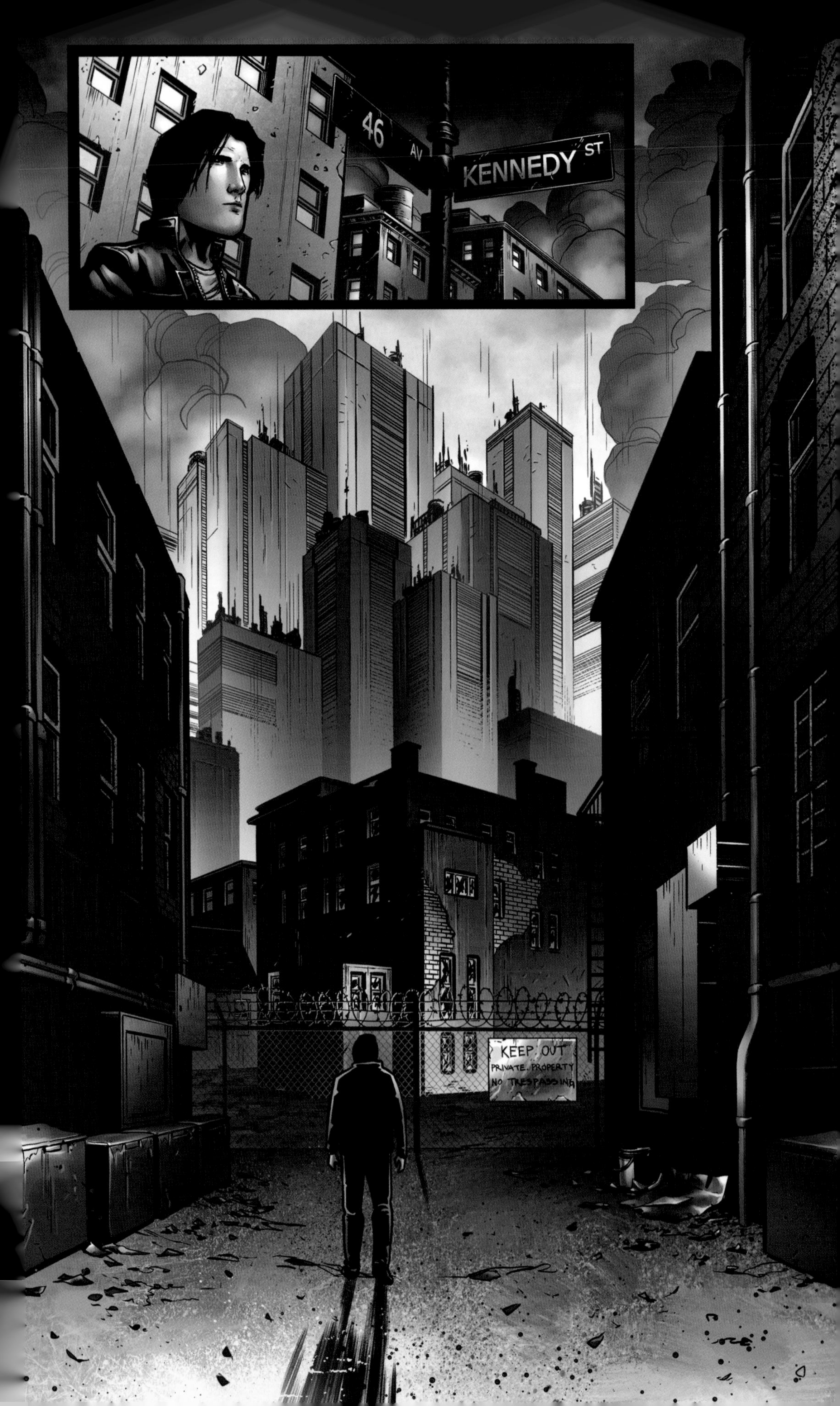
46 AV
KENNEDY ST
KEEP OUT
PRIVATE PROPERTY
NO TRESPASSING

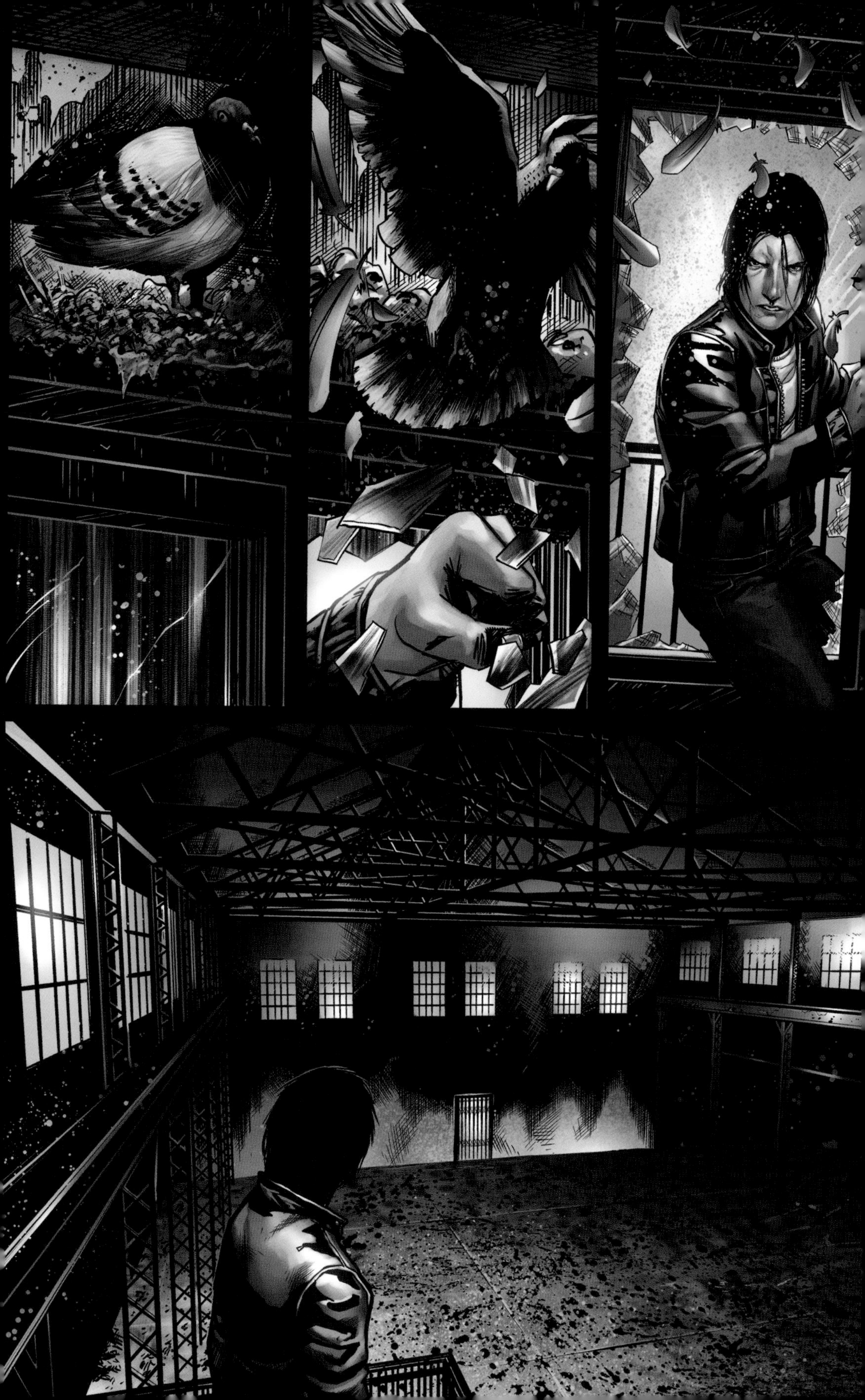

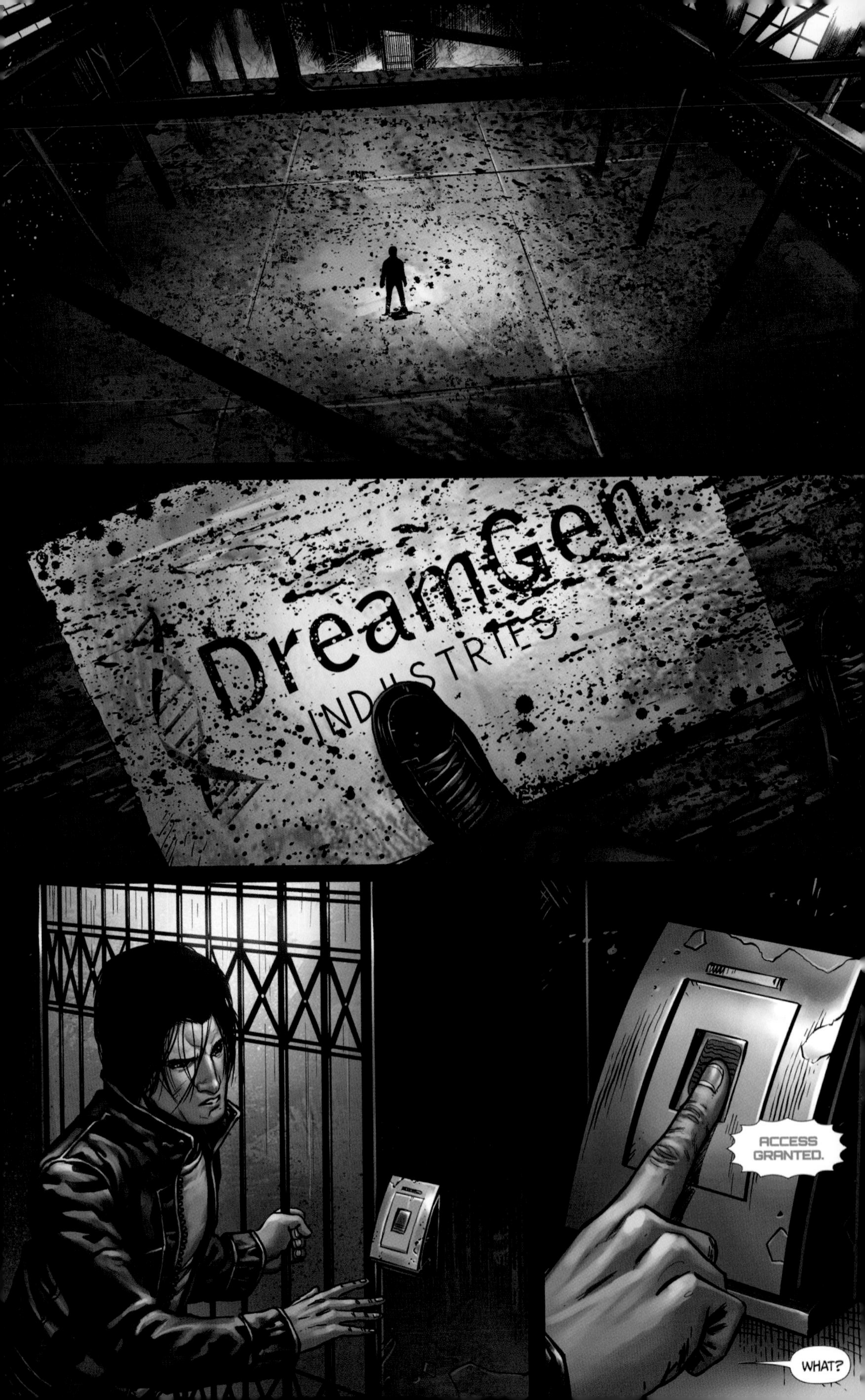
DreamGen
INDUSTRIES
ACCESS GRANTED.
WHAT?

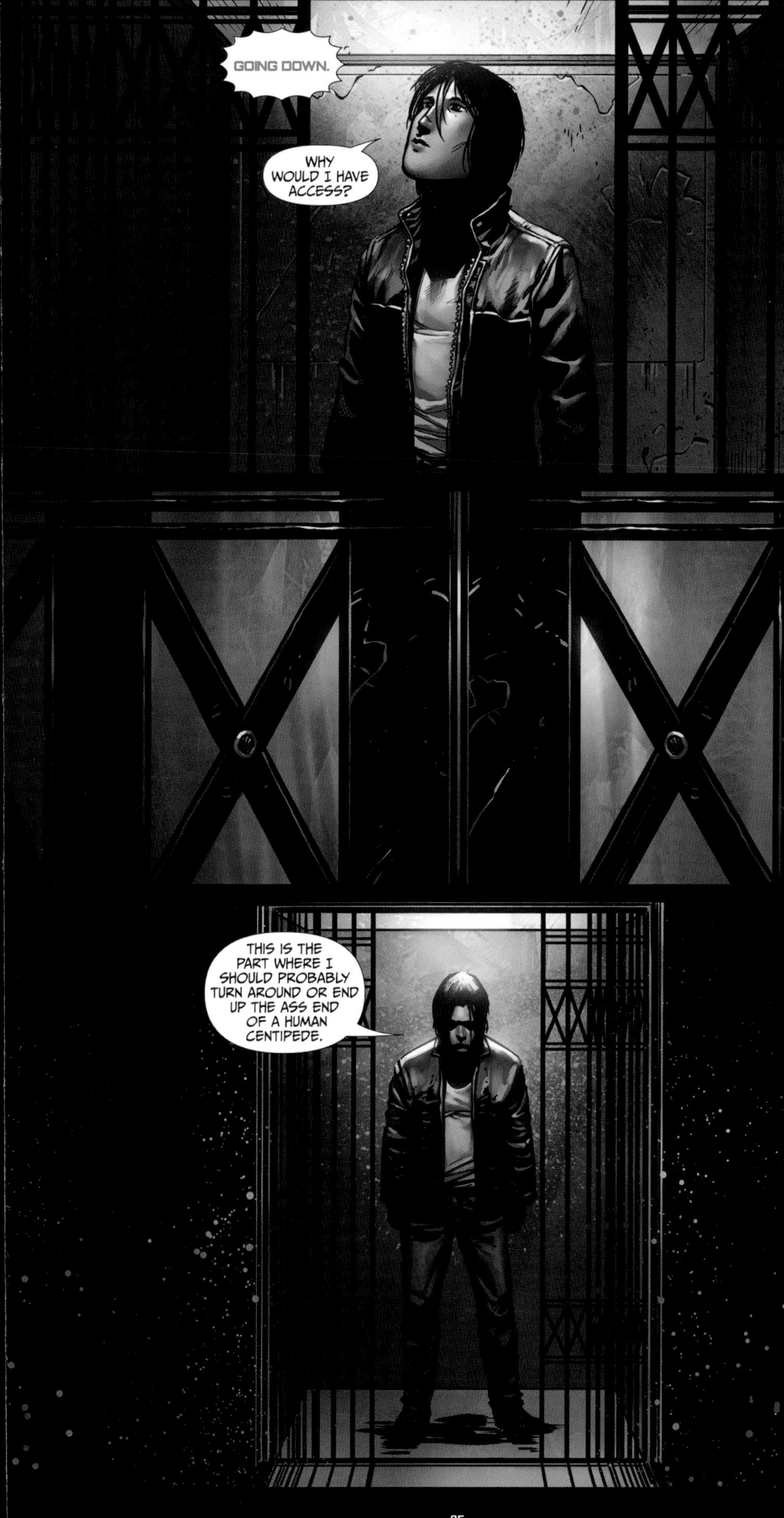
GOING DOWN.
WHY WOULD I HAVE ACCESS?
THIS IS THE PART WHERE I SHOULD PROBABLY TURN AROUND OR END UP THE ASS END OF A HUMAN CENTIPEDE.

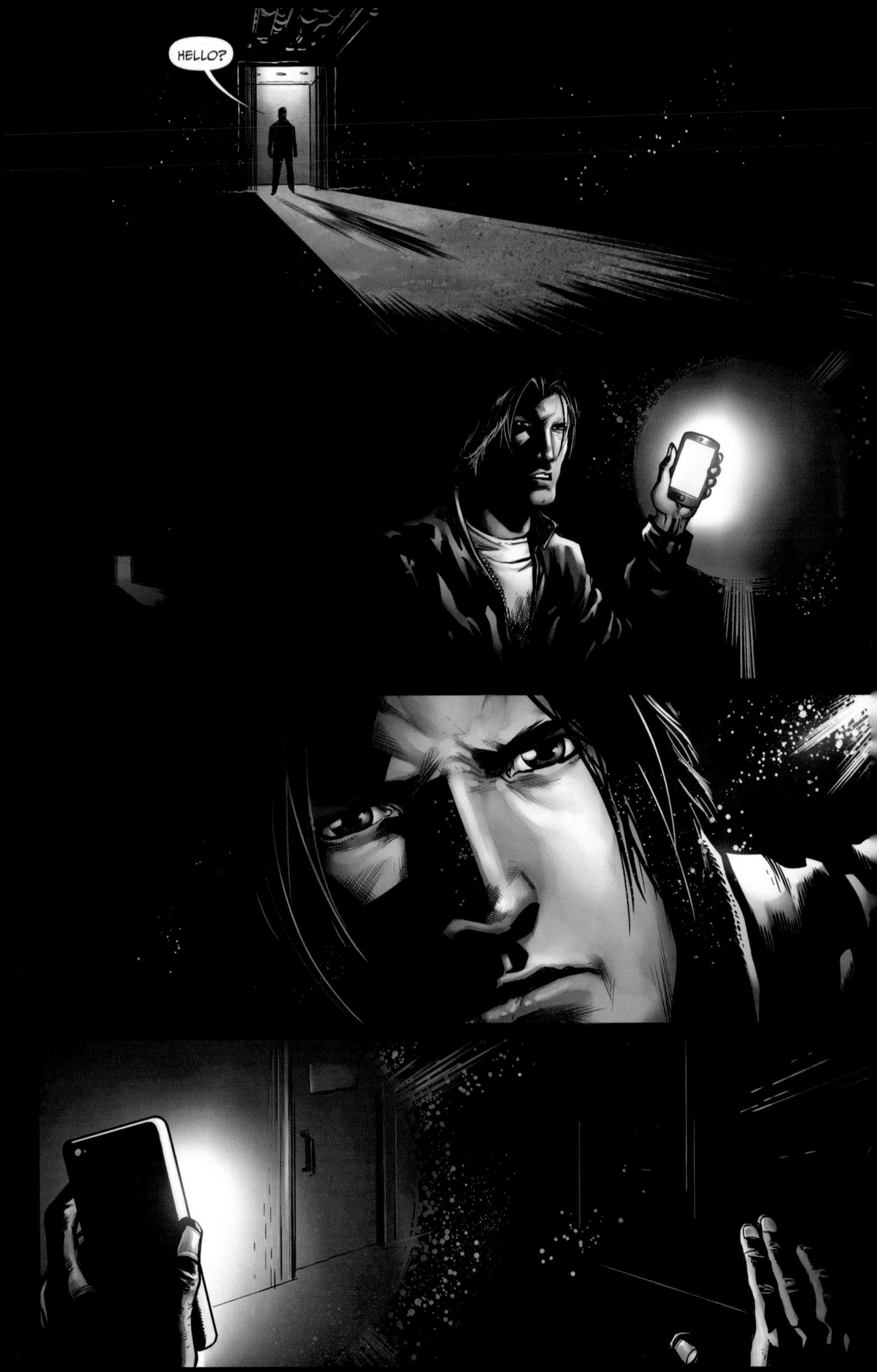
HELLO?

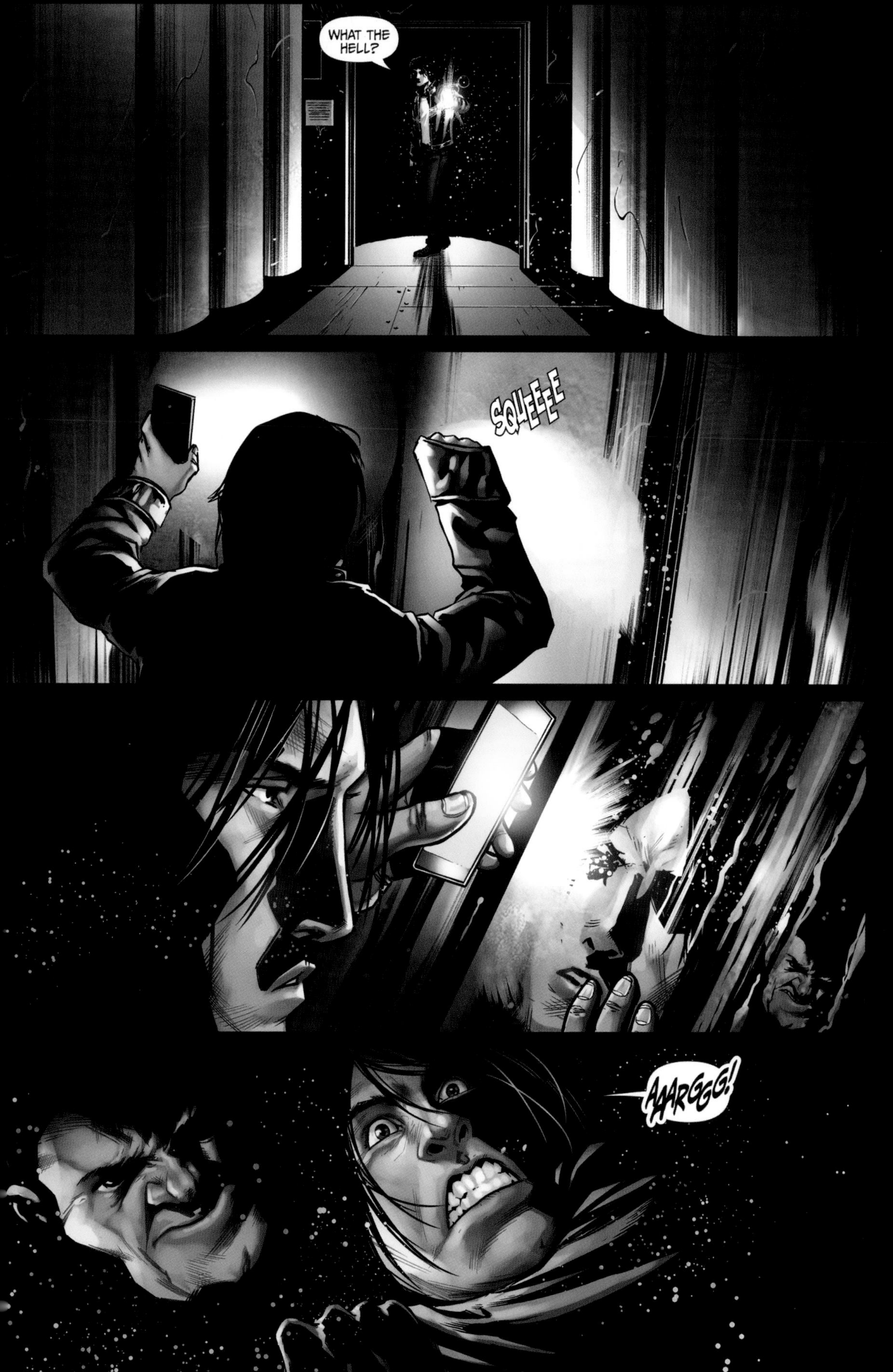
WHAT THE HELL?
SQUEEEE
AAARGGG!

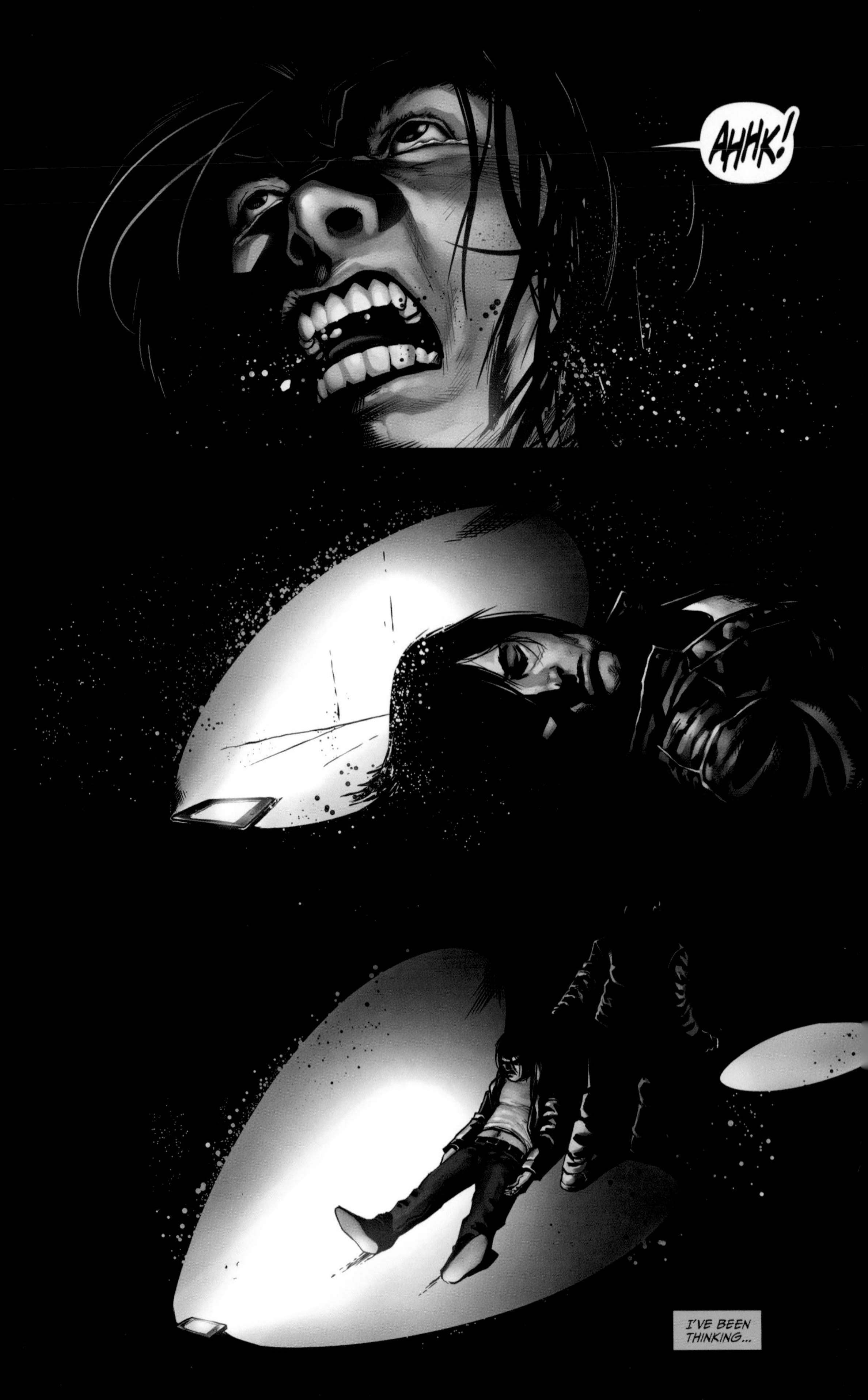
AHHK!
I'VE BEEN THINKING...

HIS STATS ARE STABLE AND EVERYTHING IS READY, BUT I'M WARNING YOU, THIS IS TOO MANY TIMES.

THOUGH MEN INDIVIDUALLY ARE UNPREDICTABLE, IF YOU LOOK AT TRENDS IN THE WHOLE OF HUMAN HISTORY YOU FIND TRAITS IN MANKIND THAT ARE STEADFAST AND AS UNCHANGING AS THE RISING SUN.

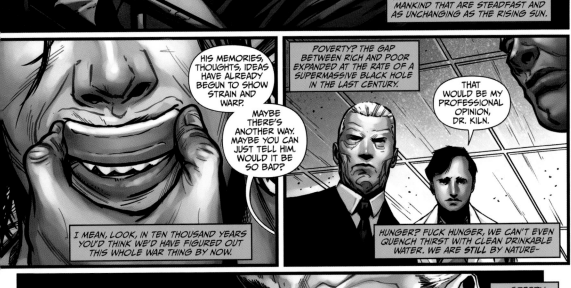

HIS MEMORIES, THOUGHTS, IDEAS HAVE ALREADY BEGUN TO SHOW STRAIN AND WARP.

MAYBE THERE'S ANOTHER WAY. MAYBE YOU CAN JUST TELL HIM. WOULD IT BE SO BAD?

I MEAN, LOOK, IN TEN THOUSAND YEARS YOU'D THINK WE'D HAVE FIGURED OUT THIS WHOLE WAR THING BY NOW.

POVERTY? THE GAP BETWEEN RICH AND POOR EXPANDED AT THE RATE OF A SUPERMASSIVE BLACK HOLE IN THE LAST CENTURY.

THAT WOULD BE MY PROFESSIONAL OPINION, DR. KILN.

HUNGER? FUCK HUNGER, WE CAN'T EVEN QUENCH THIRST WITH CLEAN DRINKABLE WATER. WE ARE STILL BY NATURE—

HE GOT TOO CLOSE THIS TIME AND WE ARE TOO FAR ALONG TO JEOPARDIZE THIS EXPERIMENT NOW. BESIDES I KNOW HIS STRENGTH.

I TOOK HIM UNDER MY WING WHEN HIS FATHER DISAPPEARED AND RAISED HIM AS MY OWN. I WOULD ONLY DO WHAT'S BEST FOR US. NOW INITIATE THE DREAMJUGGLER.

—GREEDY, TERRITORIAL, SELF-RIGHTEOUS.

MY FATHER FOUND A WAY TO ALTER THE UNALTERABLE.

IF YOU WANT A GUY TO CHANGE, YOU CHANGE HIM AT HIS CORE. YOU CHANGE HIS DNA. AND IF YOU WANT THE WORLD TO CHANGE...

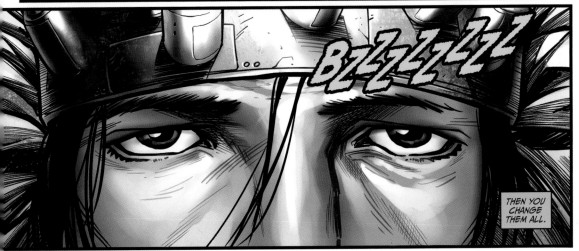

BZZZZZZ

THEN YOU CHANGE THEM ALL.

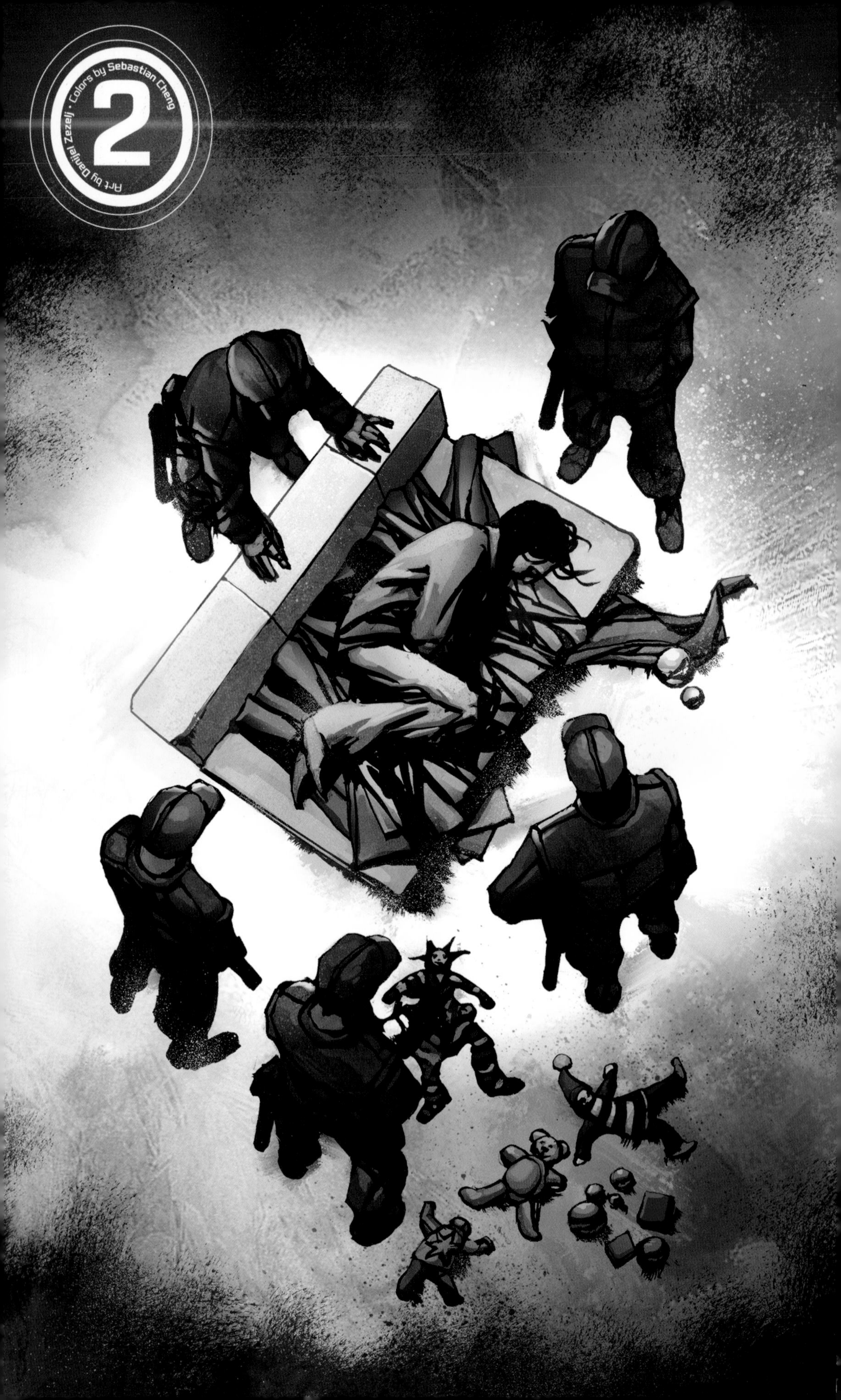
2
Art by Danijel Zezelj • Colors by Sebastian Cheng

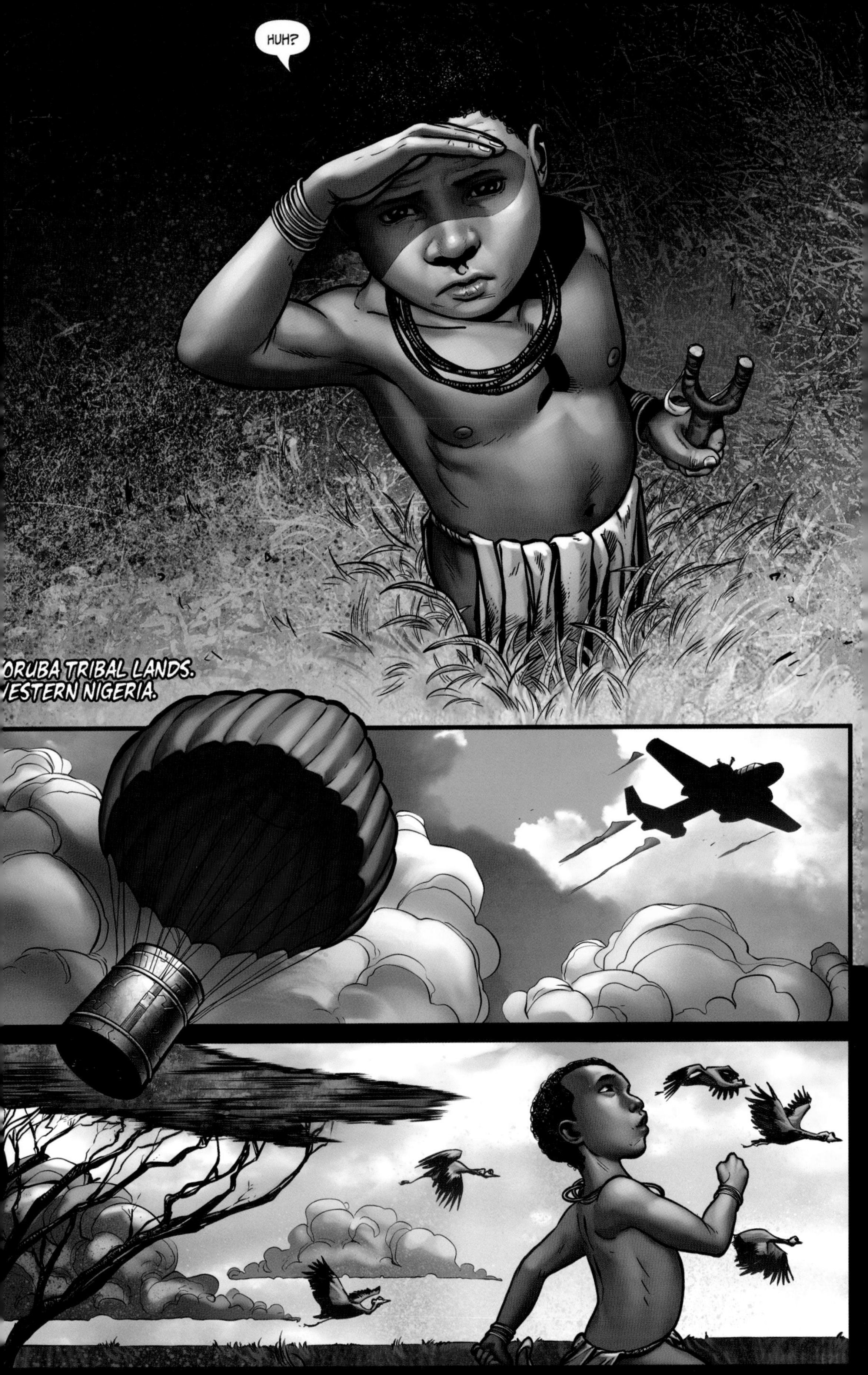
HUH?
ORUBA TRIBAL LANDS.
VESTERN NIGERIA.

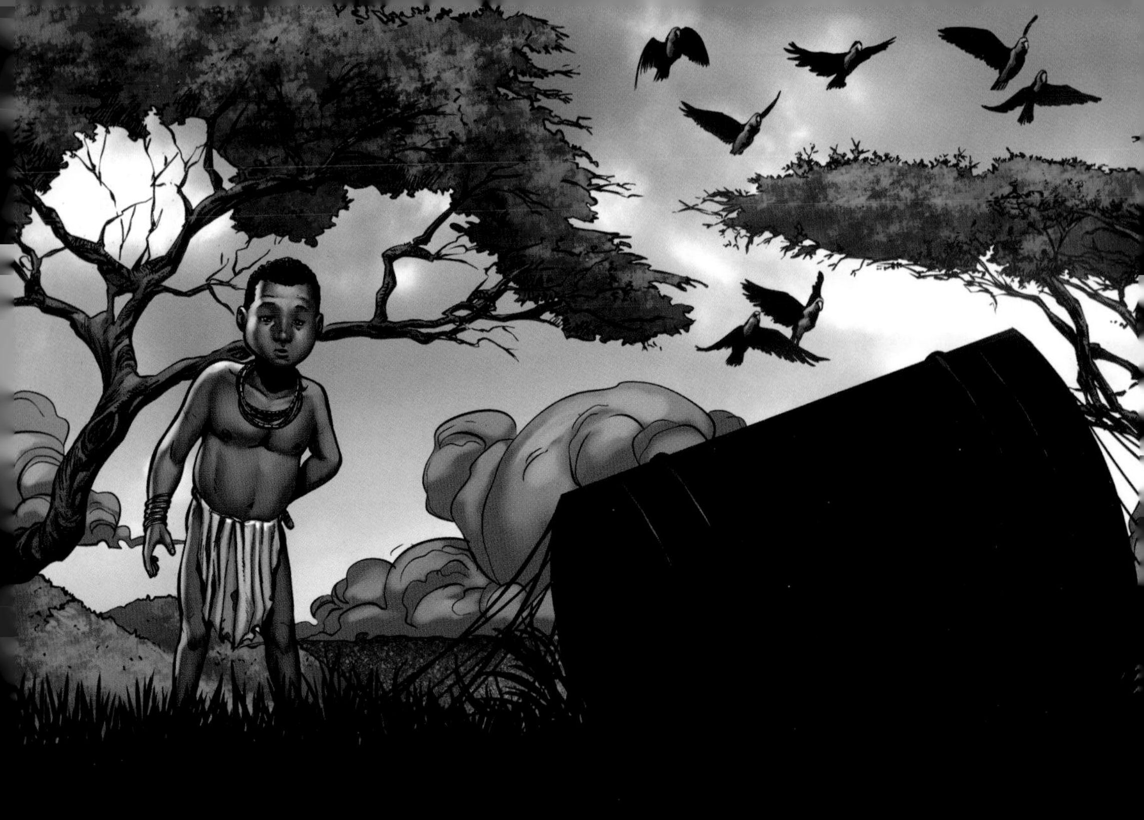

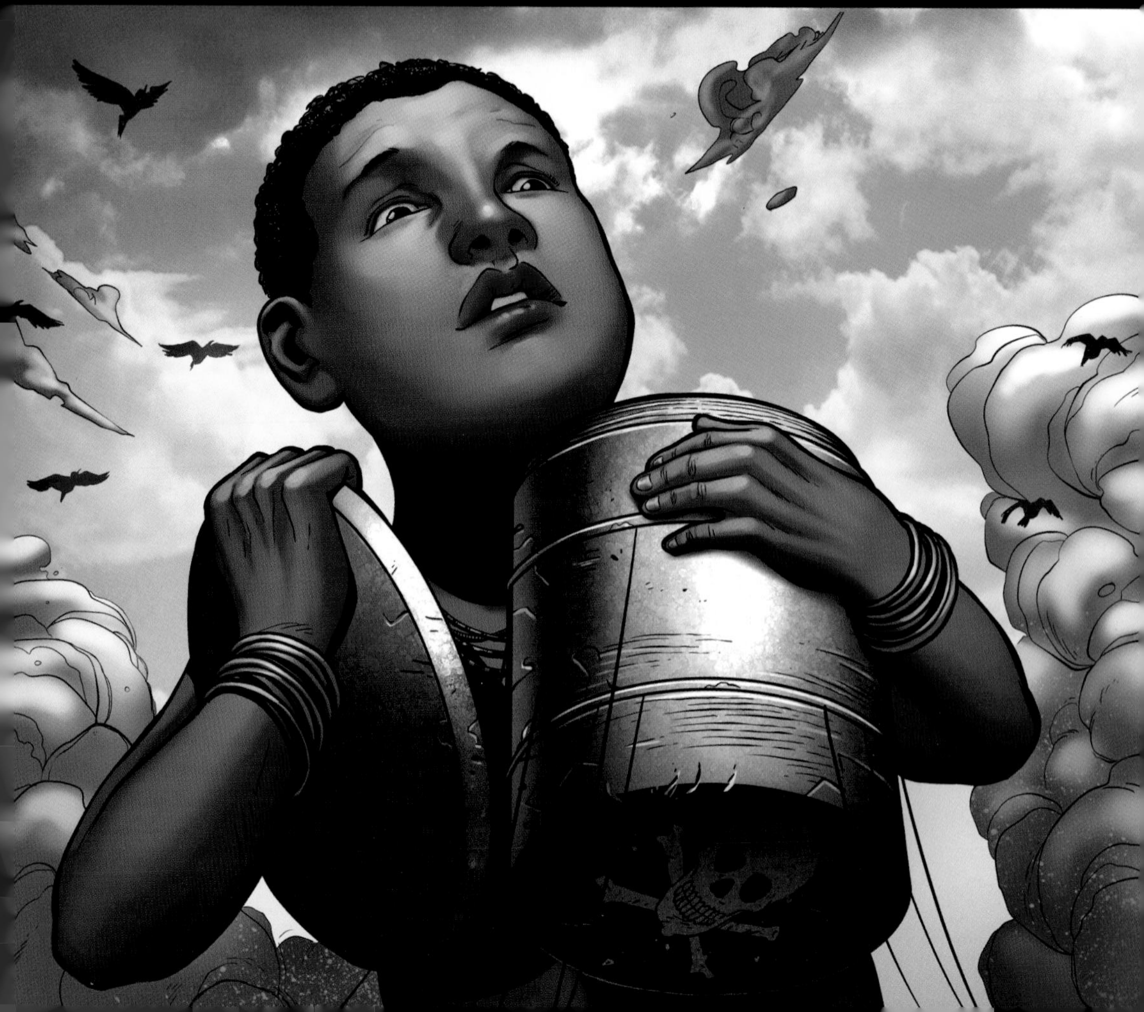

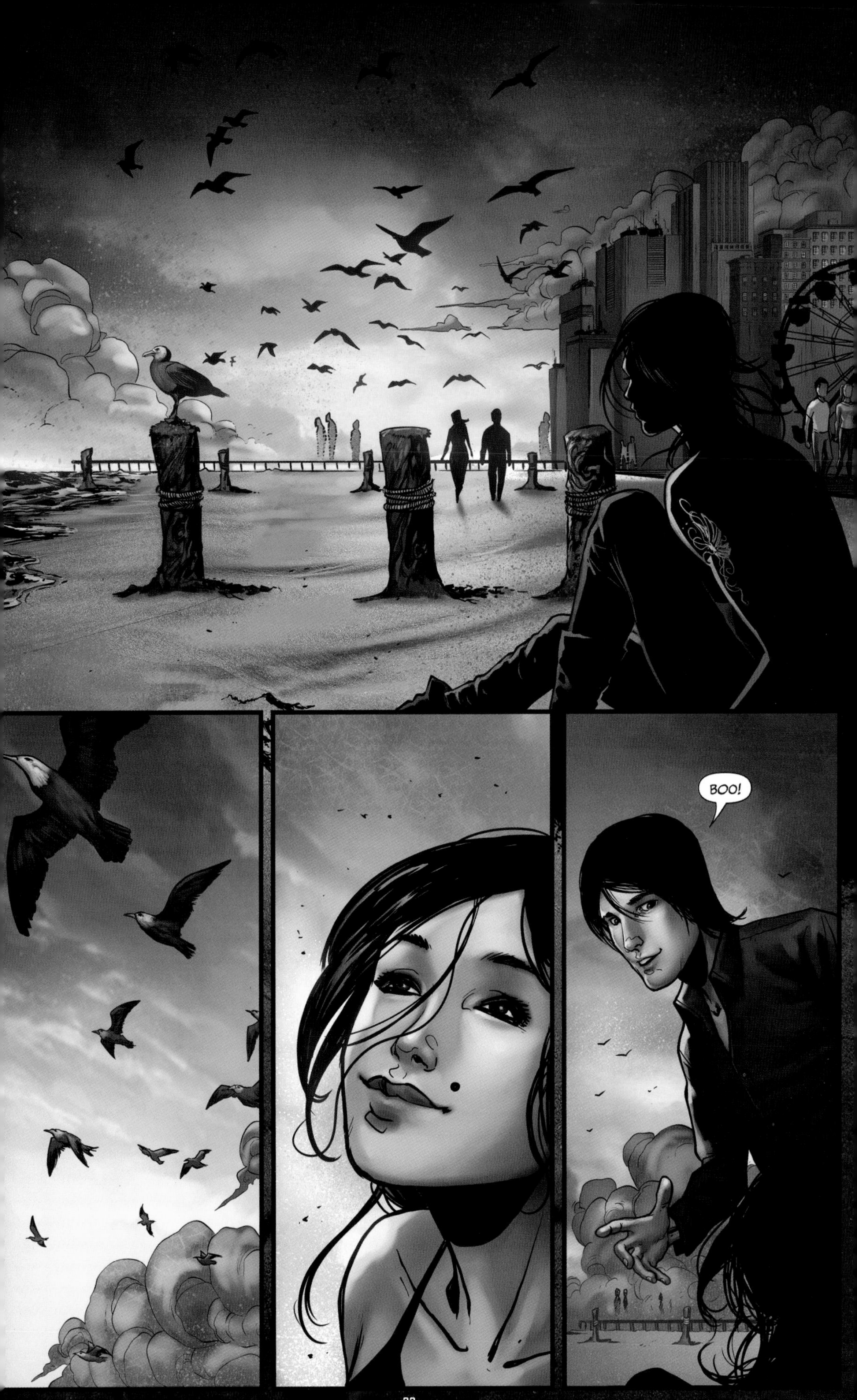
BOO!

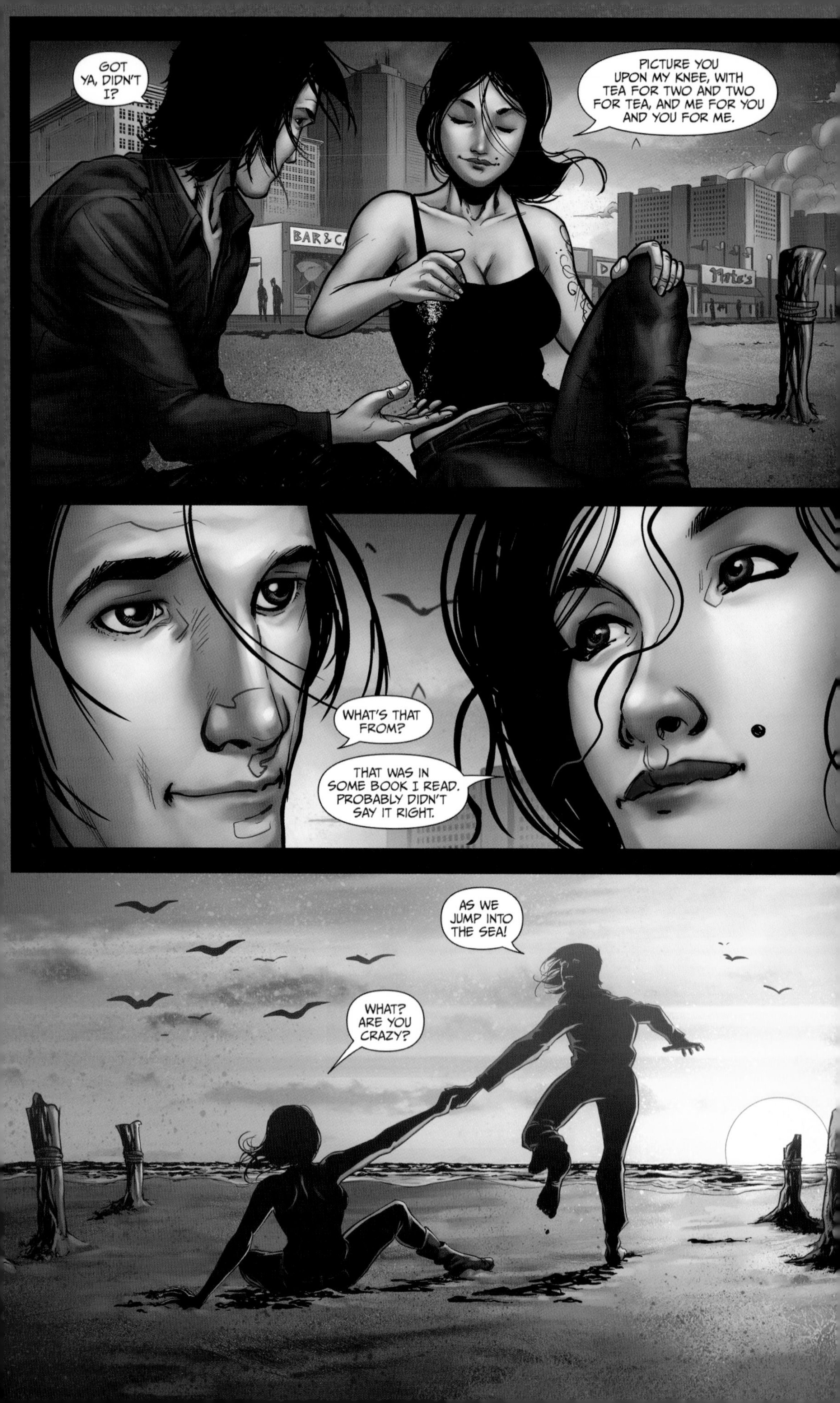
GOT YA, DIDN'T I?
PICTURE YOU UPON MY KNEE, WITH TEA FOR TWO AND TWO FOR TEA, AND ME FOR YOU AND YOU FOR ME.
BAR & CA
Nate's
WHAT'S THAT FROM?
THAT WAS IN SOME BOOK I READ. PROBABLY DIDN'T SAY IT RIGHT.
AS WE JUMP INTO THE SEA!
WHAT? ARE YOU CRAZY?

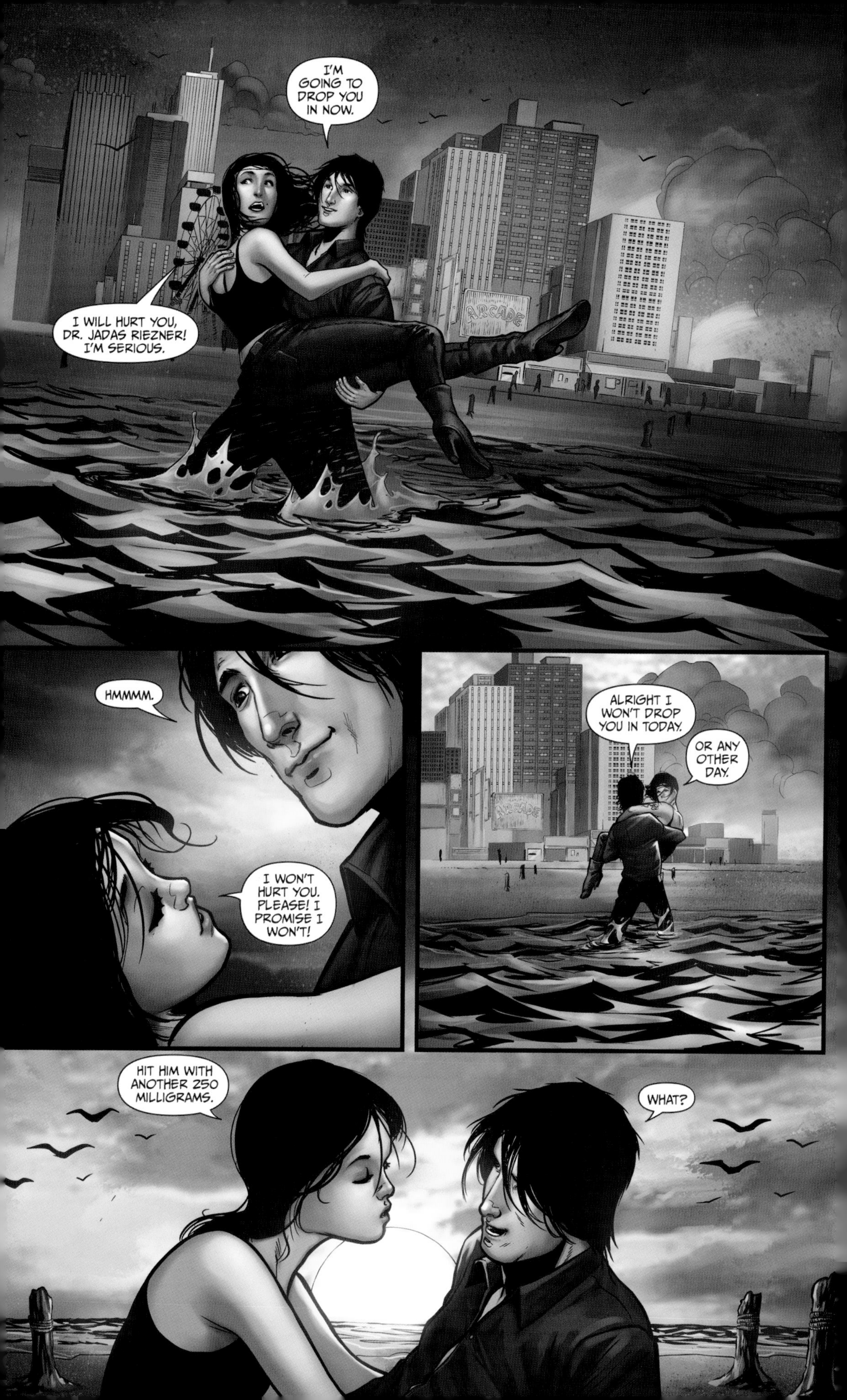
I'M GOING TO DROP YOU IN NOW.
I WILL HURT YOU, DR. JADAS RIEZNER! I'M SERIOUS.
ARCADE
HMMMM.
I WON'T HURT YOU. PLEASE! I PROMISE I WON'T!
ALRIGHT I WON'T DROP YOU IN TODAY.
OR ANY OTHER DAY.
ARCADE
HIT HIM WITH ANOTHER 250 MILLIGRAMS.
WHAT?

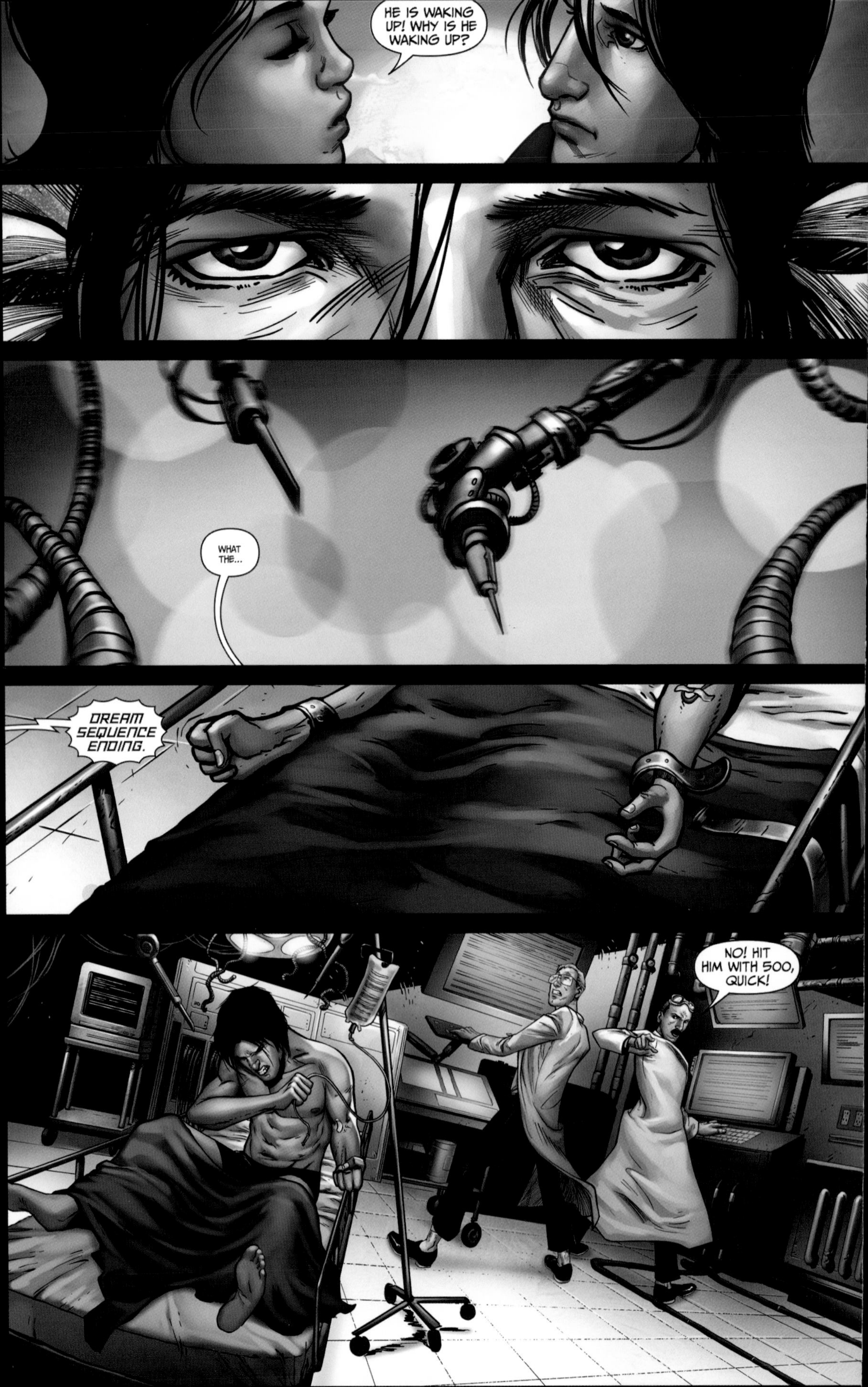
HE IS WAKING UP! WHY IS HE WAKING UP?
WHAT THE...
DREAM SEQUENCE ENDING.
NO! HIT HIM WITH 500, QUICK!

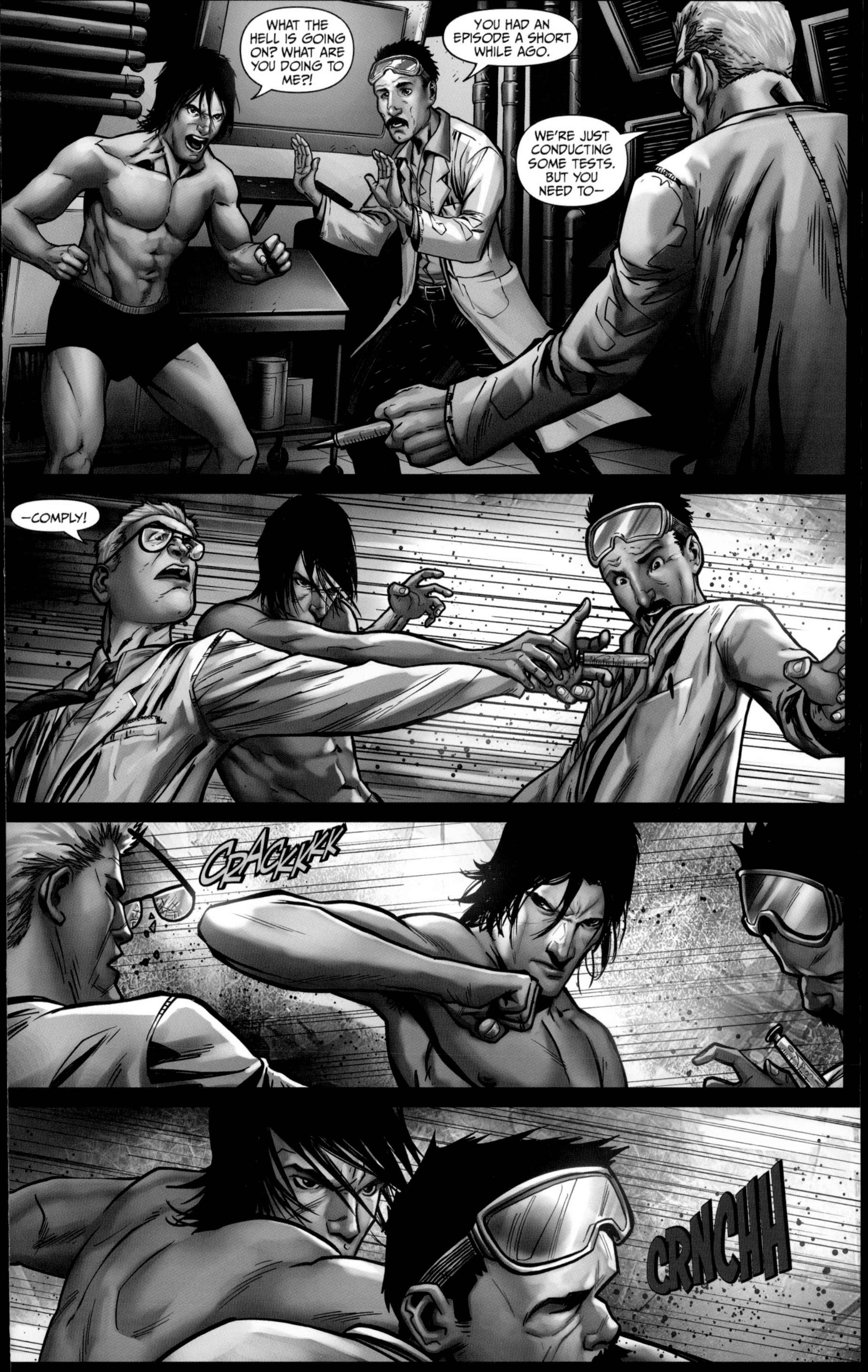
WHAT THE HELL IS GOING ON? WHAT ARE YOU DOING TO ME?!
YOU HAD AN EPISODE A SHORT WHILE AGO.
WE'RE JUST CONDUCTING SOME TESTS. BUT YOU NEED TO—
—COMPLY!
CRACKKKK
CRNCHH

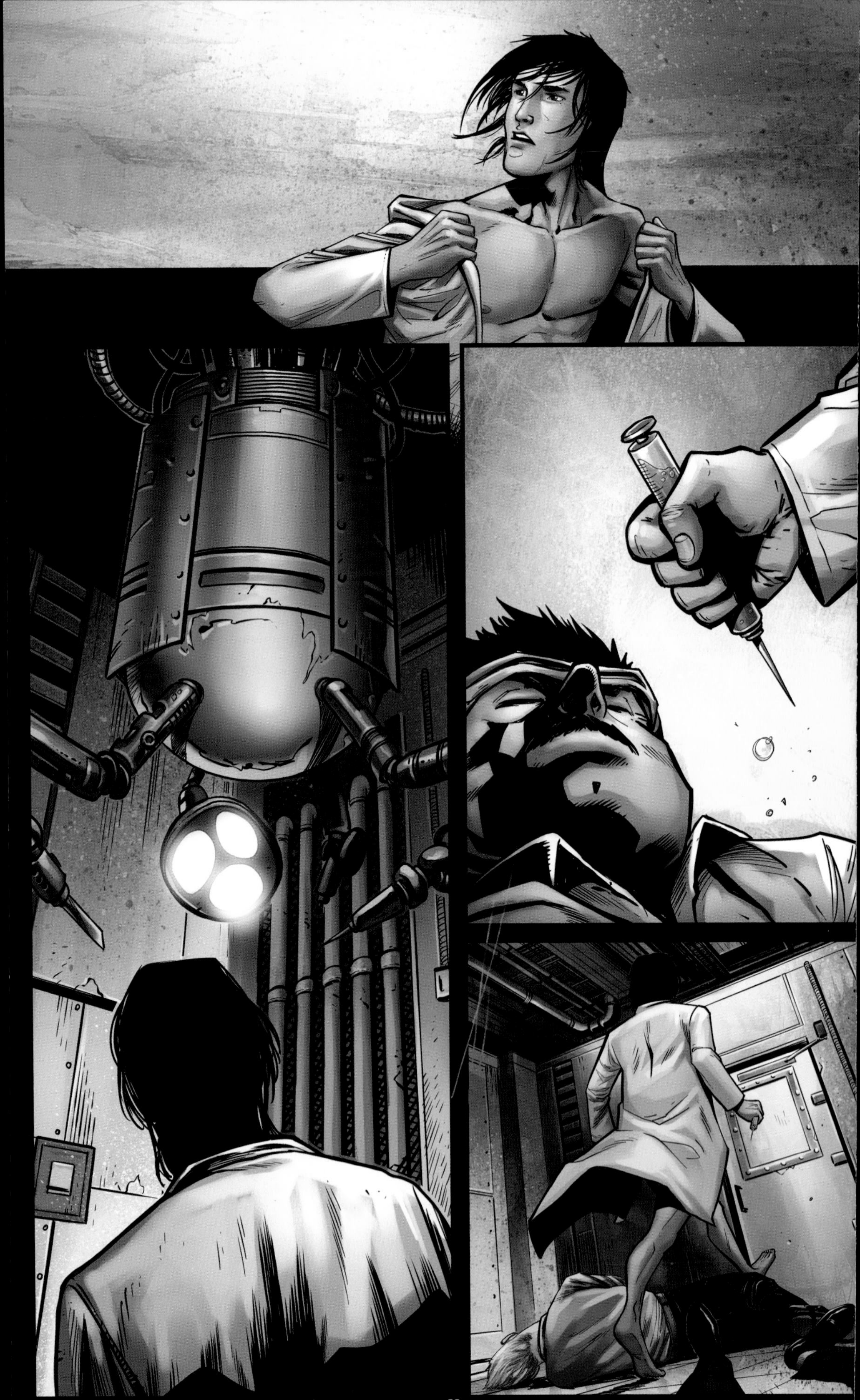

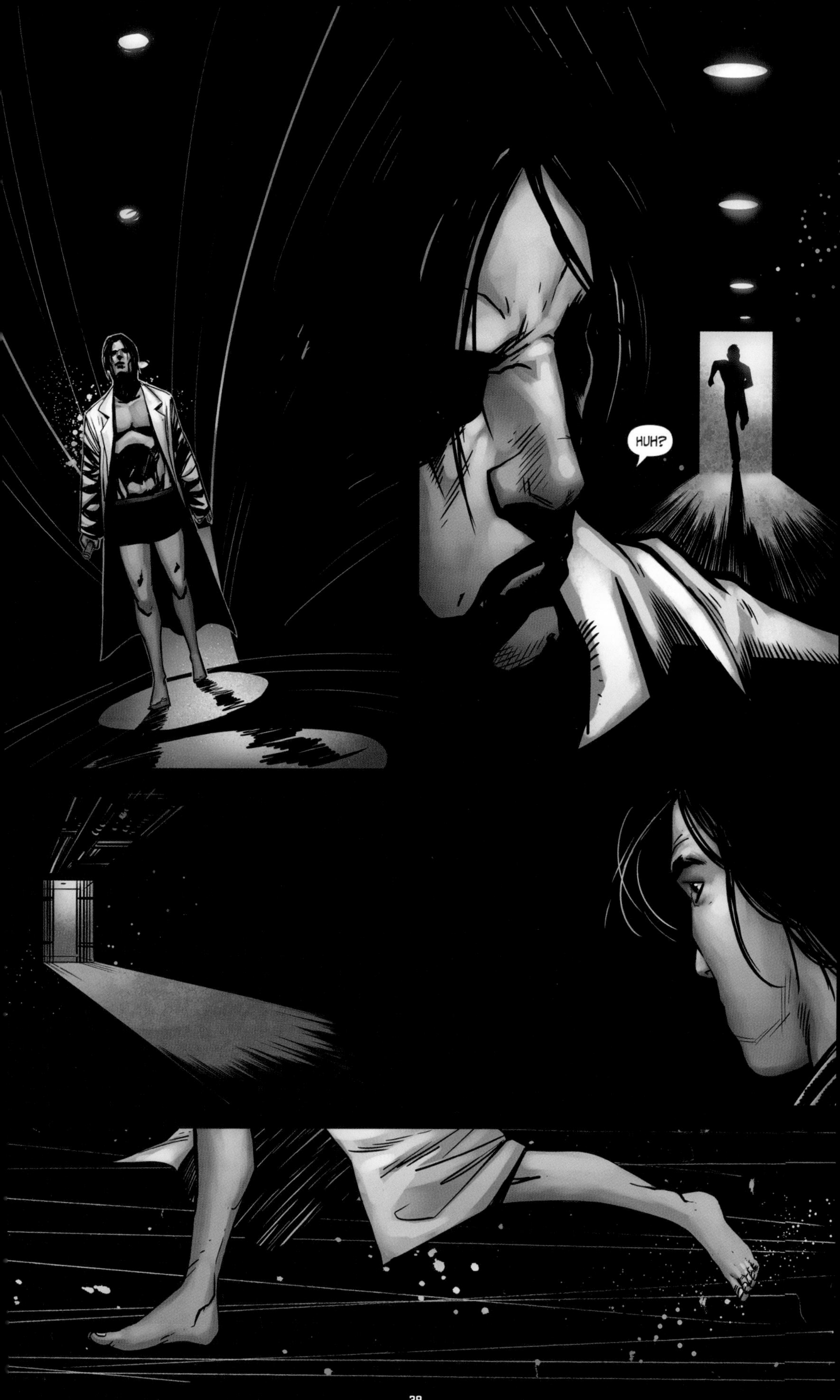
HUH?

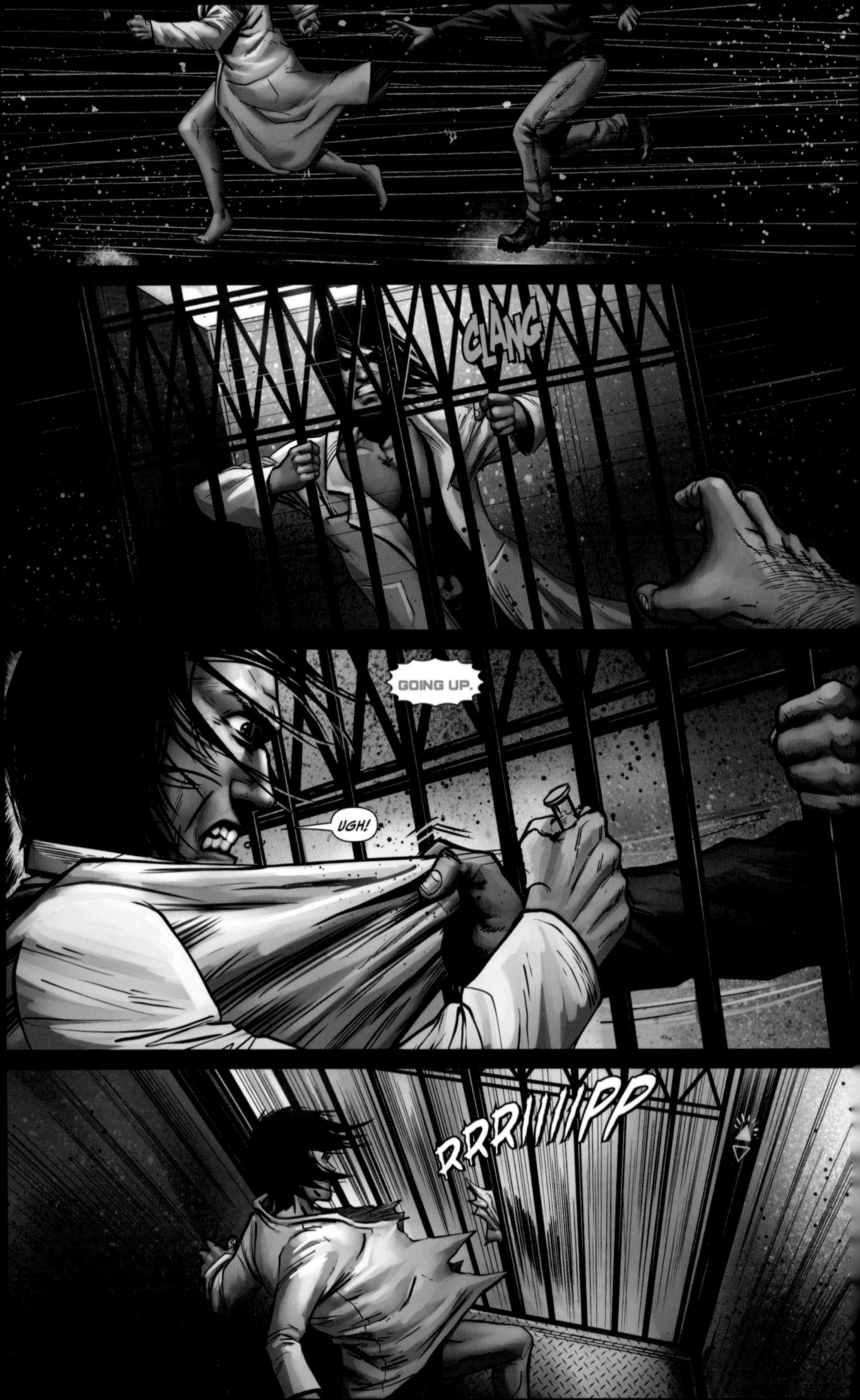
CLANG
GOING UP.
UGH!
RRRIIIIIPP

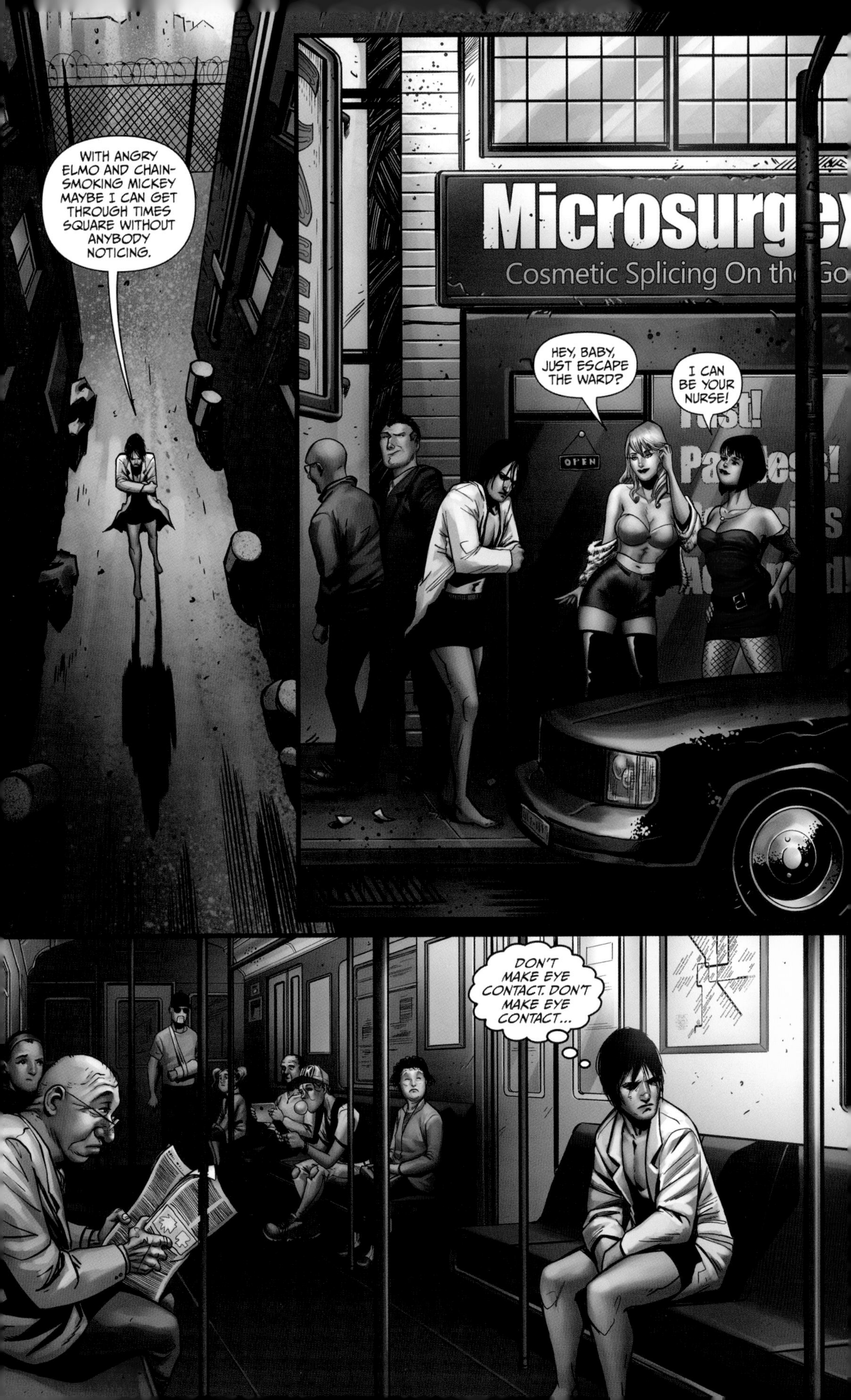
WITH ANGRY ELMO AND CHAIN-SMOKING MICKEY MAYBE I CAN GET THROUGH TIMES SQUARE WITHOUT ANYBODY NOTICING.
Microsurg
Cosmetic Splicing On th
OPEN
HEY, BABY, JUST ESCAPE THE WARD?
I CAN BE YOUR NURSE!
DON'T MAKE EYE CONTACT. DON'T MAKE EYE CONTACT...

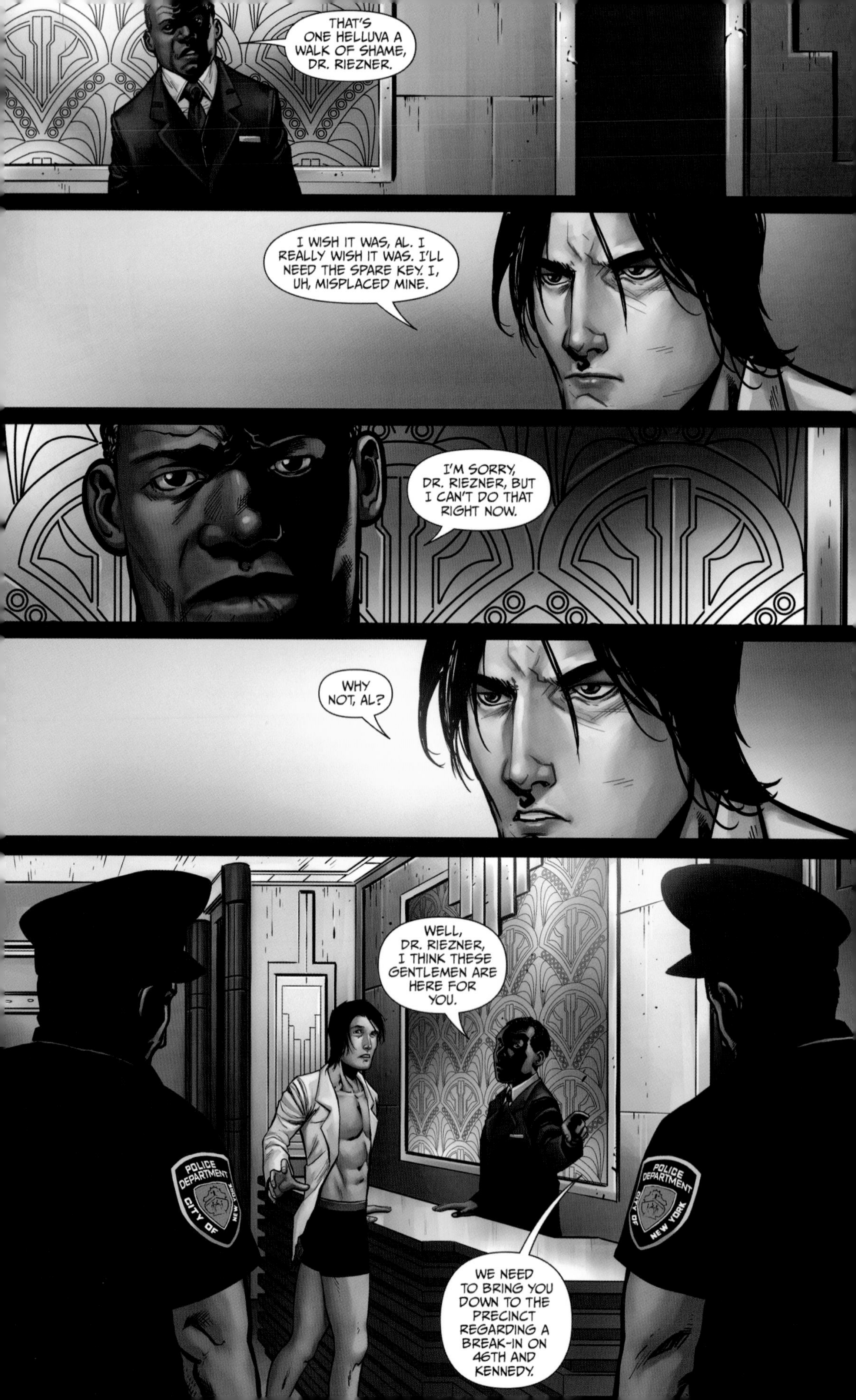
THAT'S ONE HELLUVA A WALK OF SHAME, DR. RIEZNER.
I WISH IT WAS, AL. I REALLY WISH IT WAS. I'LL NEED THE SPARE KEY. I, UH, MISPLACED MINE.
I'M SORRY, DR. RIEZNER, BUT I CAN'T DO THAT RIGHT NOW.
WHY NOT, AL?
WELL, DR. RIEZNER, I THINK THESE GENTLEMEN ARE HERE FOR YOU.
WE NEED TO BRING YOU DOWN TO THE PRECINCT REGARDING A BREAK-IN ON 46TH AND KENNEDY.
POLICE DEPARTMENT CITY OF NEW YORK

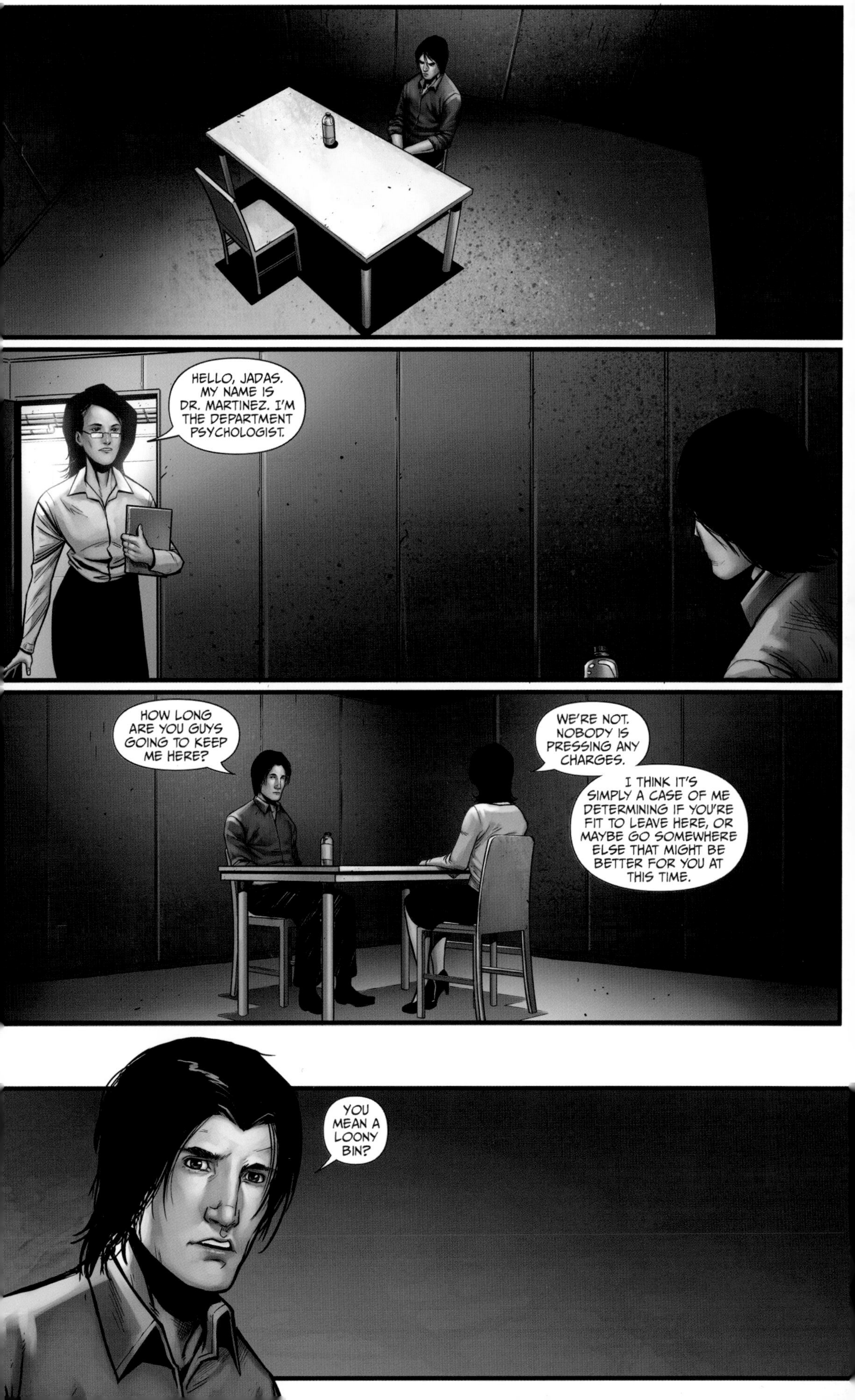
HELLO, JADAS. MY NAME IS DR. MARTINEZ. I'M THE DEPARTMENT PSYCHOLOGIST.
HOW LONG ARE YOU GUYS GOING TO KEEP ME HERE?
WE'RE NOT. NOBODY IS PRESSING ANY CHARGES.
I THINK IT'S SIMPLY A CASE OF ME DETERMINING IF YOU'RE FIT TO LEAVE HERE, OR MAYBE GO SOMEWHERE ELSE THAT MIGHT BE BETTER FOR YOU AT THIS TIME.
YOU MEAN A LOONY BIN?

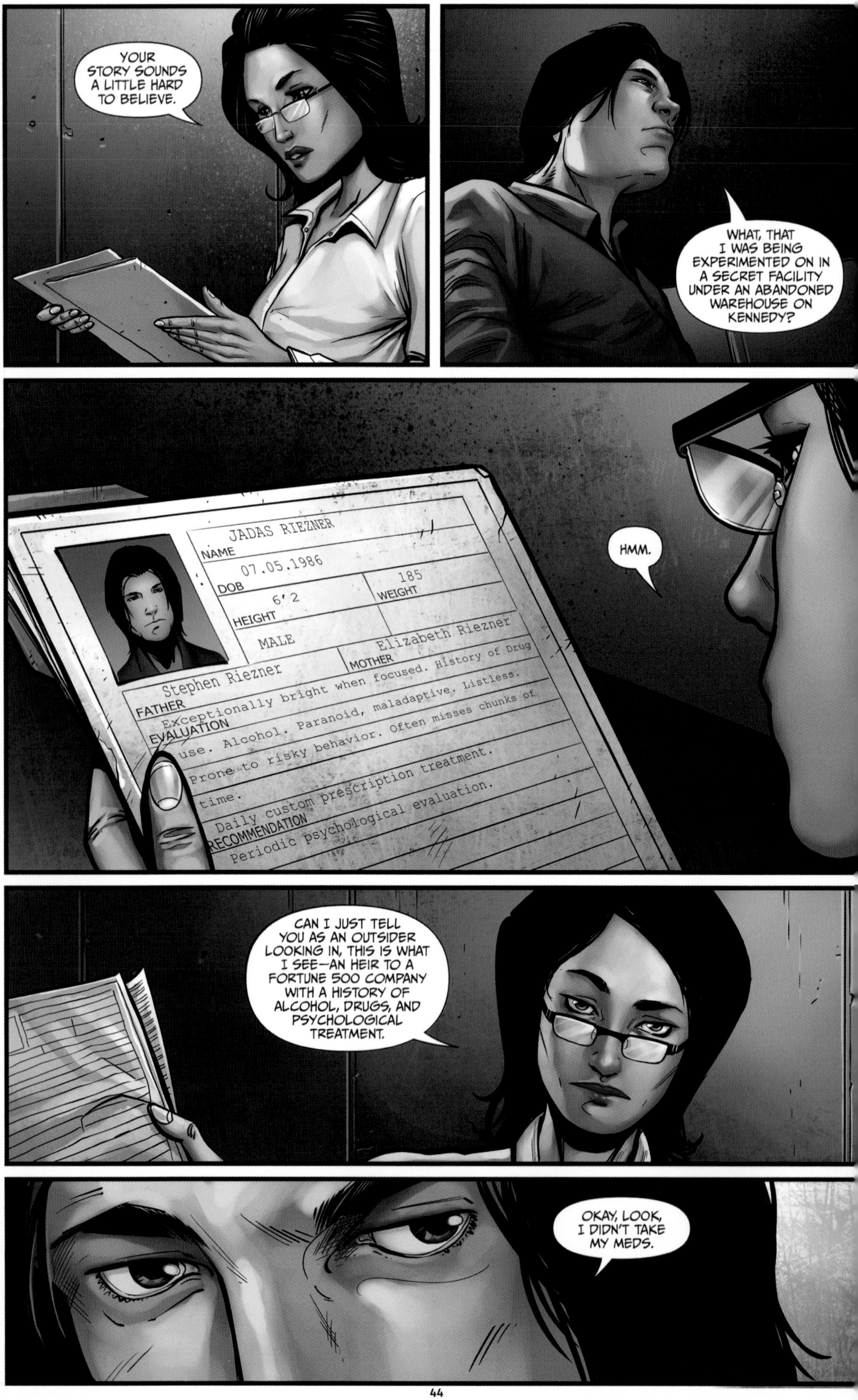
YOUR STORY SOUNDS A LITTLE HARD TO BELIEVE.
WHAT, THAT I WAS BEING EXPERIMENTED ON IN A SECRET FACILITY UNDER AN ABANDONED WAREHOUSE ON KENNEDY?
JADAS RIEZNER
NAME
07.05.1986
DOB
185
WEIGHT
6'2
HEIGHT
MALE
Elizabeth Riezner
MOTHER
Stephen Riezner
FATHER
Exceptionally bright when focused. History of Drug use. Alcohol. Paranoid, maladaptive. Listless. Prone to risky behavior. Often misses chunks of time.
EVALUATION
Daily custom prescription treatment. Periodic psychological evaluation.
RECOMMENDATION
HMM.
CAN I JUST TELL YOU AS AN OUTSIDER LOOKING IN, THIS IS WHAT I SEE—AN HEIR TO A FORTUNE 500 COMPANY WITH A HISTORY OF ALCOHOL, DRUGS, AND PSYCHOLOGICAL TREATMENT.
OKAY, LOOK, I DIDN'T TAKE MY MEDS.

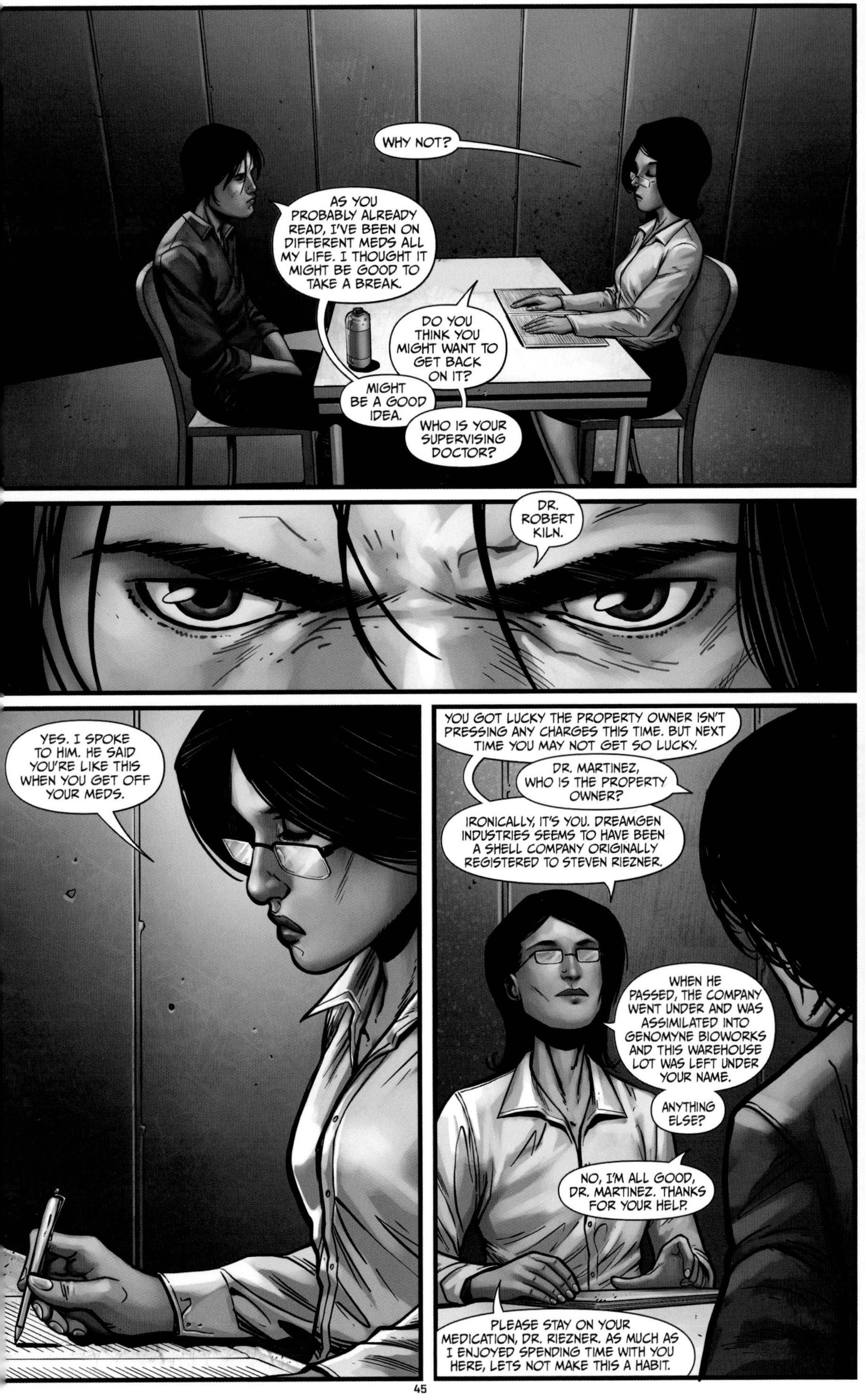
WHY NOT?
AS YOU PROBABLY ALREADY READ, I'VE BEEN ON DIFFERENT MEDS ALL MY LIFE. I THOUGHT IT MIGHT BE GOOD TO TAKE A BREAK.
DO YOU THINK YOU MIGHT WANT TO GET BACK ON IT?
MIGHT BE A GOOD IDEA.
WHO IS YOUR SUPERVISING DOCTOR?
DR. ROBERT KILN.
YES. I SPOKE TO HIM. HE SAID YOU'RE LIKE THIS WHEN YOU GET OFF YOUR MEDS.
YOU GOT LUCKY THE PROPERTY OWNER ISN'T PRESSING ANY CHARGES THIS TIME. BUT NEXT TIME YOU MAY NOT GET SO LUCKY.
DR. MARTINEZ, WHO IS THE PROPERTY OWNER?
IRONICALLY, IT'S YOU. DREAMGEN INDUSTRIES SEEMS TO HAVE BEEN A SHELL COMPANY ORIGINALLY REGISTERED TO STEVEN RIEZNER.
WHEN HE PASSED, THE COMPANY WENT UNDER AND WAS ASSIMILATED INTO GENOMYNE BIOWORKS AND THIS WAREHOUSE LOT WAS LEFT UNDER YOUR NAME.
ANYTHING ELSE?
NO, I'M ALL GOOD, DR. MARTINEZ. THANKS FOR YOUR HELP.
PLEASE STAY ON YOUR MEDICATION, DR. RIEZNER. AS MUCH AS I ENJOYED SPENDING TIME WITH YOU HERE, LETS NOT MAKE THIS A HABIT.

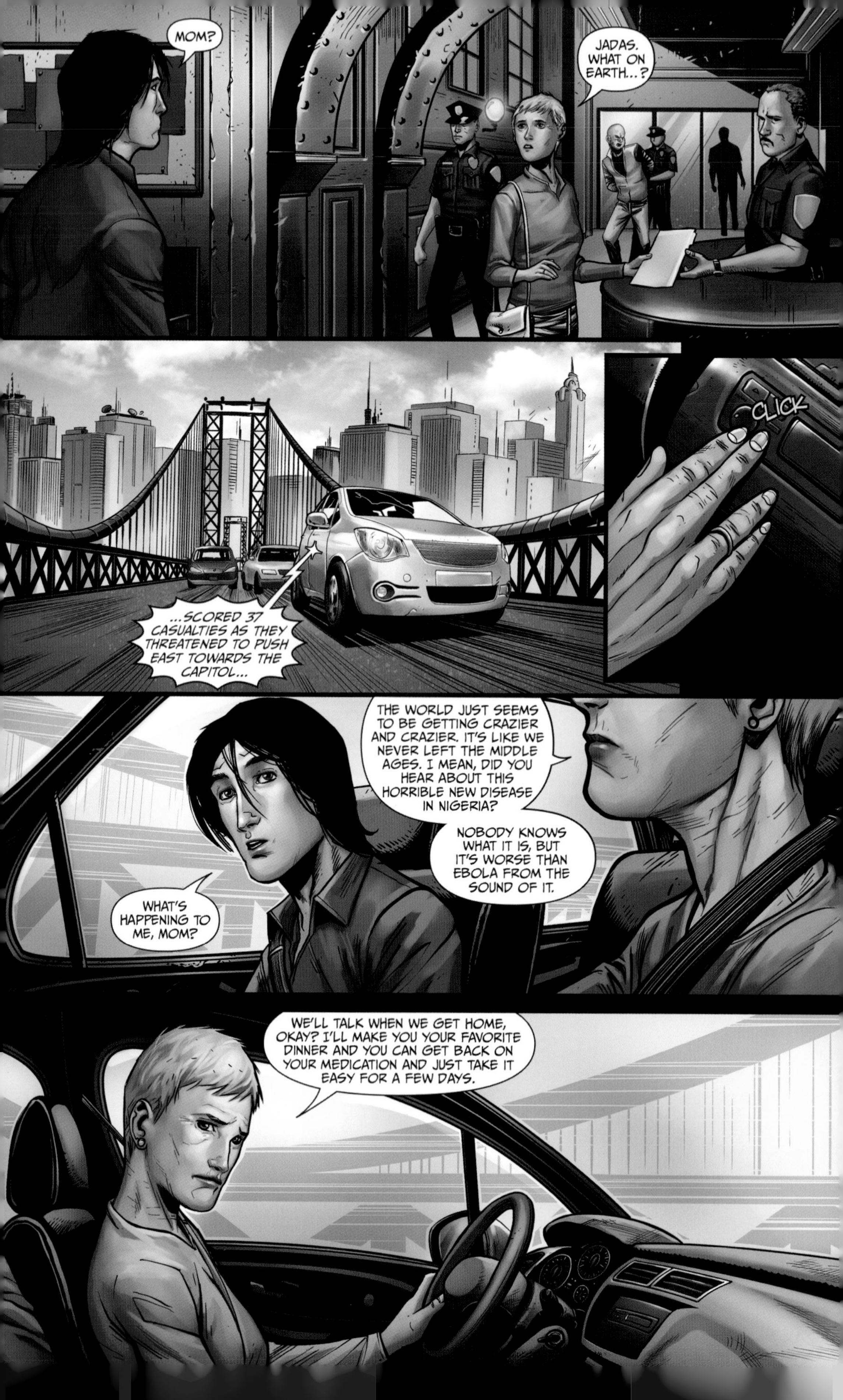
MOM?
JADAS. WHAT ON EARTH...?
CLICK
...SCORED 37 CASUALTIES AS THEY THREATENED TO PUSH EAST TOWARDS THE CAPITOL...
THE WORLD JUST SEEMS TO BE GETTING CRAZIER AND CRAZIER. IT'S LIKE WE NEVER LEFT THE MIDDLE AGES. I MEAN, DID YOU HEAR ABOUT THIS HORRIBLE NEW DISEASE IN NIGERIA?
NOBODY KNOWS WHAT IT IS, BUT IT'S WORSE THAN EBOLA FROM THE SOUND OF IT.
WHAT'S HAPPENING TO ME, MOM?
WE'LL TALK WHEN WE GET HOME, OKAY? I'LL MAKE YOU YOUR FAVORITE DINNER AND YOU CAN GET BACK ON YOUR MEDICATION AND JUST TAKE IT EASY FOR A FEW DAYS.

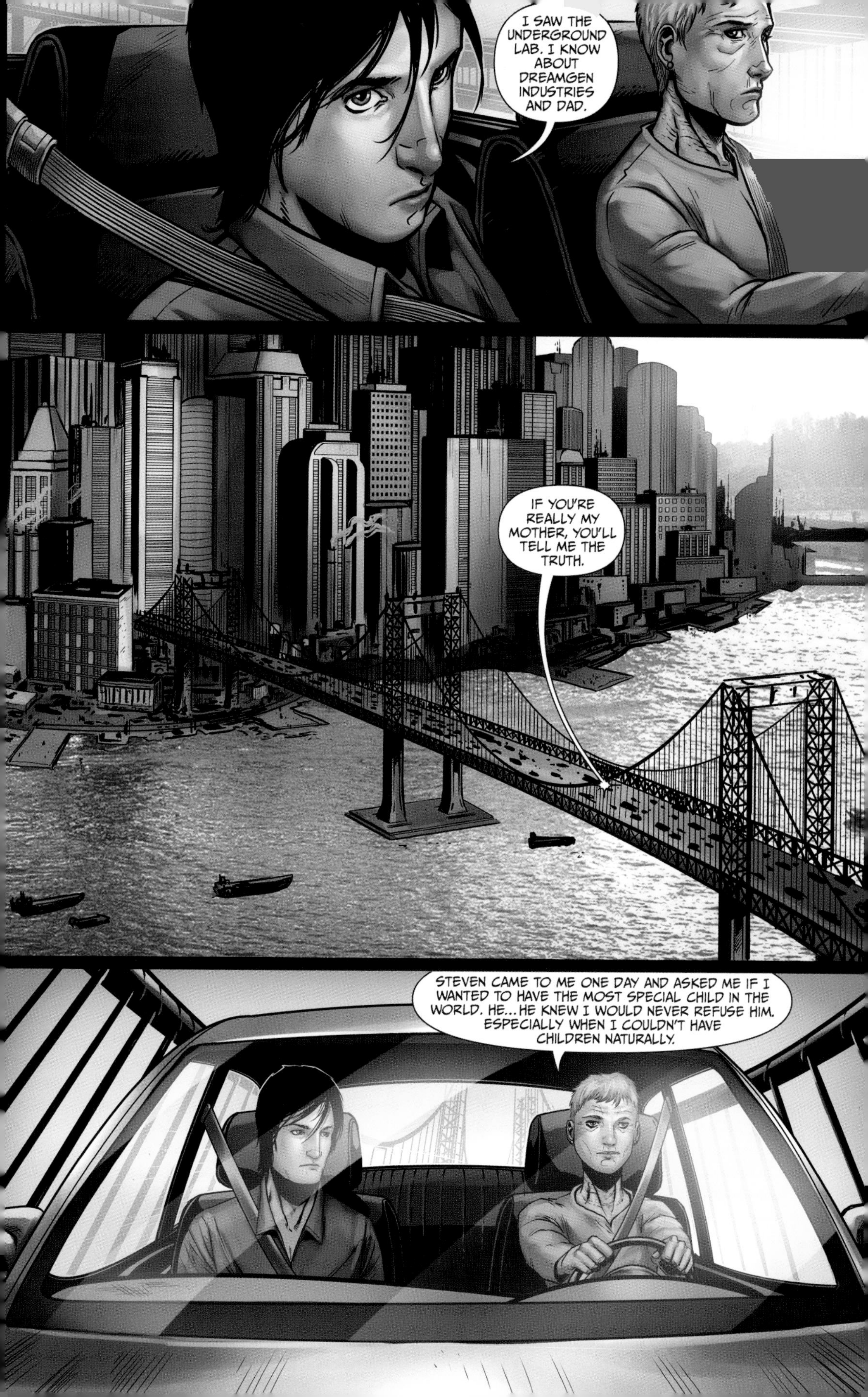
I SAW THE UNDERGROUND LAB. I KNOW ABOUT DREAMGEN INDUSTRIES AND DAD.
IF YOU'RE REALLY MY MOTHER, YOU'LL TELL ME THE TRUTH.
STEVEN CAME TO ME ONE DAY AND ASKED ME IF I WANTED TO HAVE THE MOST SPECIAL CHILD IN THE WORLD. HE... HE KNEW I WOULD NEVER REFUSE HIM. ESPECIALLY WHEN I COULDN'T HAVE CHILDREN NATURALLY.

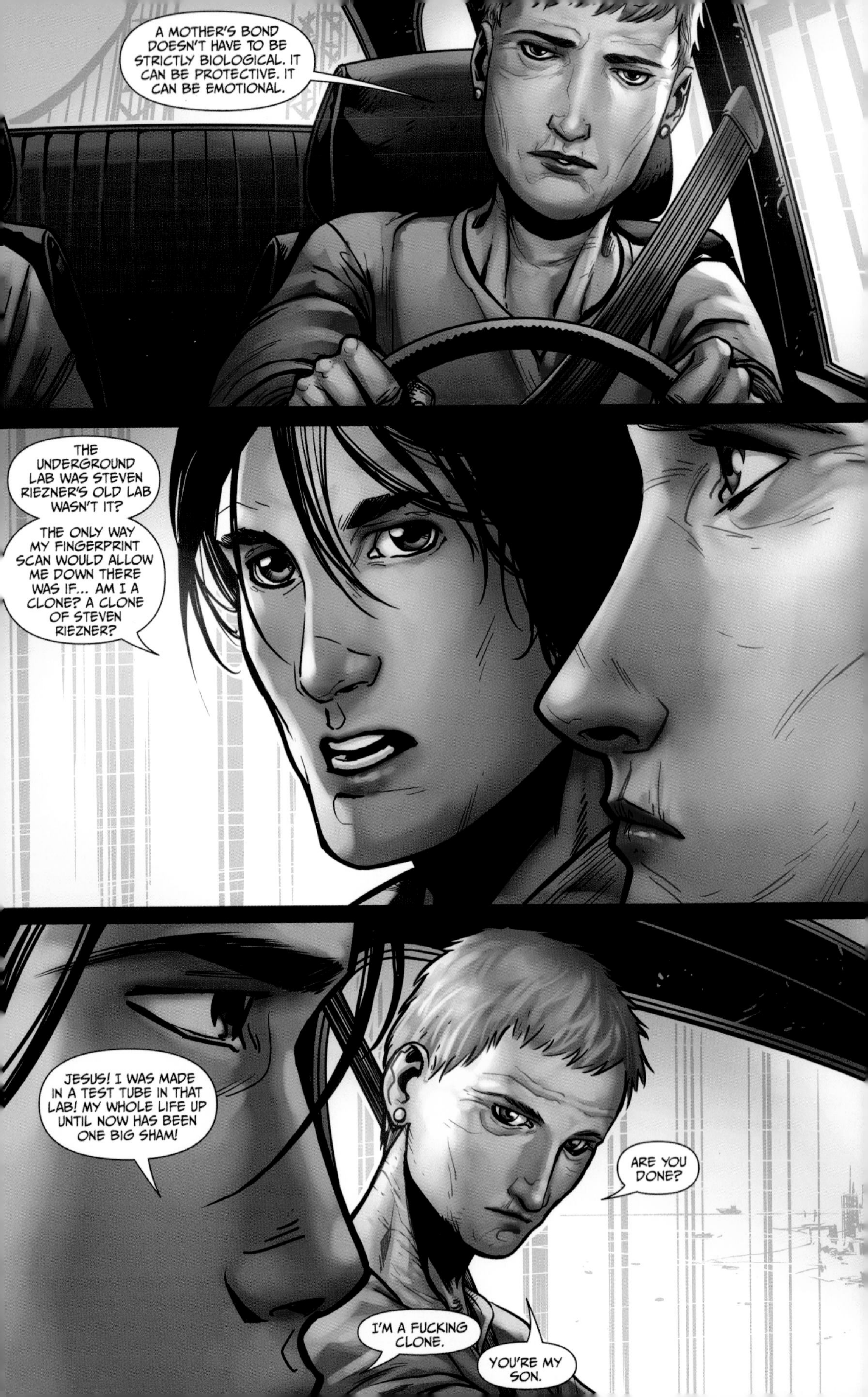
A MOTHER'S BOND DOESN'T HAVE TO BE STRICTLY BIOLOGICAL. IT CAN BE PROTECTIVE. IT CAN BE EMOTIONAL.
THE UNDERGROUND LAB WAS STEVEN RIEZNER'S OLD LAB WASN'T IT?
THE ONLY WAY MY FINGERPRINT SCAN WOULD ALLOW ME DOWN THERE WAS IF... AM I A CLONE? A CLONE OF STEVEN RIEZNER?
JESUS! I WAS MADE IN A TEST TUBE IN THAT LAB! MY WHOLE LIFE UP UNTIL NOW HAS BEEN ONE BIG SHAM!
ARE YOU DONE?
I'M A FUCKING CLONE.
YOU'RE MY SON.

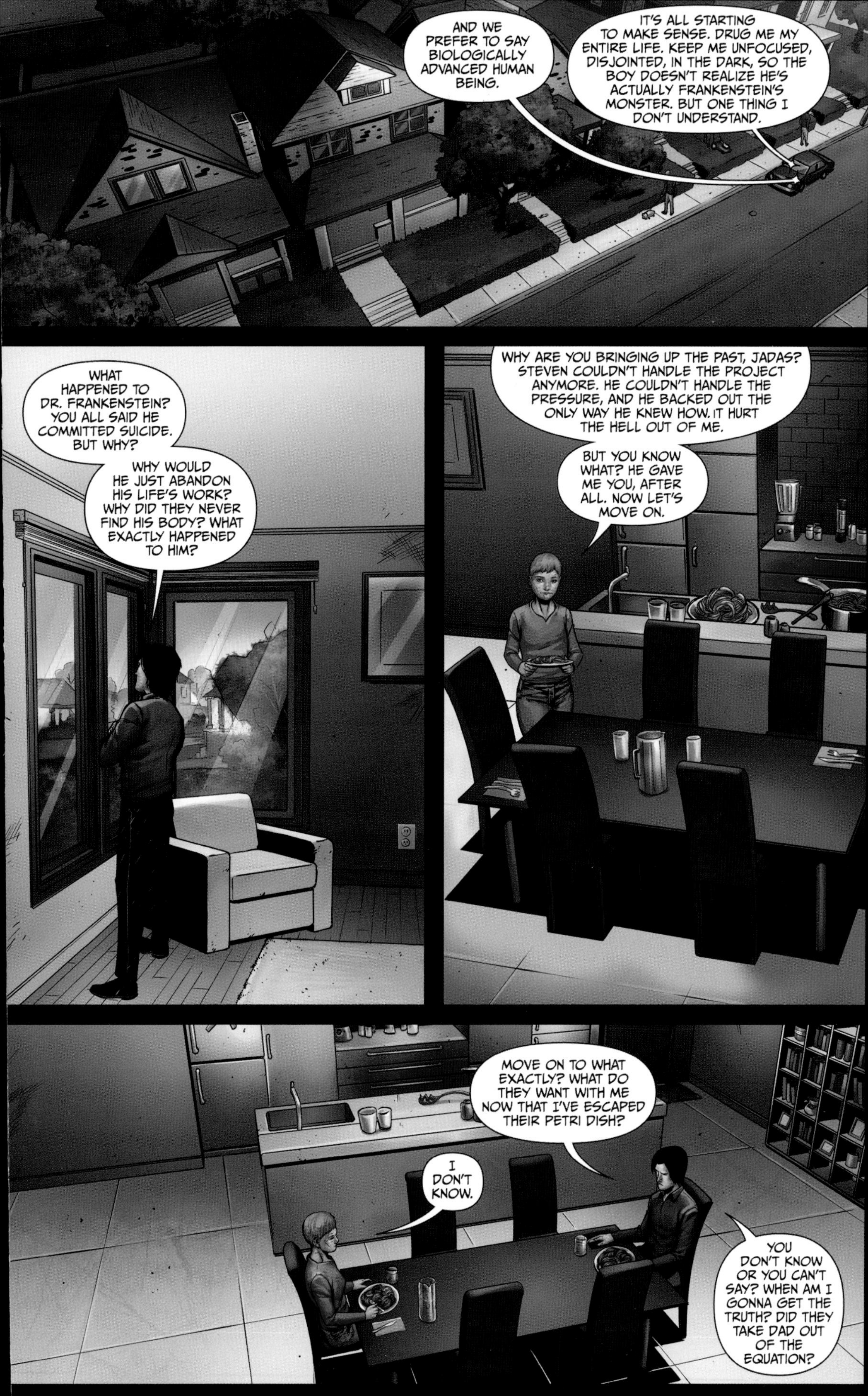
IT'S ALL STARTING TO MAKE SENSE. DRUG ME MY ENTIRE LIFE. KEEP ME UNFOCUSED, DISJOINTED, IN THE DARK, SO THE BOY DOESN'T REALIZE HE'S ACTUALLY FRANKENSTEIN'S MONSTER. BUT ONE THING I DON'T UNDERSTAND.
AND WE PREFER TO SAY BIOLOGICALLY ADVANCED HUMAN BEING.
WHAT HAPPENED TO DR. FRANKENSTEIN? YOU ALL SAID HE COMMITTED SUICIDE. BUT WHY?
WHY WOULD HE JUST ABANDON HIS LIFE'S WORK? WHY DID THEY NEVER FIND HIS BODY? WHAT EXACTLY HAPPENED TO HIM?
WHY ARE YOU BRINGING UP THE PAST, JADAS? STEVEN COULDN'T HANDLE THE PROJECT ANYMORE. HE COULDN'T HANDLE THE PRESSURE, AND HE BACKED OUT THE ONLY WAY HE KNEW HOW. IT HURT THE HELL OUT OF ME.
BUT YOU KNOW WHAT? HE GAVE ME YOU, AFTER ALL. NOW LET'S MOVE ON.
MOVE ON TO WHAT EXACTLY? WHAT DO THEY WANT WITH ME NOW THAT I'VE ESCAPED THEIR PETRI DISH?
I DON'T KNOW.
YOU DON'T KNOW OR YOU CAN'T SAY? WHEN AM I GONNA GET THE TRUTH? DID THEY TAKE DAD OUT OF THE EQUATION?

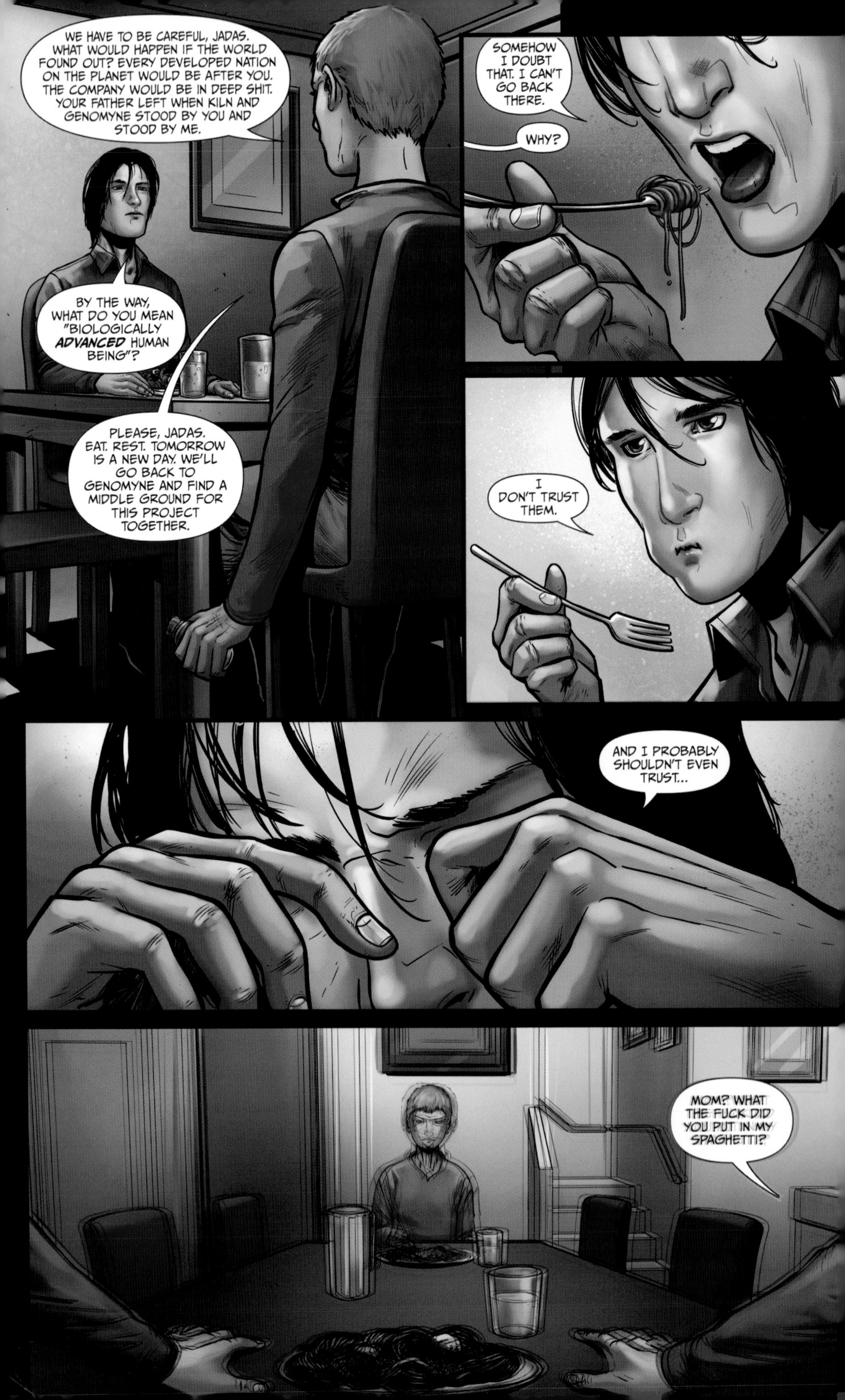
WE HAVE TO BE CAREFUL, JADAS. WHAT WOULD HAPPEN IF THE WORLD FOUND OUT? EVERY DEVELOPED NATION ON THE PLANET WOULD BE AFTER YOU. THE COMPANY WOULD BE IN DEEP SHIT. YOUR FATHER LEFT WHEN KILN AND GENOMYNE STOOD BY YOU AND STOOD BY ME.
BY THE WAY, WHAT DO YOU MEAN "BIOLOGICALLY ADVANCED HUMAN BEING"?
PLEASE, JADAS. EAT. REST. TOMORROW IS A NEW DAY. WE'LL GO BACK TO GENOMYNE AND FIND A MIDDLE GROUND FOR THIS PROJECT TOGETHER.
SOMEHOW I DOUBT THAT. I CAN'T GO BACK THERE.
WHY?
I DON'T TRUST THEM.
AND I PROBABLY SHOULDN'T EVEN TRUST...
MOM? WHAT THE FUCK DID YOU PUT IN MY SPAGHETTI?

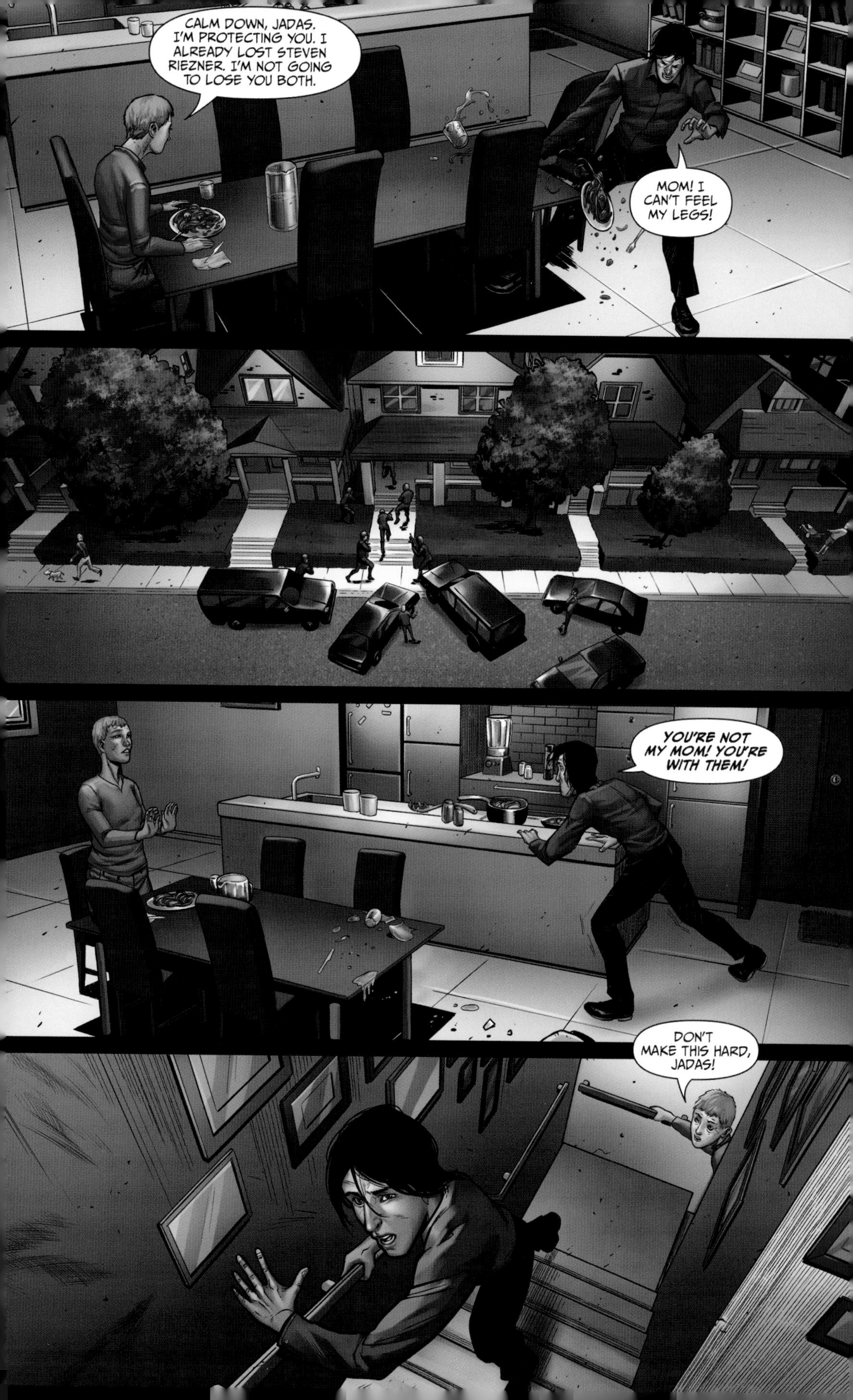
CALM DOWN, JADAS. I'M PROTECTING YOU. I ALREADY LOST STEVEN RIEZNER. I'M NOT GOING TO LOSE YOU BOTH.
MOM! I CAN'T FEEL MY LEGS!
YOU'RE NOT MY MOM! YOU'RE WITH THEM!
DON'T MAKE THIS HARD, JADAS!

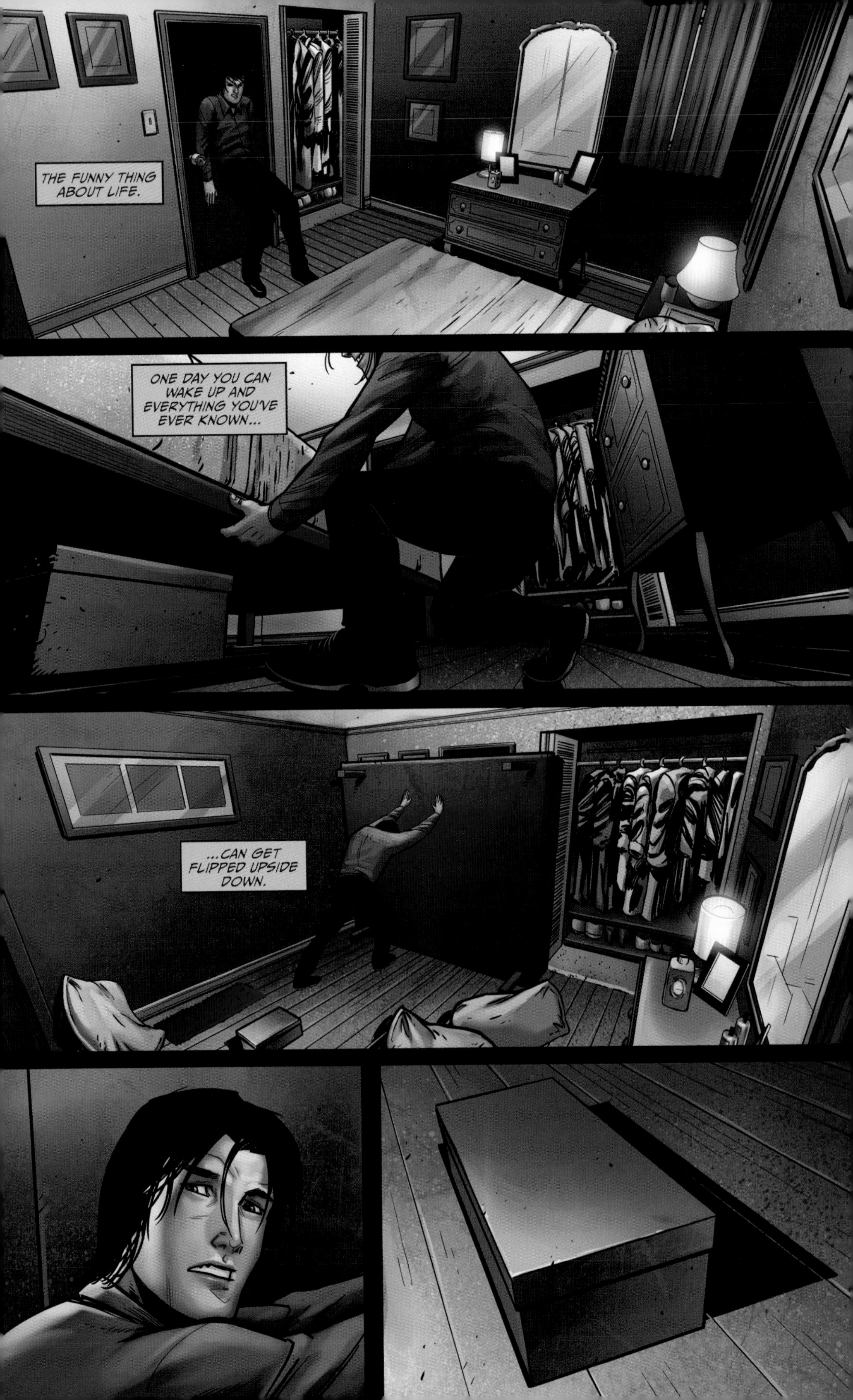
THE FUNNY THING ABOUT LIFE.
ONE DAY YOU CAN WAKE UP AND EVERYTHING YOU'VE EVER KNOWN...
...CAN GET FLIPPED UPSIDE DOWN.

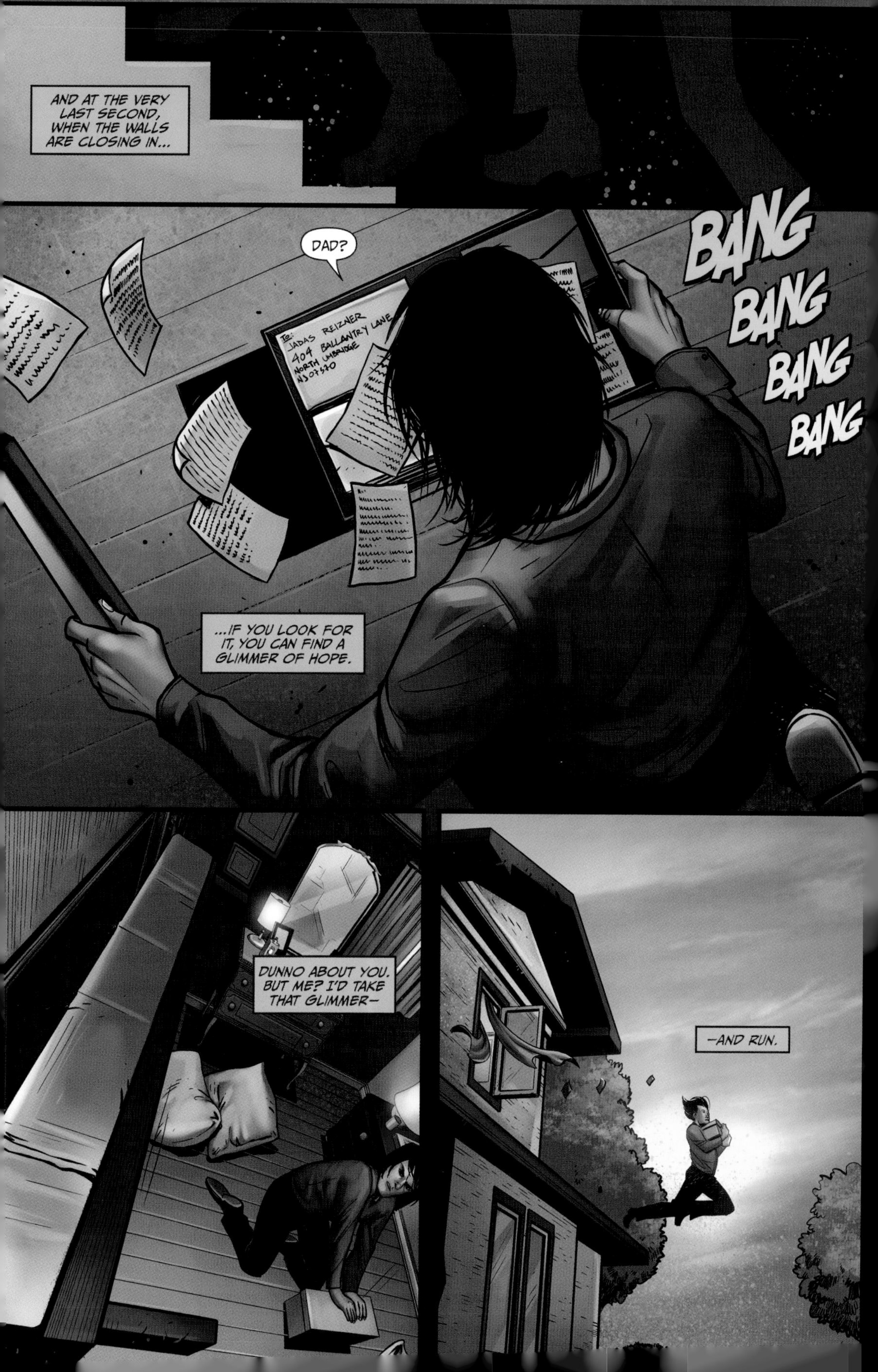
AND AT THE VERY LAST SECOND, WHEN THE WALLS ARE CLOSING IN...
DAD?
To: JADAS REIZNER
404 BALLANTRY LANE
NORTH UMBRIDGE
NJ07320
BANG
BANG
BANG
BANG
...IF YOU LOOK FOR IT, YOU CAN FIND A GLIMMER OF HOPE.
DUNNO ABOUT YOU. BUT ME? I'D TAKE THAT GLIMMER—
—AND RUN.

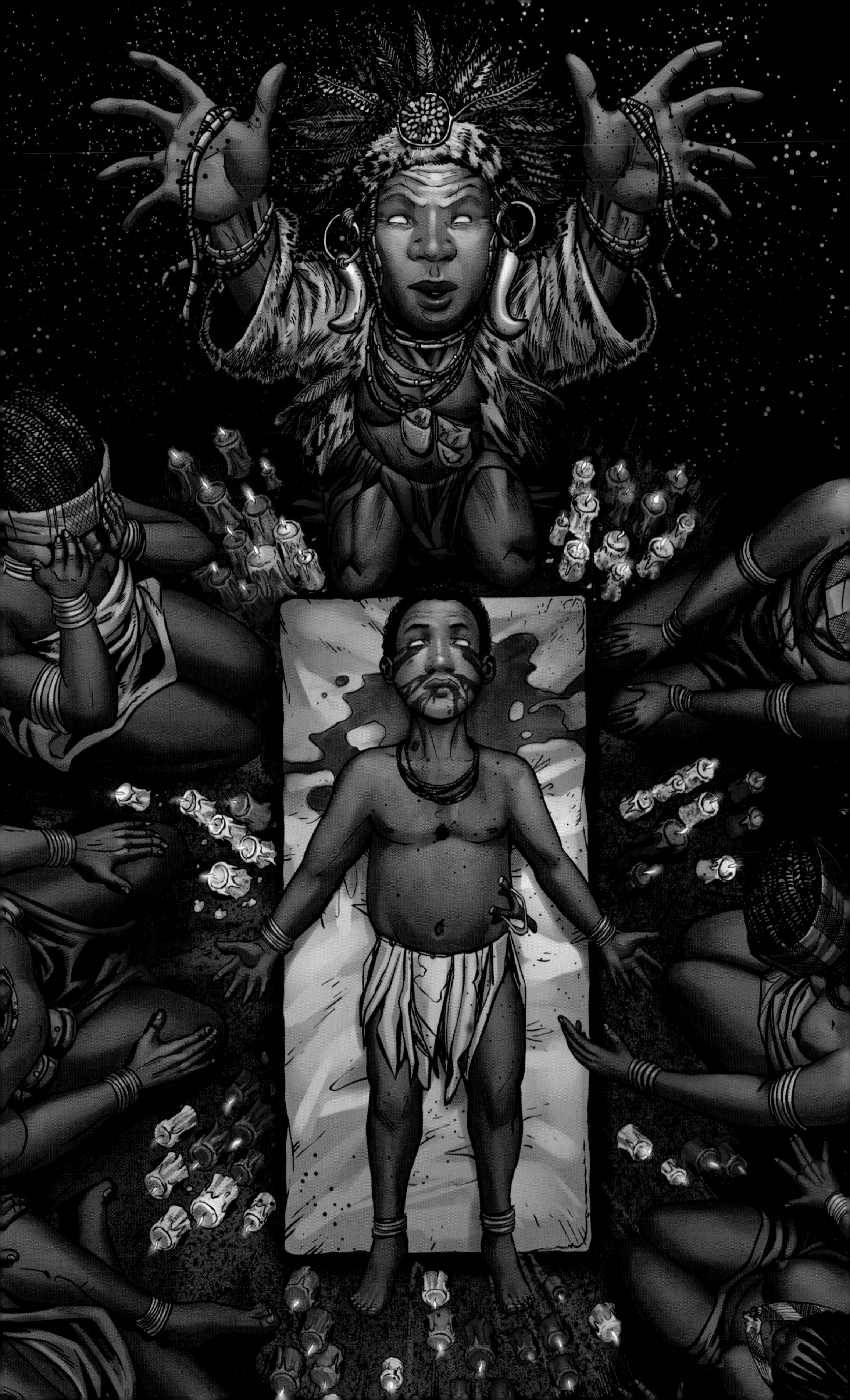

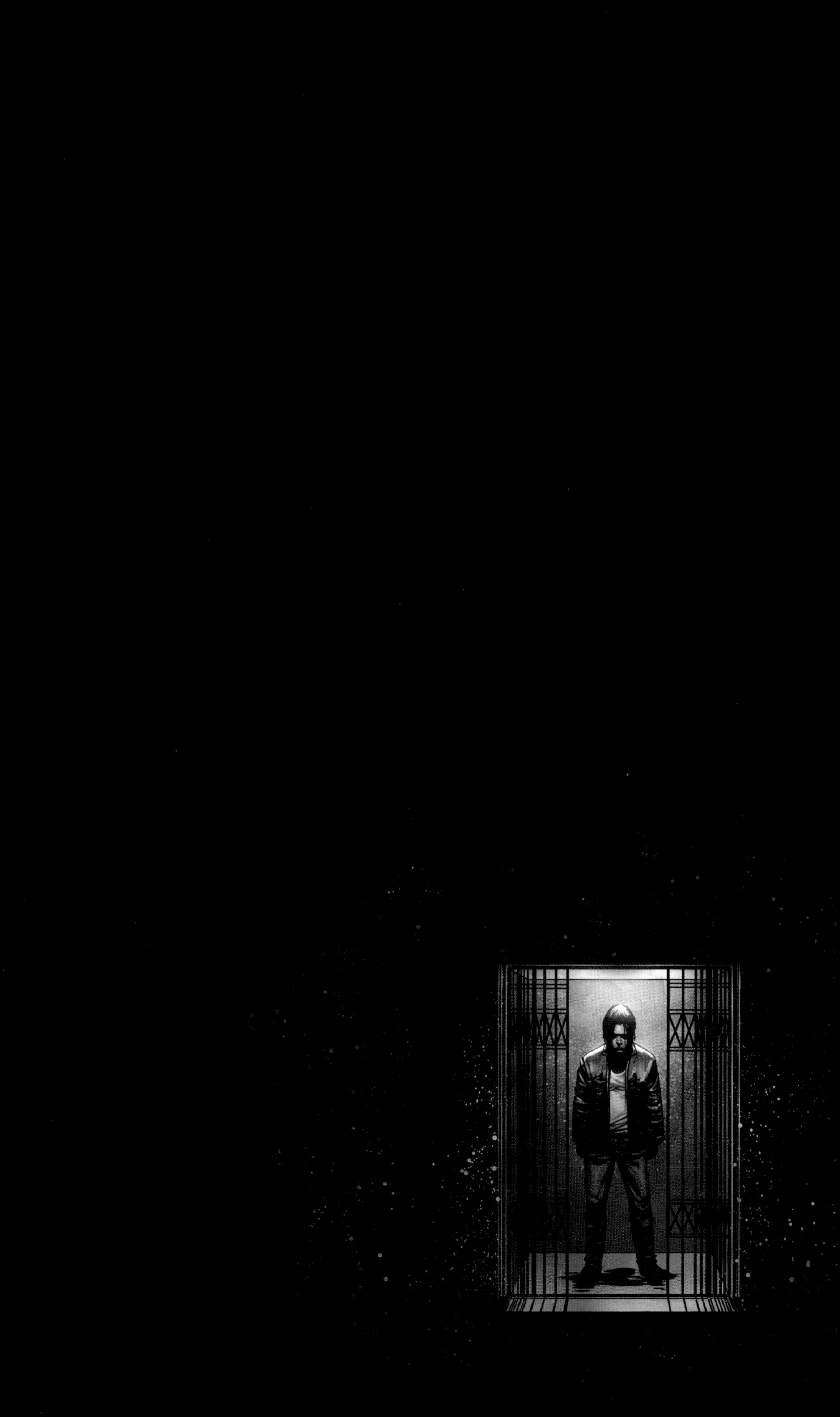

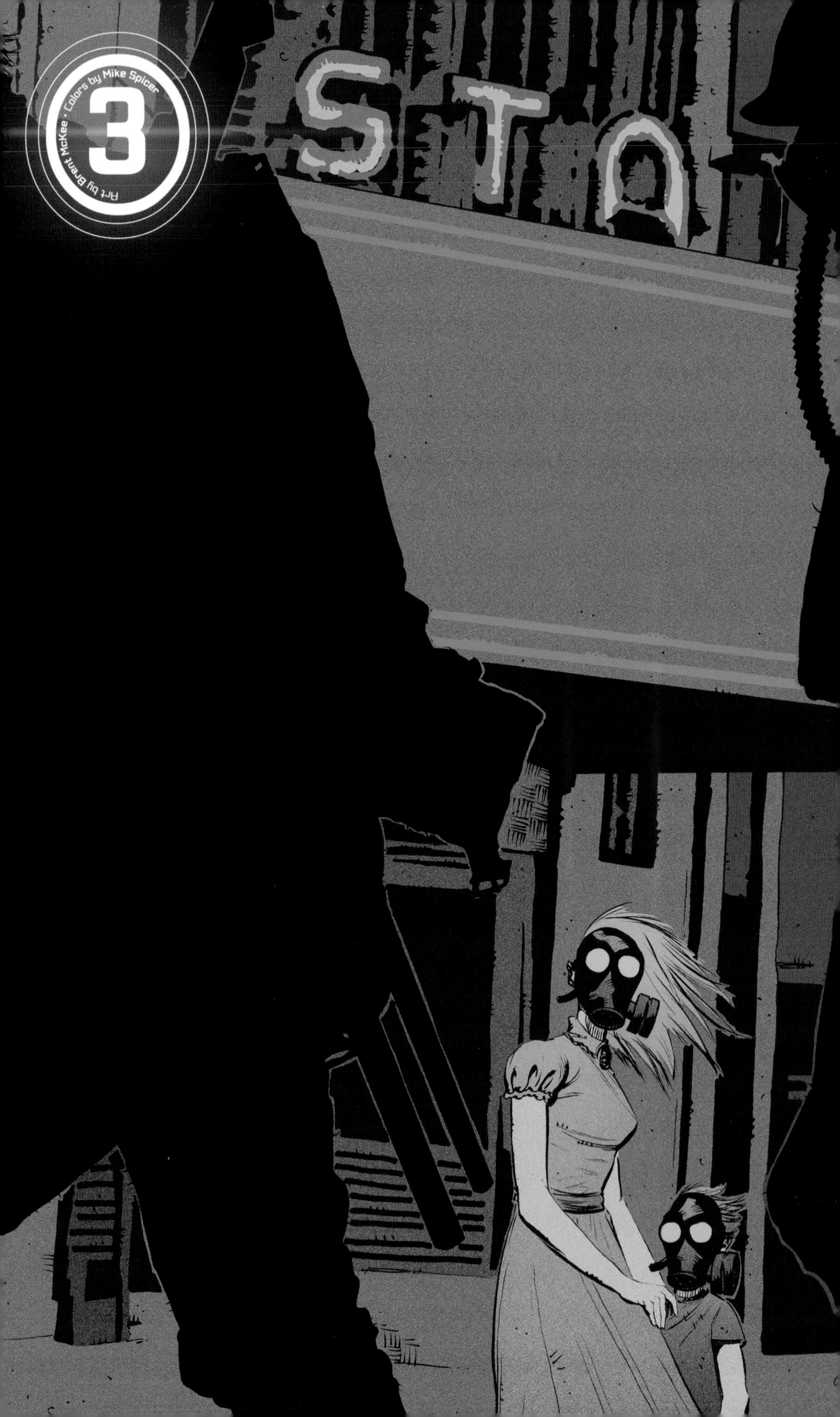
3
Art by Brent McKee • Colors by Mike Spicer
STO

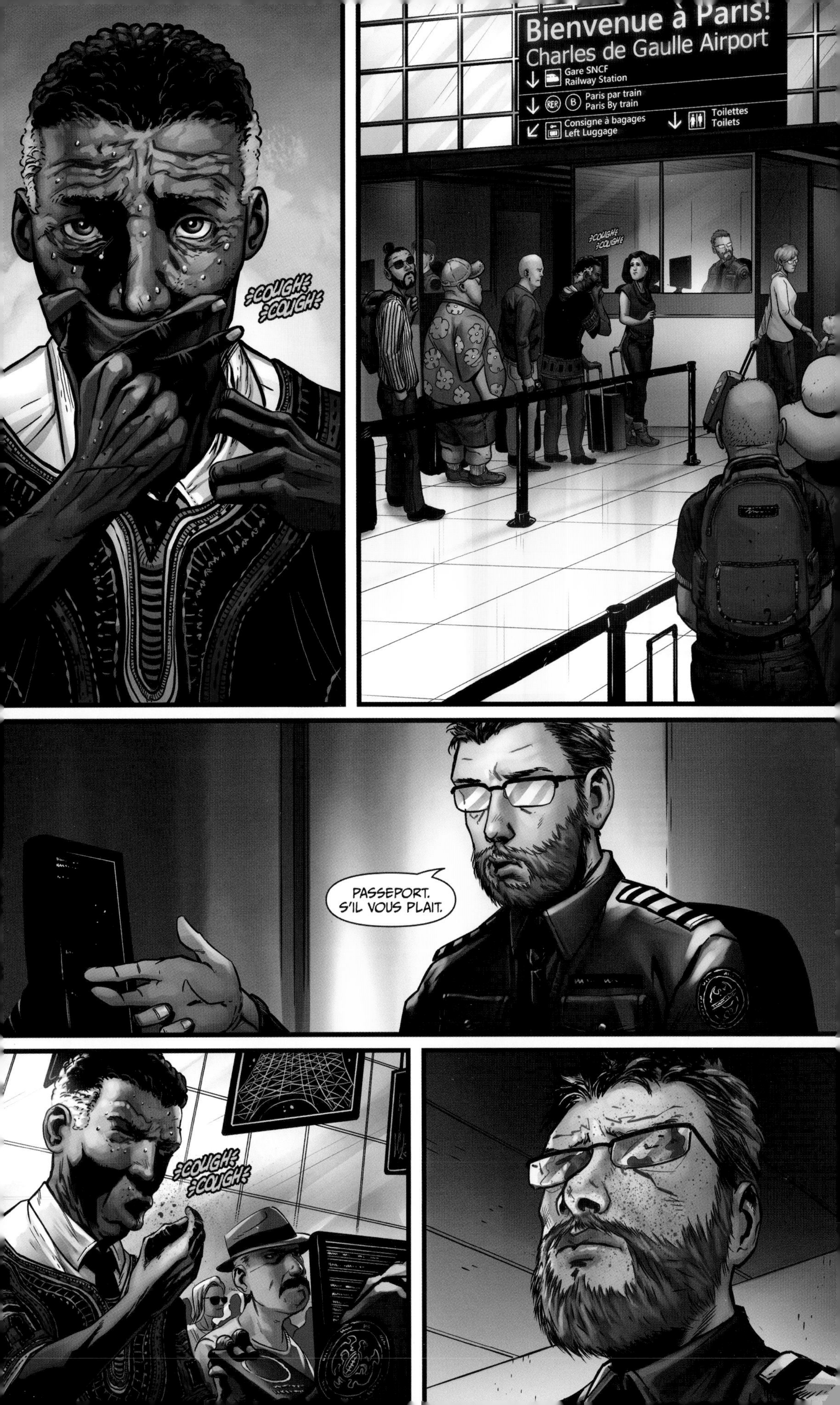
COUGH COUGH
Bienvenue à Paris!
Charles de Gaulle Airport
Gare SNCF
Railway Station
Paris par train
Paris By train
Consigne à bagages
Left Luggage
Toilettes
Toilets
COUGH COUGH
PASSEPORT. S'IL VOUS PLAIT.
COUGH COUGH

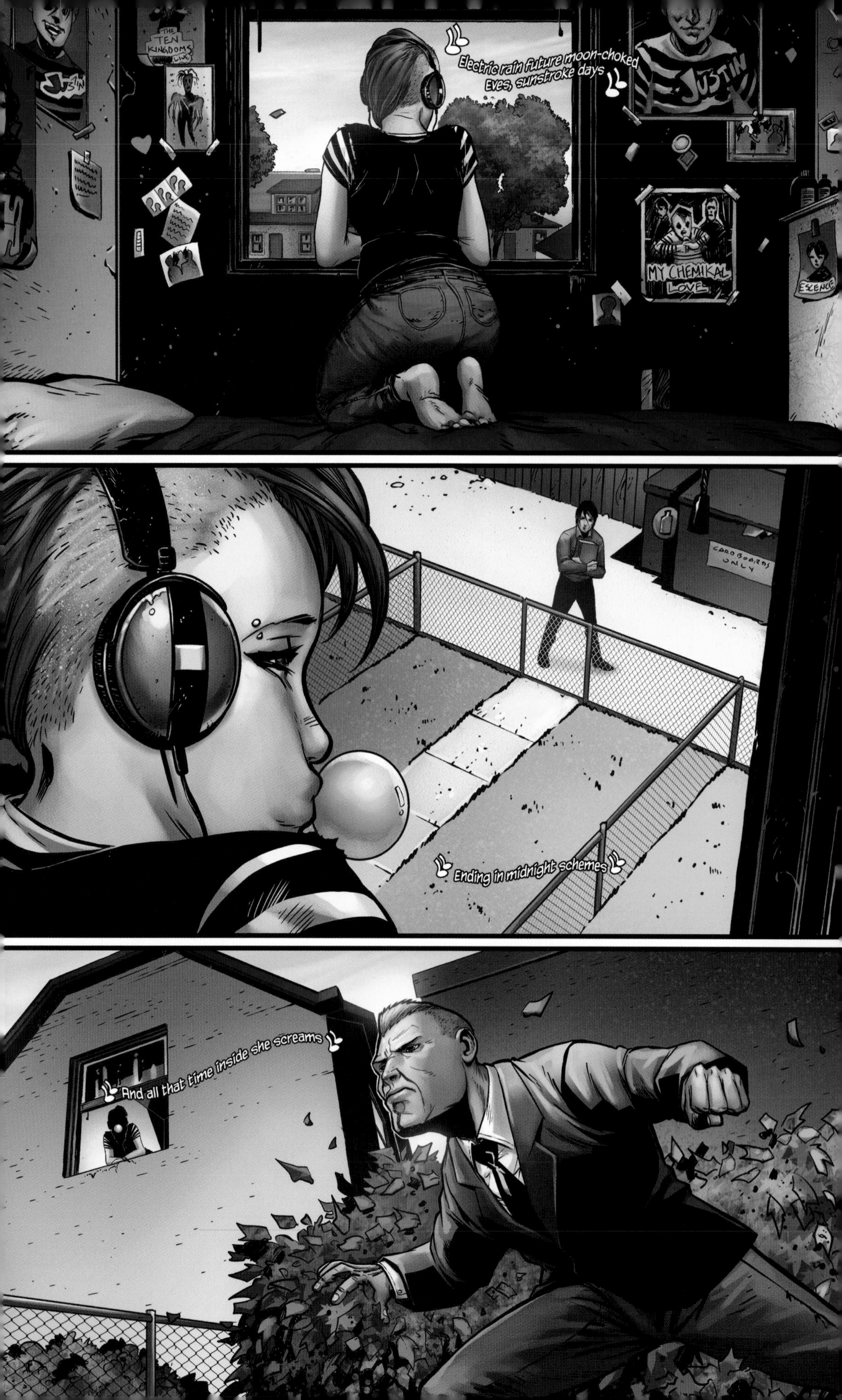
THE TEN KINGDOMS LIVE
JUSTIN
Electric rain future moon-choked
Eves, sunstroke days
MY CHEMIKAL LOVE
ESCENCE
CARDBOARDS ONLY
Ending in midnight schemes
All that time inside she screams
And all that time inside she screams

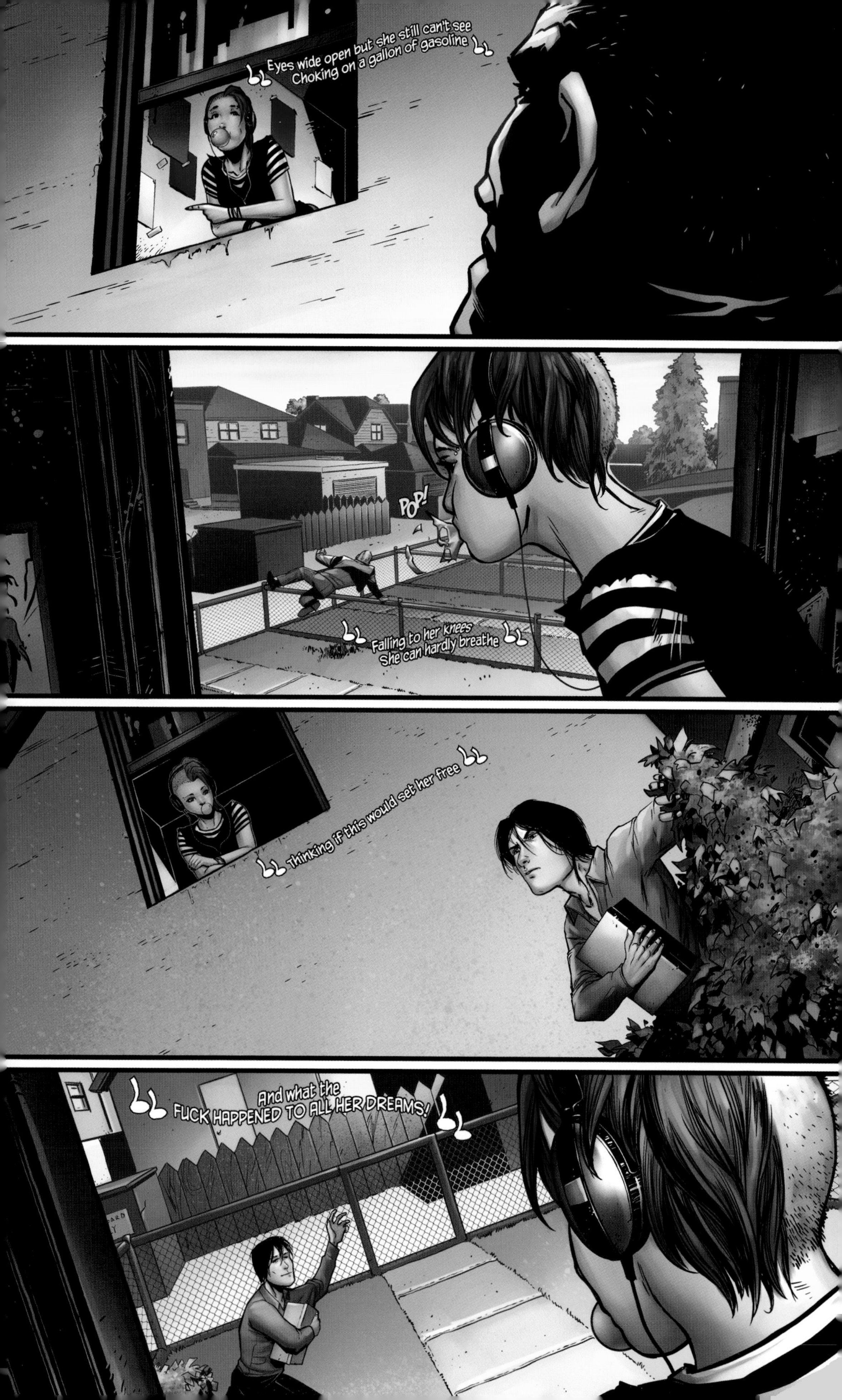
Eyes wide open but she still can't see
Choking on a gallon of gasoline
POP!
Falling to her knees
She can hardly breathe
Thinking if this would set her free
And what the
FUCK HAPPENED TO ALL HER DREAMS!

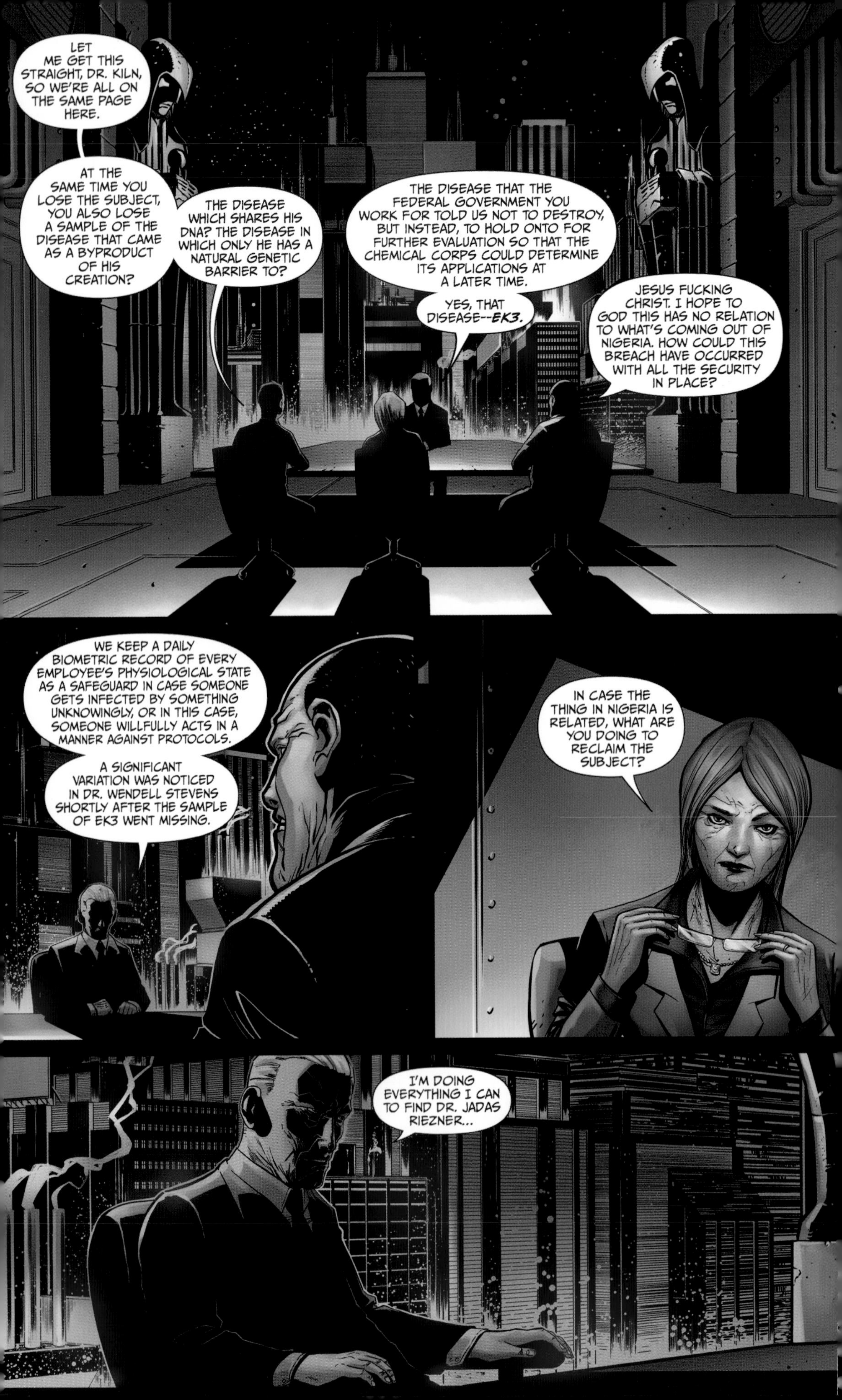
LET ME GET THIS STRAIGHT, DR. KILN, SO WE'RE ALL ON THE SAME PAGE HERE.
AT THE SAME TIME YOU LOSE THE SUBJECT, YOU ALSO LOSE A SAMPLE OF THE DISEASE THAT CAME AS A BYPRODUCT OF HIS CREATION?
THE DISEASE WHICH SHARES HIS DNA? THE DISEASE IN WHICH ONLY HE HAS A NATURAL GENETIC BARRIER TO?
THE DISEASE THAT THE FEDERAL GOVERNMENT YOU WORK FOR TOLD US NOT TO DESTROY, BUT INSTEAD, TO HOLD ONTO FOR FURTHER EVALUATION SO THAT THE CHEMICAL CORPS COULD DETERMINE ITS APPLICATIONS AT A LATER TIME.
YES, THAT DISEASE--*EK3.*
JESUS FUCKING CHRIST. I HOPE TO GOD THIS HAS NO RELATION TO WHAT'S COMING OUT OF NIGERIA. HOW COULD THIS BREACH HAVE OCCURRED WITH ALL THE SECURITY IN PLACE?
WE KEEP A DAILY BIOMETRIC RECORD OF EVERY EMPLOYEE'S PHYSIOLOGICAL STATE AS A SAFEGUARD IN CASE SOMEONE GETS INFECTED BY SOMETHING UNKNOWINGLY, OR IN THIS CASE, SOMEONE WILLFULLY ACTS IN A MANNER AGAINST PROTOCOLS.
A SIGNIFICANT VARIATION WAS NOTICED IN DR. WENDELL STEVENS SHORTLY AFTER THE SAMPLE OF EK3 WENT MISSING.
IN CASE THE THING IN NIGERIA IS RELATED, WHAT ARE YOU DOING TO RECLAIM THE SUBJECT?
I'M DOING EVERYTHING I CAN TO FIND DR. JADAS RIEZNER...

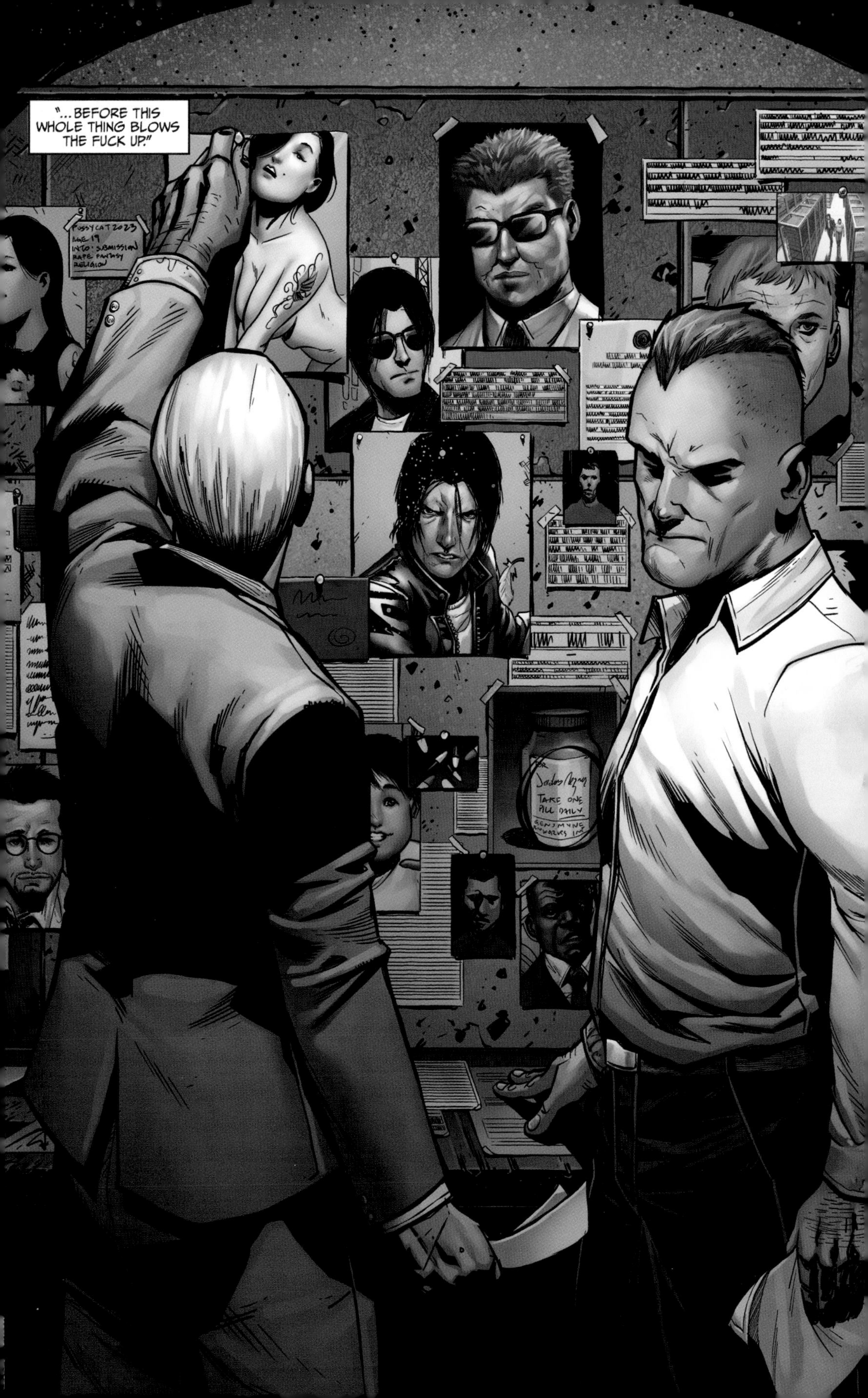
"...BEFORE THIS WHOLE THING BLOWS THE FUCK UP."
PUSSYCAT2023 AGE 19 INTO: SUBMISSION RAPE FANTASY RELIGION
TAKE ONE PILL DAILY

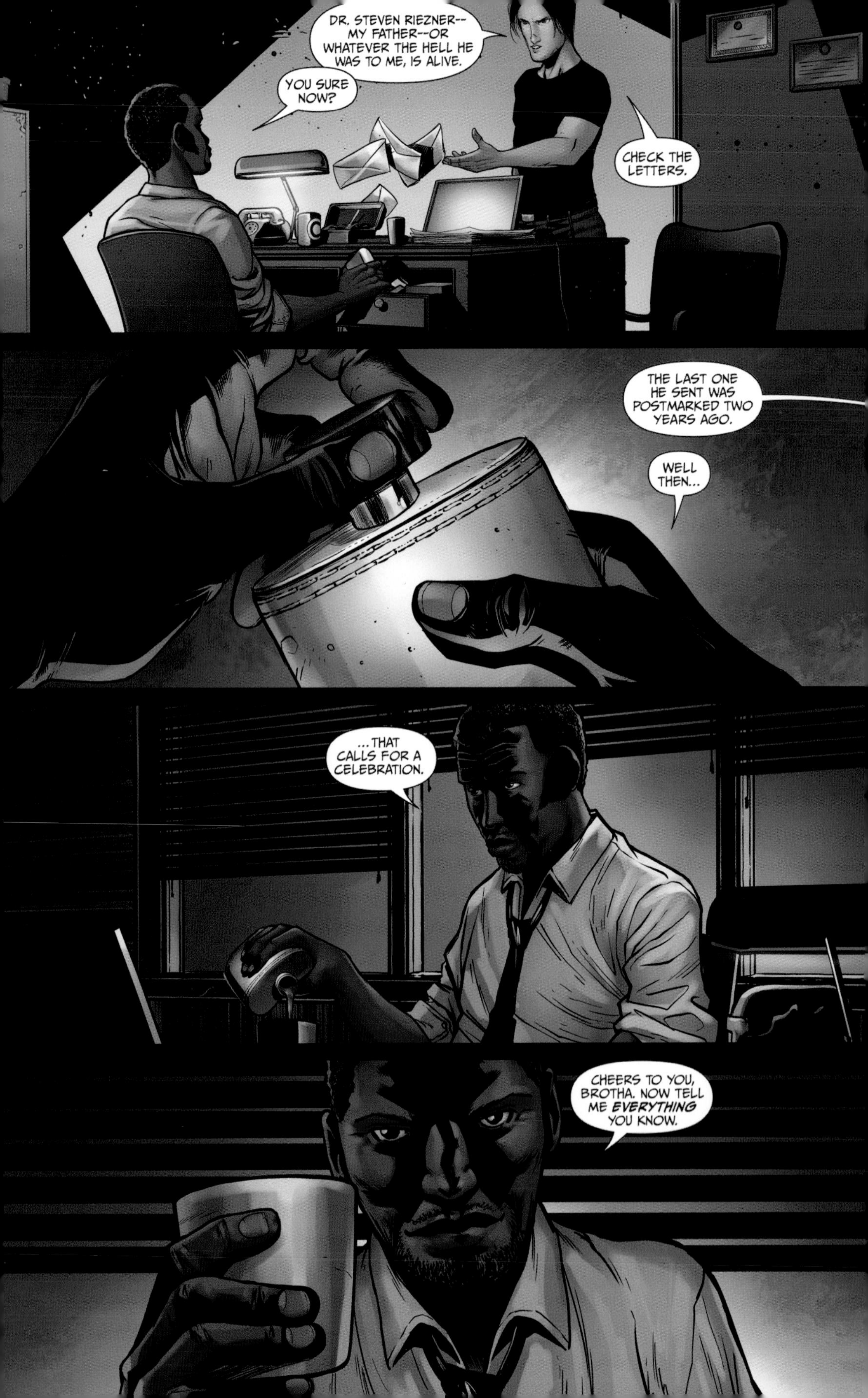

DR. STEVEN RIEZNER-- MY FATHER--OR WHATEVER THE HELL HE WAS TO ME, IS ALIVE.
YOU SURE NOW?
CHECK THE LETTERS.
THE LAST ONE HE SENT WAS POSTMARKED TWO YEARS AGO.
WELL THEN...
...THAT CALLS FOR A CELEBRATION.
CHEERS TO YOU, BROTHA. NOW TELL ME *EVERYTHING* YOU KNOW.

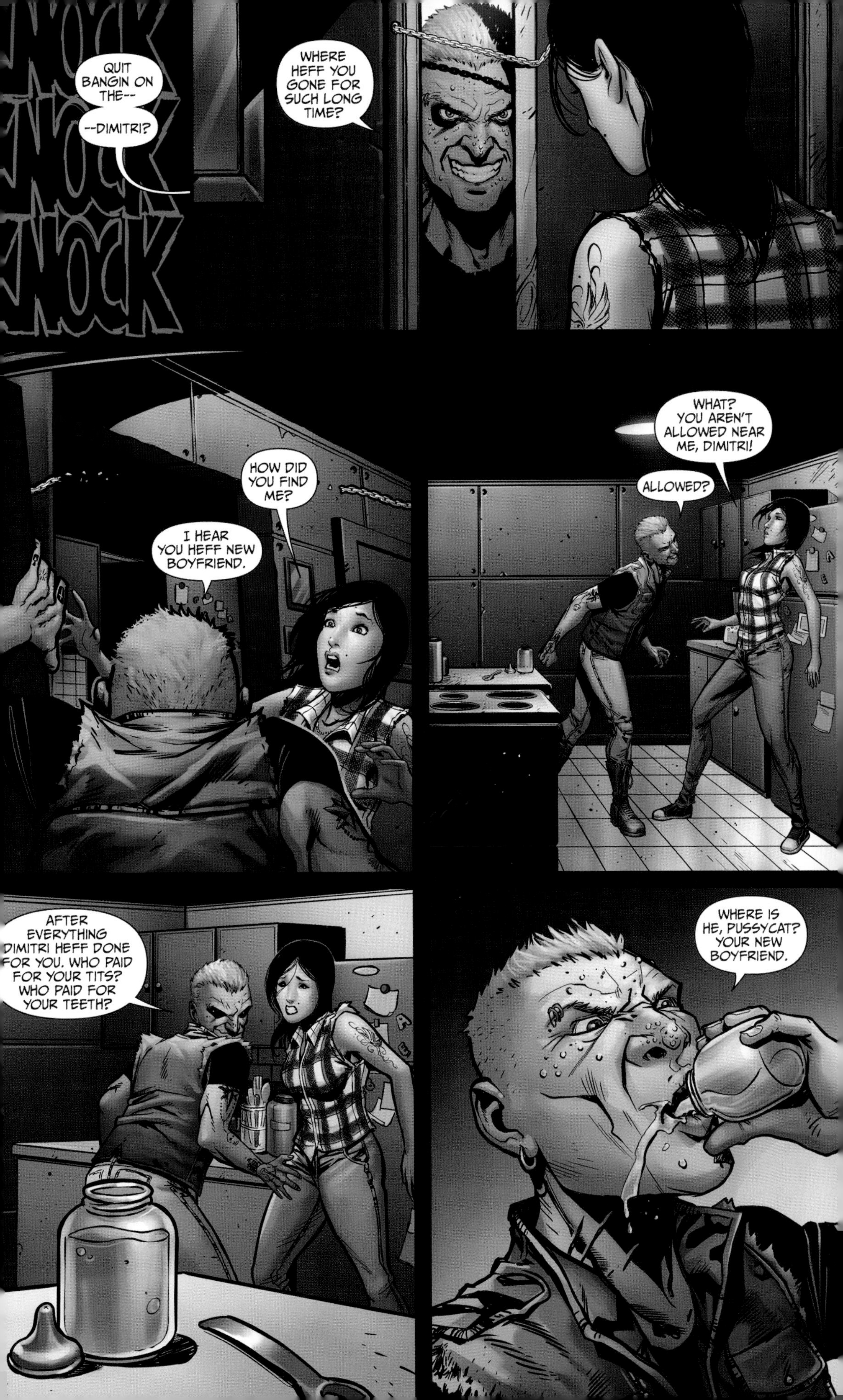

KNOCK KNOCK KNOCK
QUIT BANGIN ON THE--
--DIMITRI?
WHERE HEFF YOU GONE FOR SUCH LONG TIME?
HOW DID YOU FIND ME?
I HEAR YOU HEFF NEW BOYFRIEND.
WHAT? YOU AREN'T ALLOWED NEAR ME, DIMITRI!
ALLOWED?
AFTER EVERYTHING DIMITRI HEFF DONE FOR YOU. WHO PAID FOR YOUR TITS? WHO PAID FOR YOUR TEETH?
WHERE IS HE, PUSSYCAT? YOUR NEW BOYFRIEND.

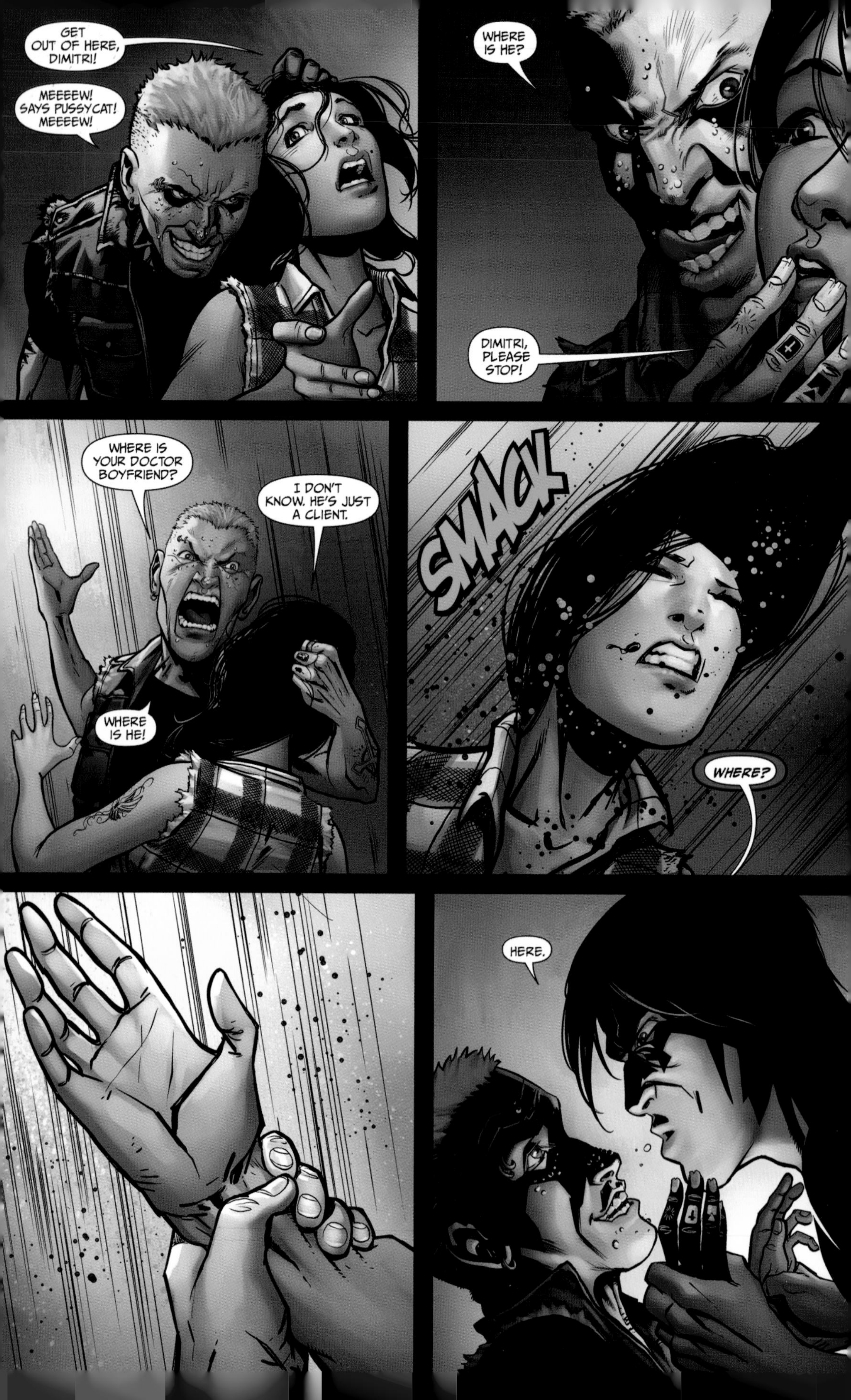
GET OUT OF HERE, DIMITRI!
MEEEEW! SAYS PUSSYCAT! MEEEEW!
WHERE IS HE?
DIMITRI, PLEASE STOP!
WHERE IS YOUR DOCTOR BOYFRIEND?
I DON'T KNOW. HE'S JUST A CLIENT.
WHERE IS HE!
SMACK
WHERE?
HERE.

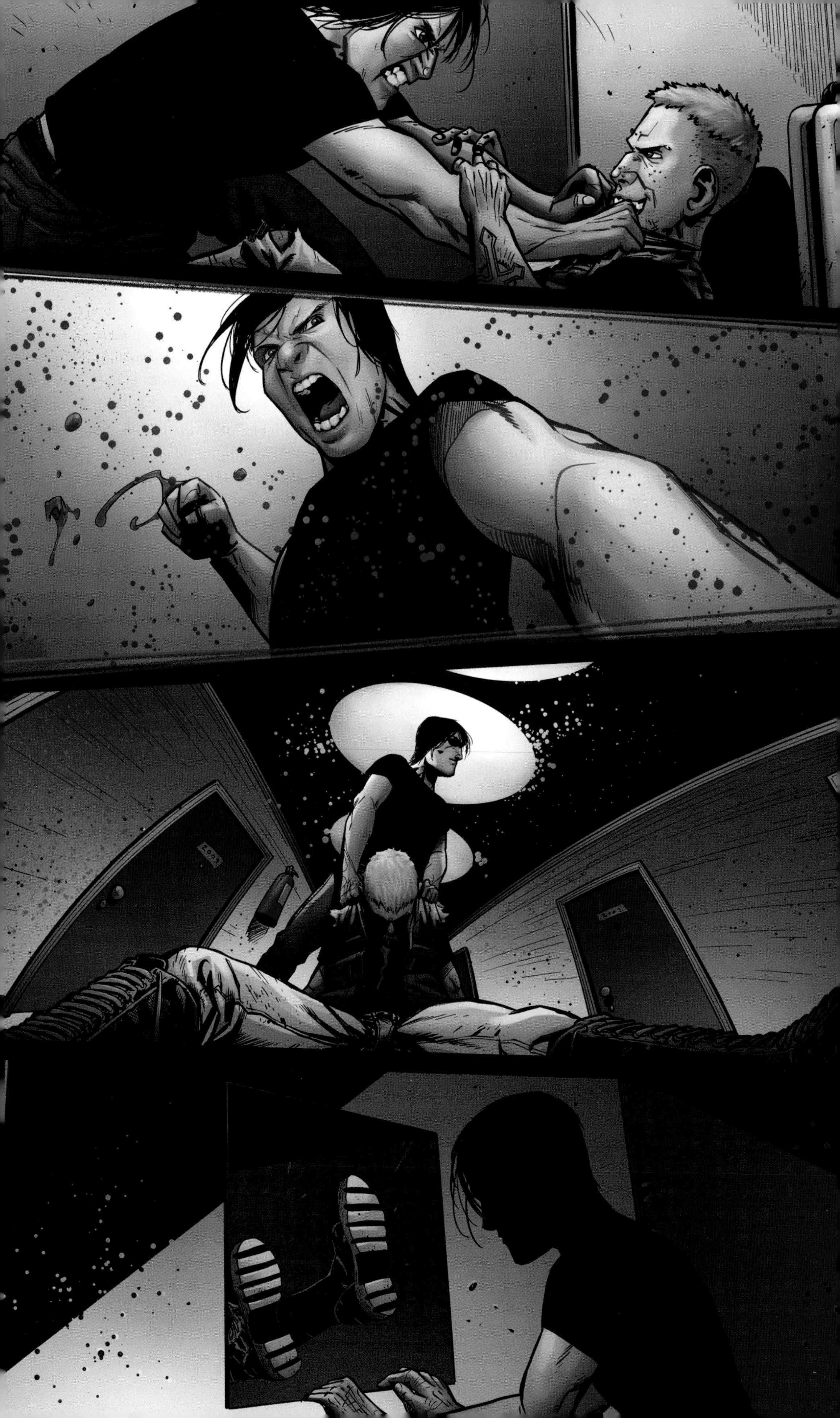

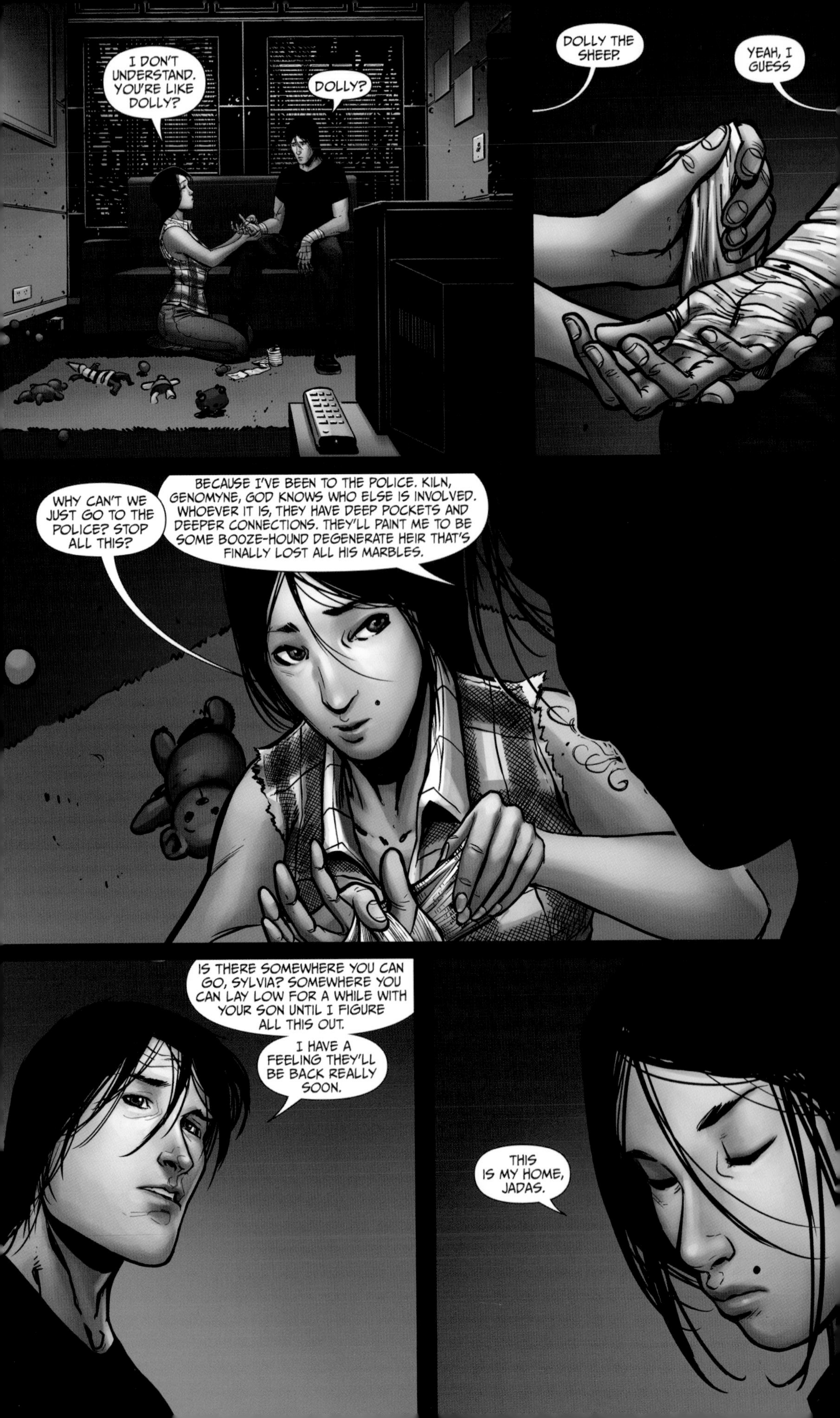
I DON'T UNDERSTAND. YOU'RE LIKE DOLLY?
DOLLY?
DOLLY THE SHEEP.
YEAH, I GUESS
WHY CAN'T WE JUST GO TO THE POLICE? STOP ALL THIS?
BECAUSE I'VE BEEN TO THE POLICE. KILN, GENOMYNE, GOD KNOWS WHO ELSE IS INVOLVED. WHOEVER IT IS, THEY HAVE DEEP POCKETS AND DEEPER CONNECTIONS. THEY'LL PAINT ME TO BE SOME BOOZE-HOUND DEGENERATE HEIR THAT'S FINALLY LOST ALL HIS MARBLES.
IS THERE SOMEWHERE YOU CAN GO, SYLVIA? SOMEWHERE YOU CAN LAY LOW FOR A WHILE WITH YOUR SON UNTIL I FIGURE ALL THIS OUT.
I HAVE A FEELING THEY'LL BE BACK REALLY SOON.
THIS IS MY HOME, JADAS.

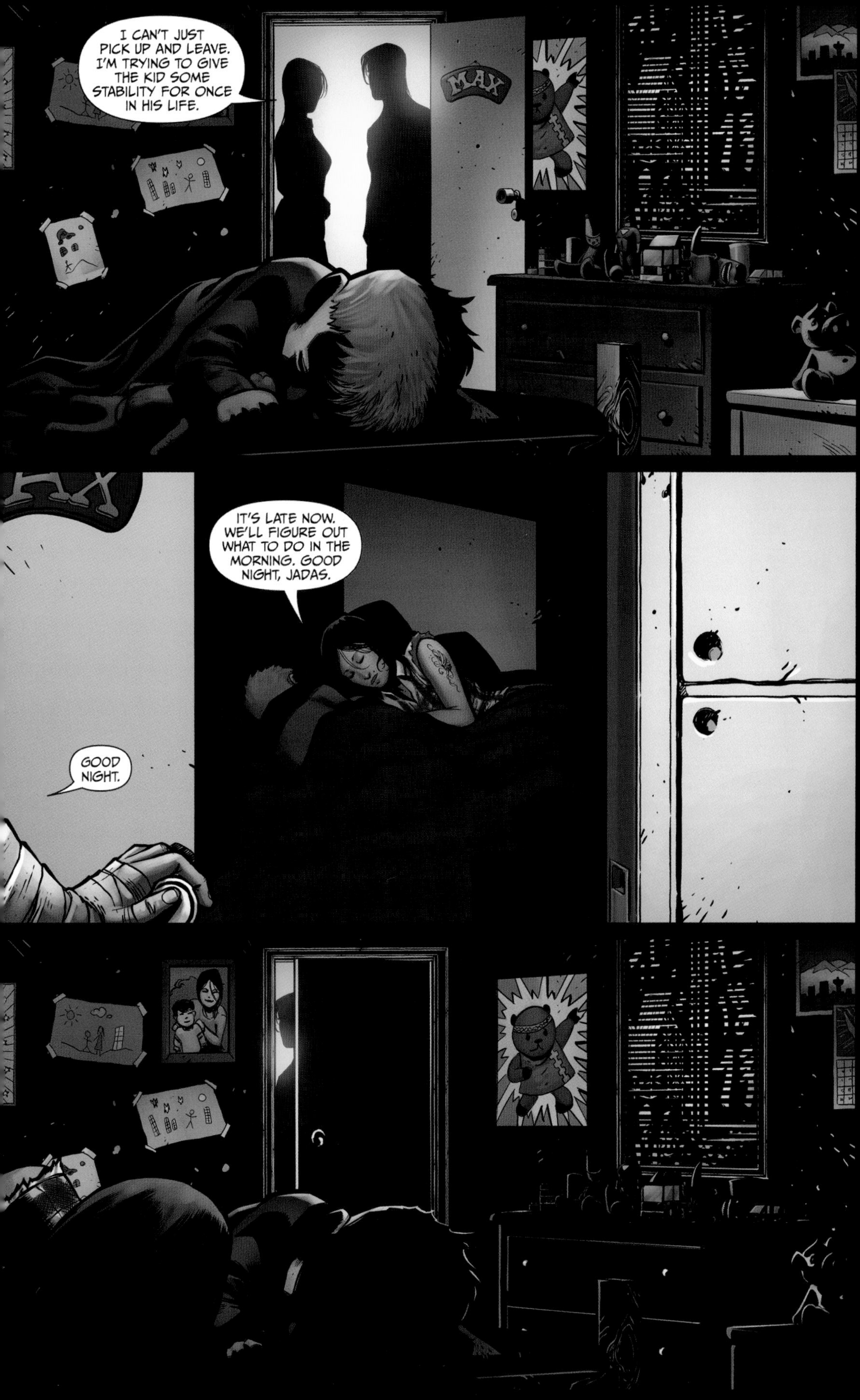

I CAN'T JUST PICK UP AND LEAVE. I'M TRYING TO GIVE THE KID SOME STABILITY FOR ONCE IN HIS LIFE.
MAX
IT'S LATE NOW. WE'LL FIGURE OUT WHAT TO DO IN THE MORNING. GOOD NIGHT, JADAS.
GOOD NIGHT.

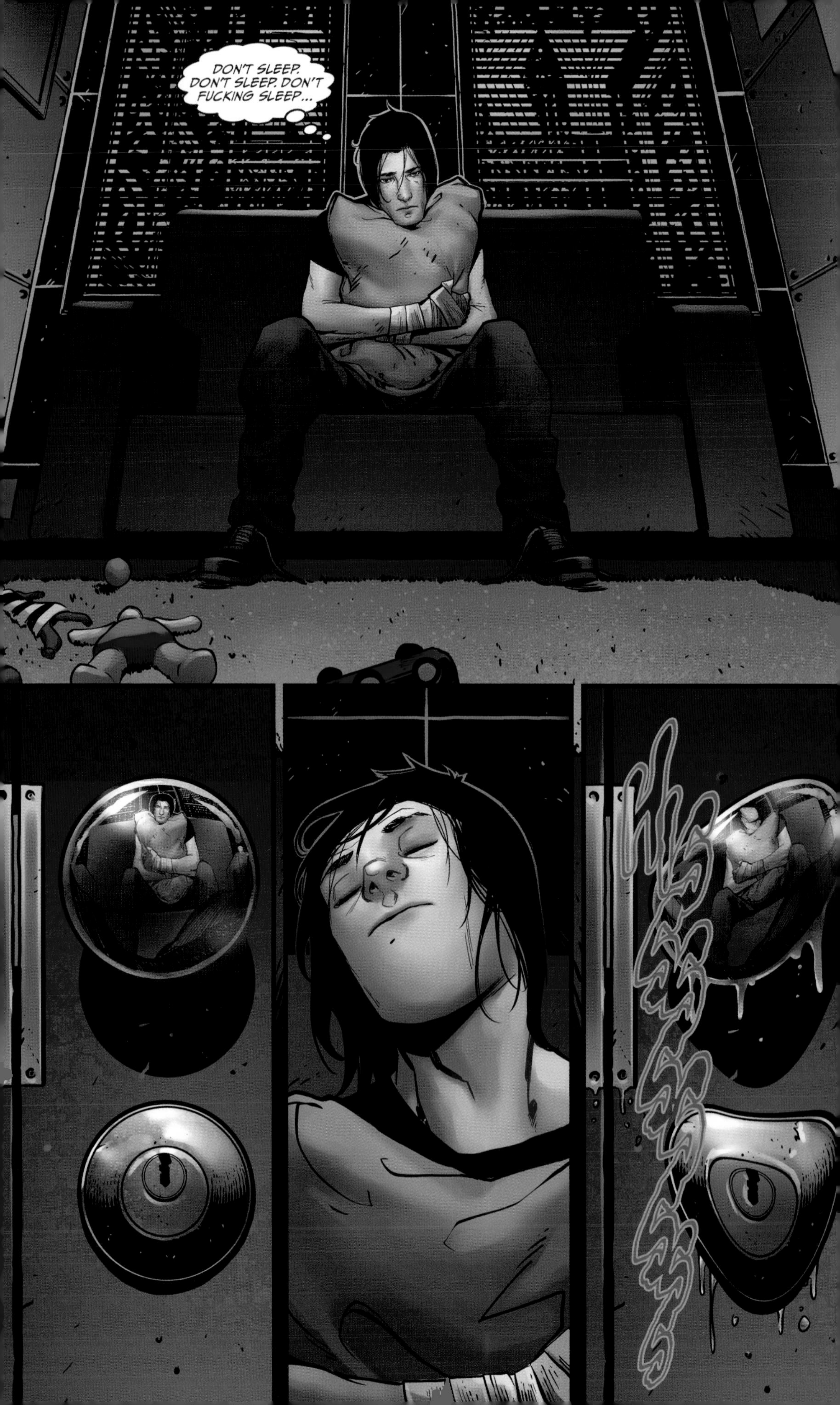
DON'T SLEEP. DON'T SLEEP. DON'T FUCKING SLEEP...

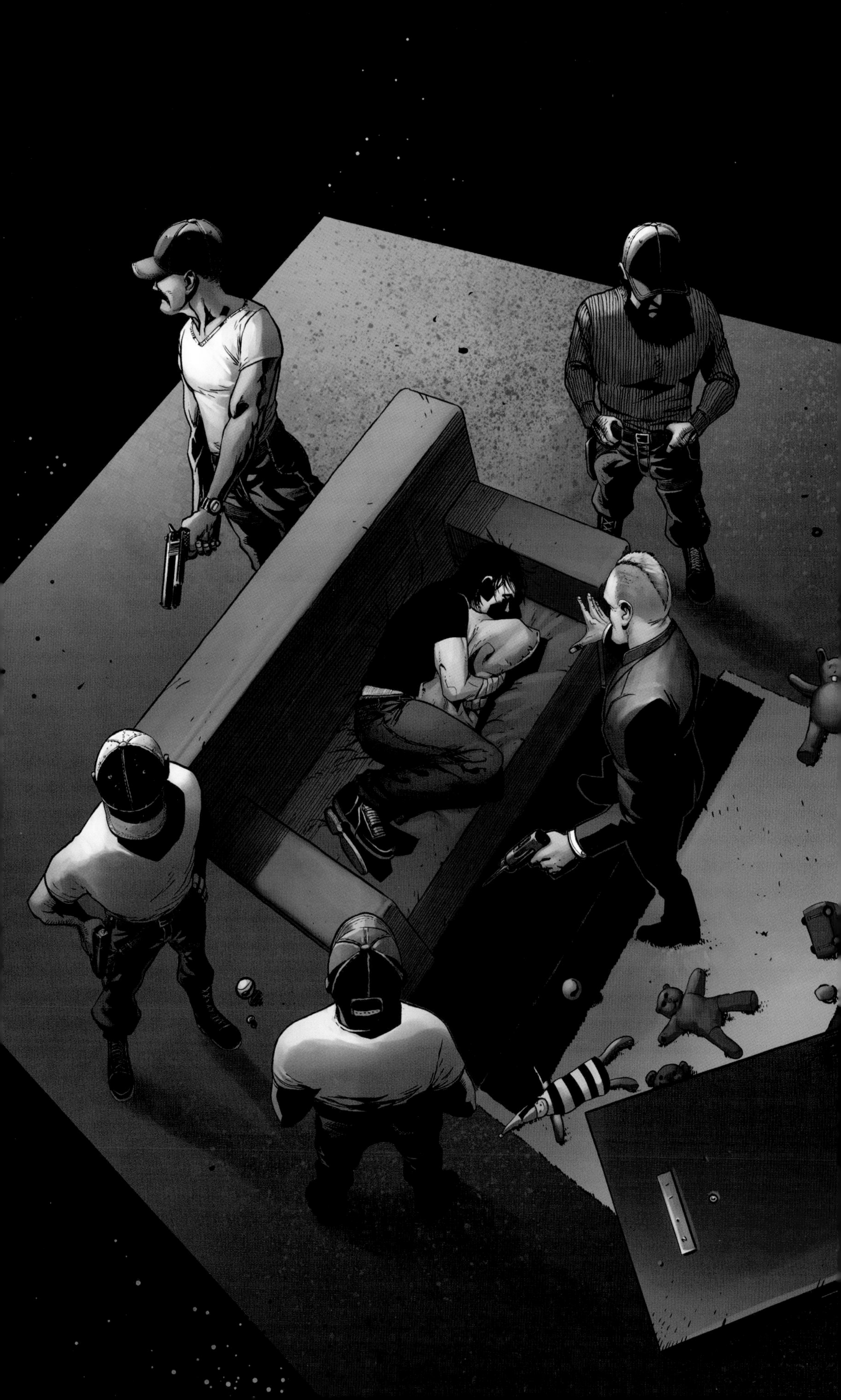

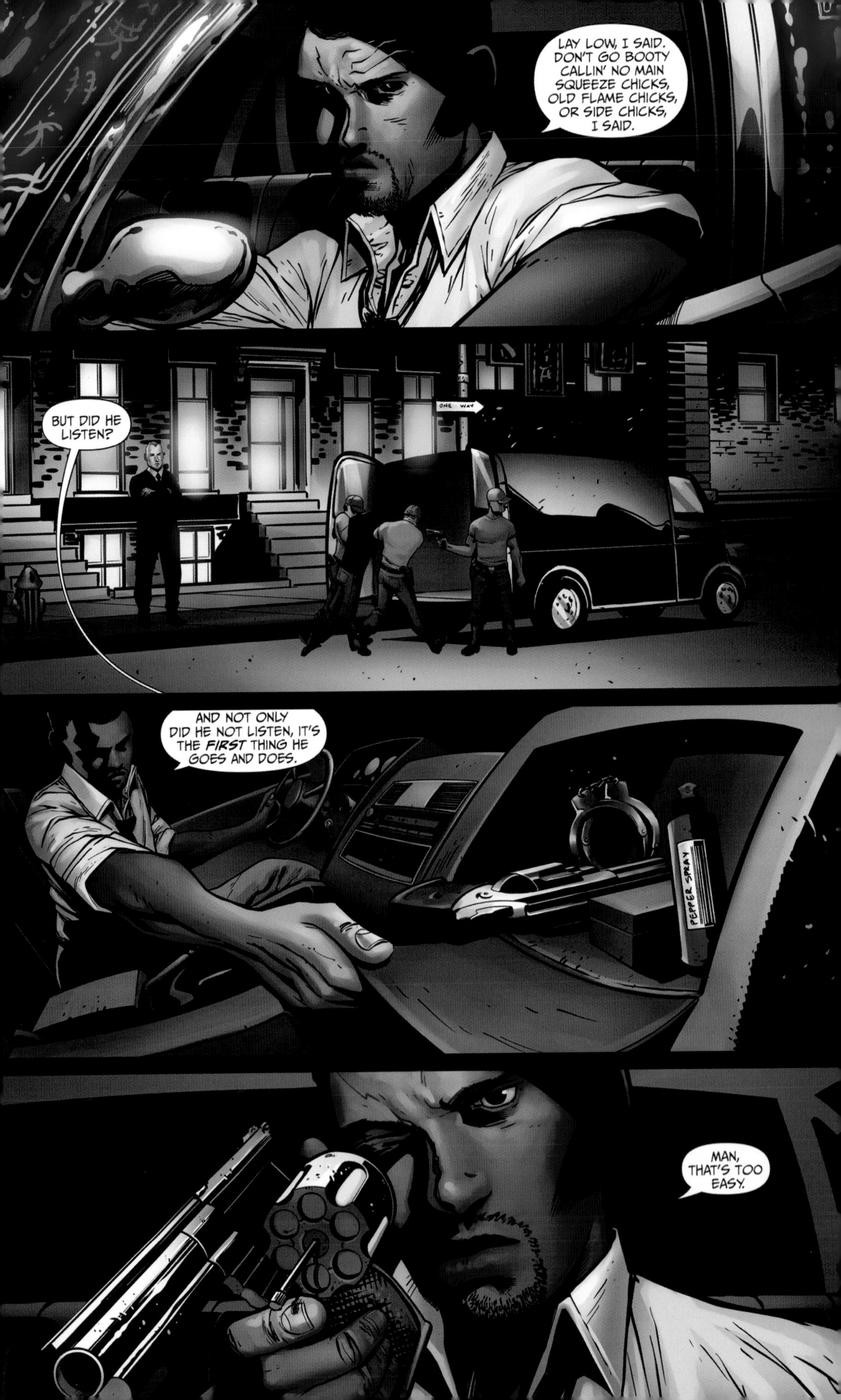
LAY LOW, I SAID. DON'T GO BOOTY CALLIN' NO MAIN SQUEEZE CHICKS, OLD FLAME CHICKS, OR SIDE CHICKS, I SAID.
BUT DID HE LISTEN?
ONE WAY
AND NOT ONLY DID HE NOT LISTEN, IT'S THE FIRST THING HE GOES AND DOES.
PEPPER SPRAY
MAN, THAT'S TOO EASY.

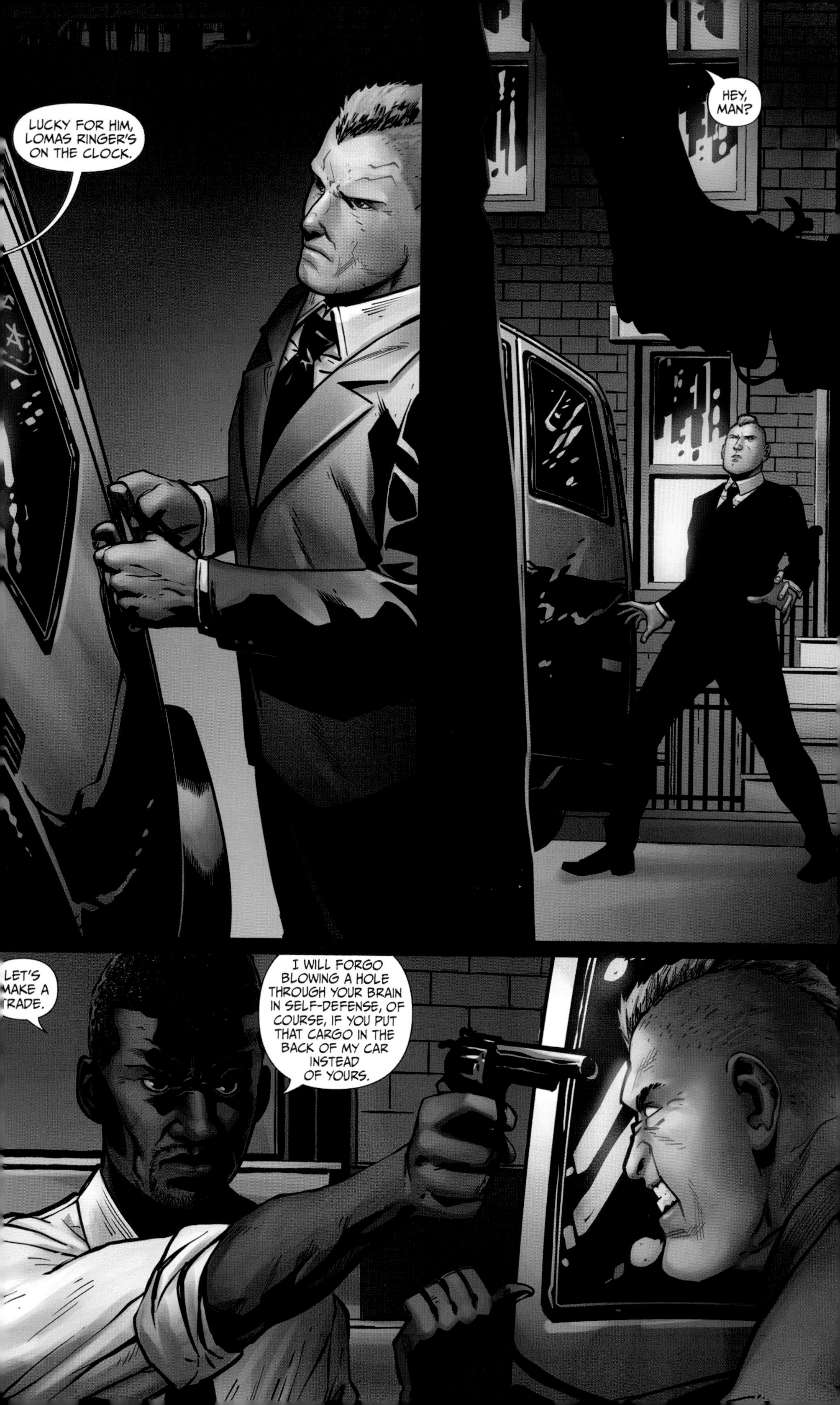
LUCKY FOR HIM, LOMAS RINGER'S ON THE CLOCK.
HEY, MAN?
LET'S MAKE A TRADE.
I WILL FORGO BLOWING A HOLE THROUGH YOUR BRAIN IN SELF-DEFENSE, OF COURSE, IF YOU PUT THAT CARGO IN THE BACK OF MY CAR INSTEAD OF YOURS.

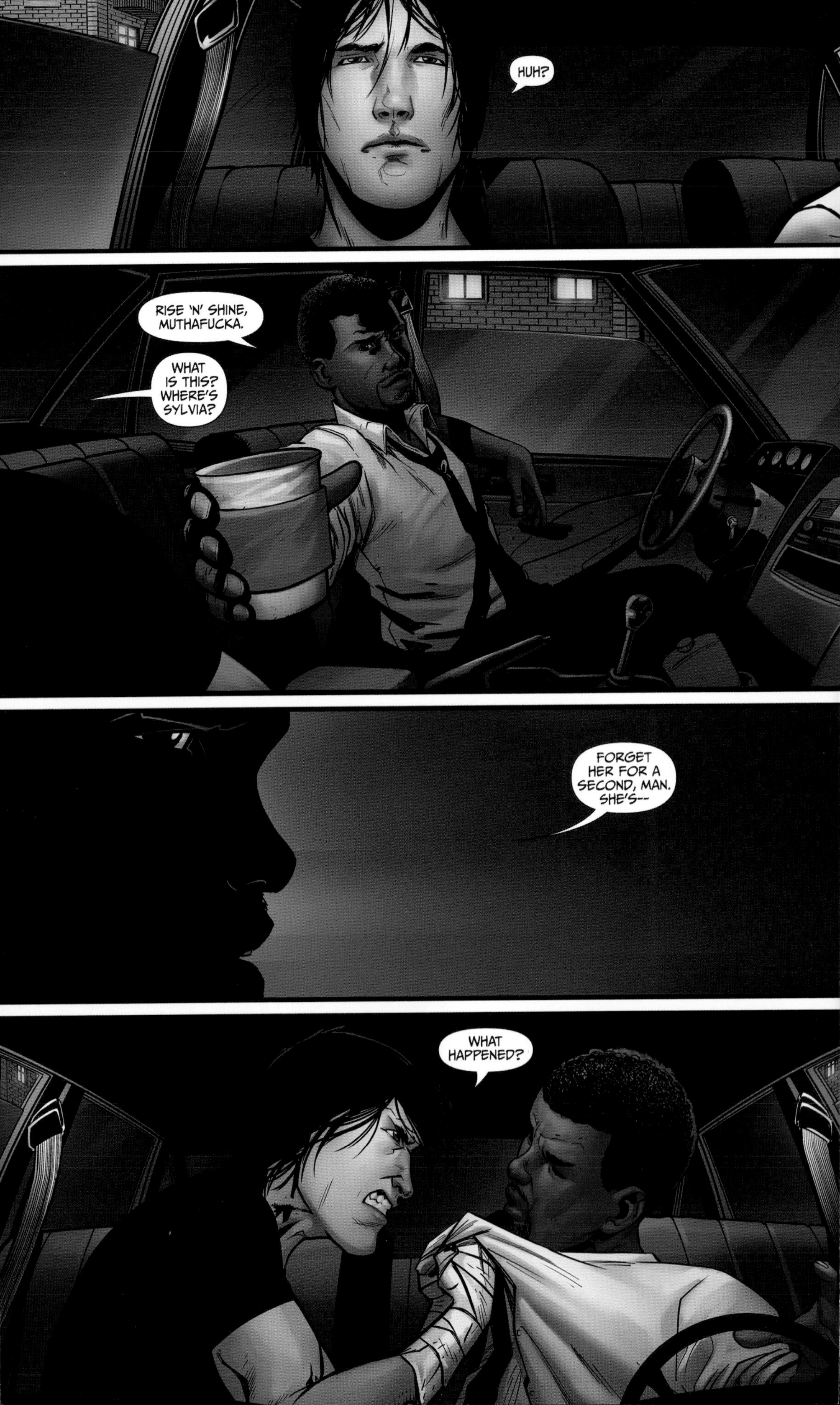
HUH?
RISE 'N' SHINE, MUTHAFUCKA.
WHAT IS THIS? WHERE'S SYLVIA?
FORGET HER FOR A SECOND, MAN. SHE'S--
WHAT HAPPENED?

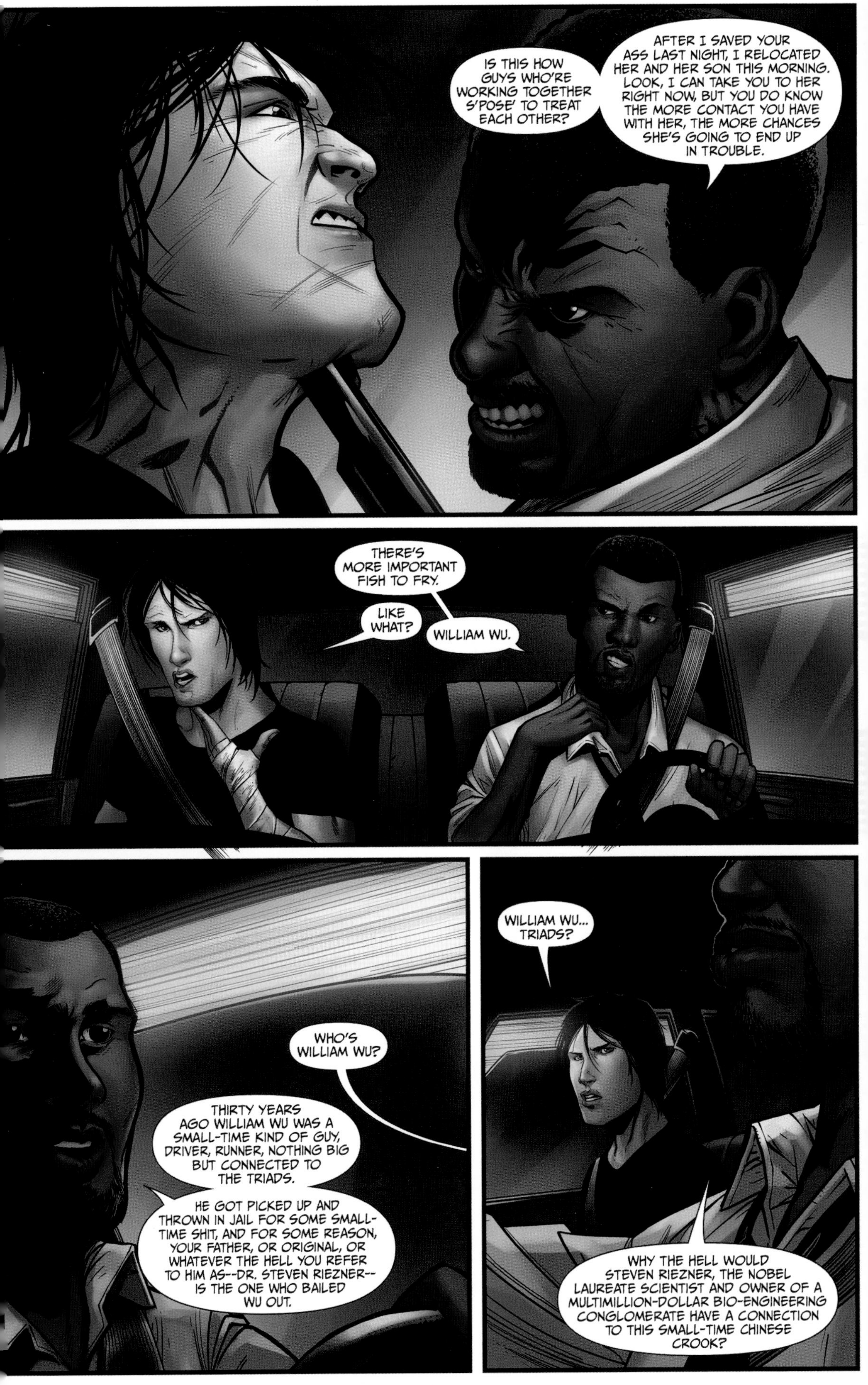
IS THIS HOW GUYS WHO'RE WORKING TOGETHER S'POSE' TO TREAT EACH OTHER?
AFTER I SAVED YOUR ASS LAST NIGHT, I RELOCATED HER AND HER SON THIS MORNING. LOOK, I CAN TAKE YOU TO HER RIGHT NOW, BUT YOU DO KNOW THE MORE CONTACT YOU HAVE WITH HER, THE MORE CHANCES SHE'S GOING TO END UP IN TROUBLE.
THERE'S MORE IMPORTANT FISH TO FRY.
LIKE WHAT?
WILLIAM WU.
WHO'S WILLIAM WU?
THIRTY YEARS AGO WILLIAM WU WAS A SMALL-TIME KIND OF GUY, DRIVER, RUNNER, NOTHING BIG BUT CONNECTED TO THE TRIADS.
HE GOT PICKED UP AND THROWN IN JAIL FOR SOME SMALL-TIME SHIT, AND FOR SOME REASON, YOUR FATHER, OR ORIGINAL, OR WHATEVER THE HELL YOU REFER TO HIM AS--DR. STEVEN RIEZNER--IS THE ONE WHO BAILED WU OUT.
WILLIAM WU... TRIADS?
WHY THE HELL WOULD STEVEN RIEZNER, THE NOBEL LAUREATE SCIENTIST AND OWNER OF A MULTIMILLION-DOLLAR BIO-ENGINEERING CONGLOMERATE HAVE A CONNECTION TO THIS SMALL-TIME CHINESE CROOK?

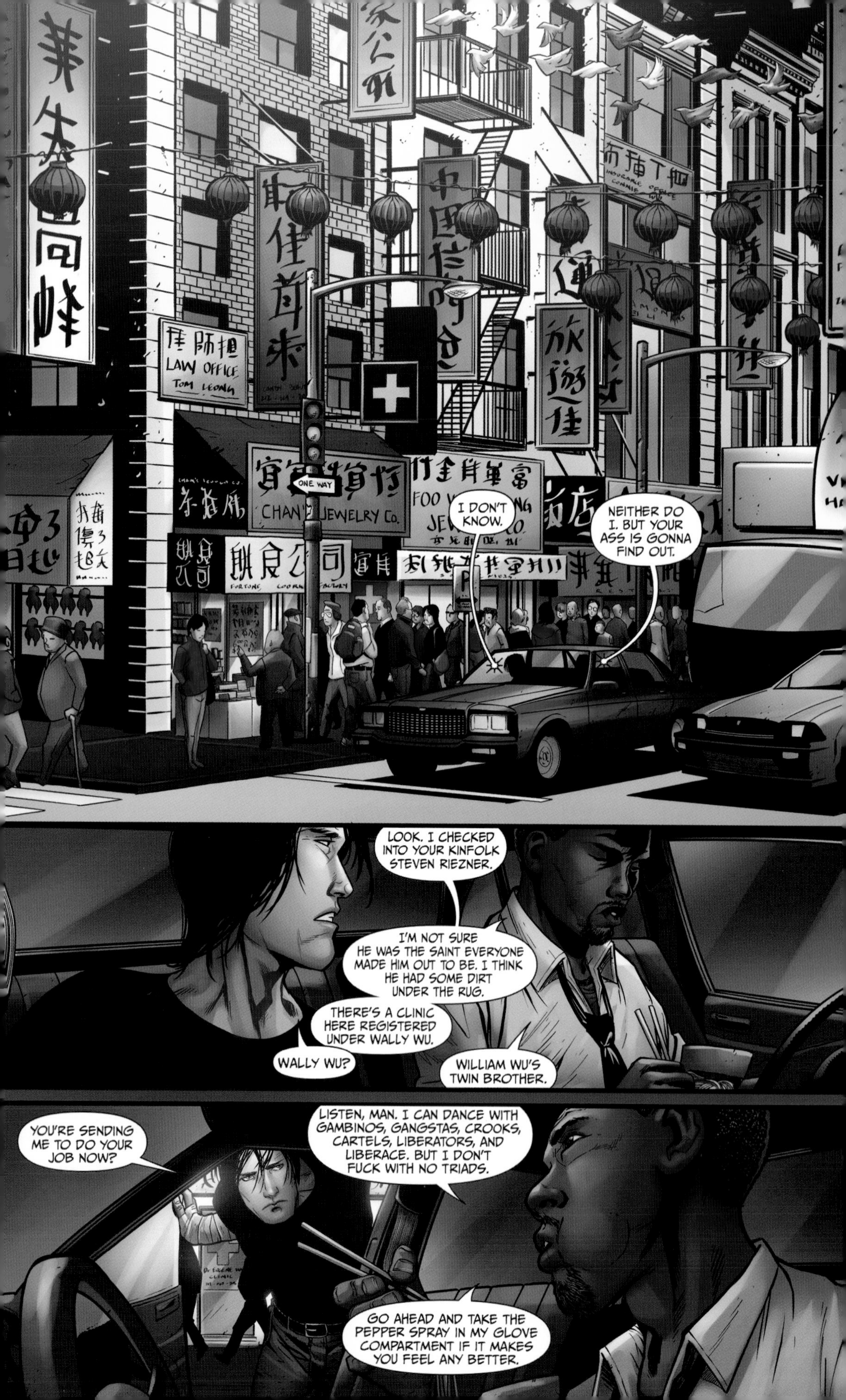
LAW OFFICE
TOM LEONG
ONE WAY
CHAN'S JEWELRY CO.
I DON'T KNOW.
NEITHER DO I. BUT YOUR ASS IS GONNA FIND OUT.
LOOK. I CHECKED INTO YOUR KINFOLK STEVEN RIEZNER.
I'M NOT SURE HE WAS THE SAINT EVERYONE MADE HIM OUT TO BE. I THINK HE HAD SOME DIRT UNDER THE RUG.
THERE'S A CLINIC HERE REGISTERED UNDER WALLY WU.
WALLY WU?
WILLIAM WU'S TWIN BROTHER.
YOU'RE SENDING ME TO DO YOUR JOB NOW?
LISTEN, MAN. I CAN DANCE WITH GAMBINOS, GANGSTAS, CROOKS, CARTELS, LIBERATORS, AND LIBERACE. BUT I DON'T FUCK WITH NO TRIADS.
GO AHEAD AND TAKE THE PEPPER SPRAY IN MY GLOVE COMPARTMENT IF IT MAKES YOU FEEL ANY BETTER.

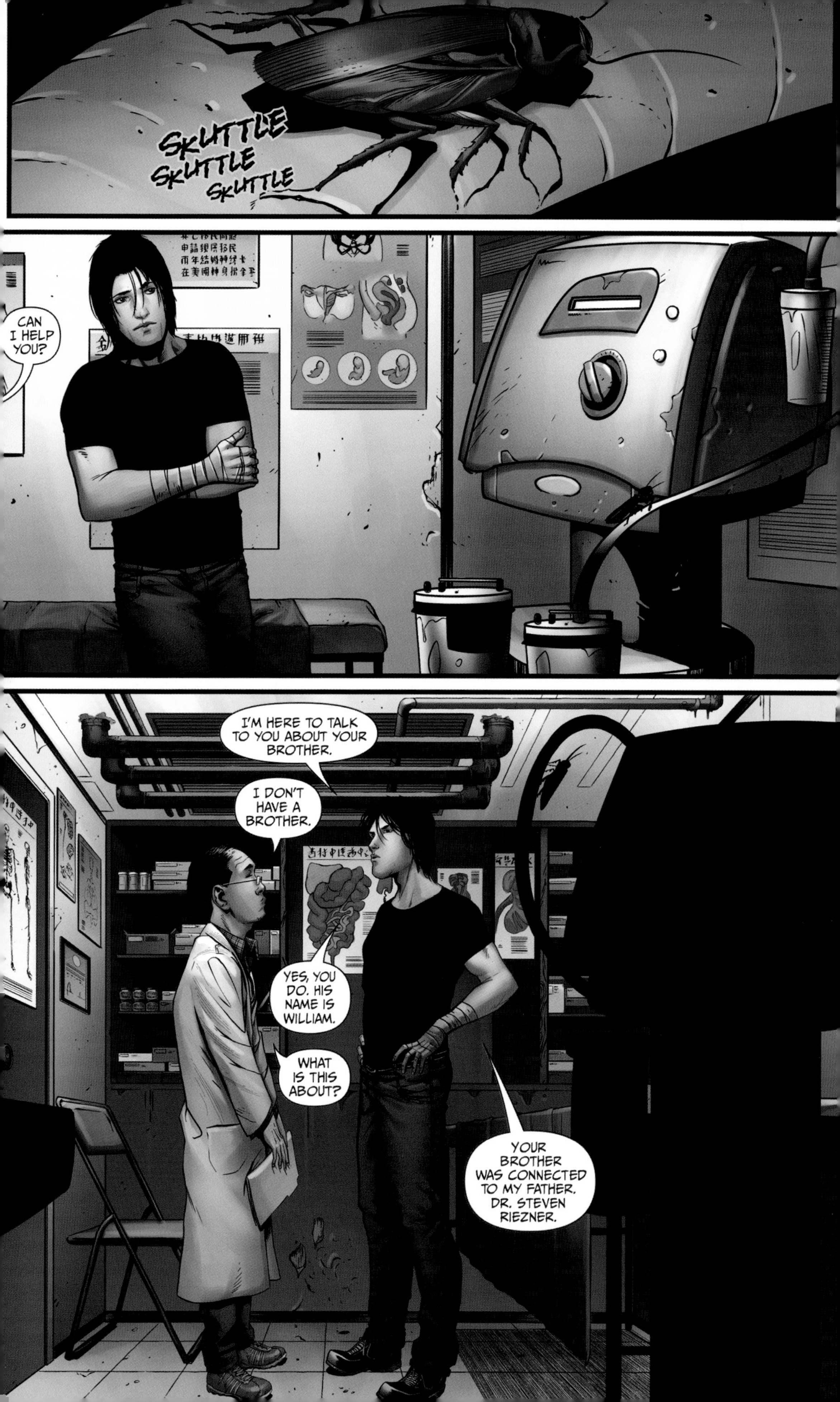
SKUTTLE
SKUTTLE
SKUTTLE
CAN I HELP YOU?
I'M HERE TO TALK TO YOU ABOUT YOUR BROTHER.
I DON'T HAVE A BROTHER.
YES, YOU DO. HIS NAME IS WILLIAM.
WHAT IS THIS ABOUT?
YOUR BROTHER WAS CONNECTED TO MY FATHER. DR. STEVEN RIEZNER.

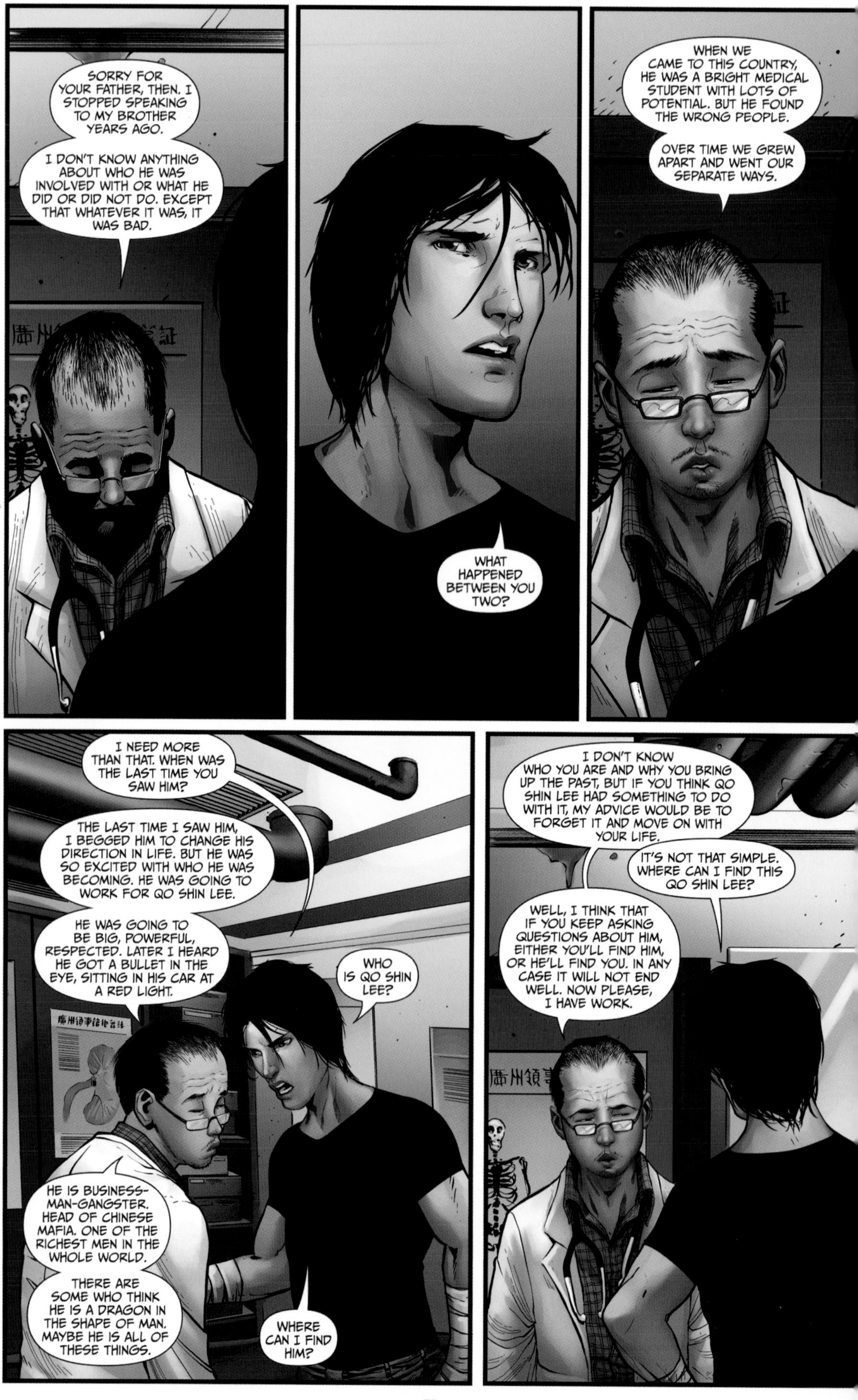

SORRY FOR YOUR FATHER, THEN. I STOPPED SPEAKING TO MY BROTHER YEARS AGO.
I DON'T KNOW ANYTHING ABOUT WHO HE WAS INVOLVED WITH OR WHAT HE DID OR DID NOT DO. EXCEPT THAT WHATEVER IT WAS, IT WAS BAD.
WHAT HAPPENED BETWEEN YOU TWO?
WHEN WE CAME TO THIS COUNTRY, HE WAS A BRIGHT MEDICAL STUDENT WITH LOTS OF POTENTIAL. BUT HE FOUND THE WRONG PEOPLE.
OVER TIME WE GREW APART AND WENT OUR SEPARATE WAYS.
I NEED MORE THAN THAT. WHEN WAS THE LAST TIME YOU SAW HIM?
THE LAST TIME I SAW HIM, I BEGGED HIM TO CHANGE HIS DIRECTION IN LIFE. BUT HE WAS SO EXCITED WITH WHO HE WAS BECOMING. HE WAS GOING TO WORK FOR QO SHIN LEE.
HE WAS GOING TO BE BIG, POWERFUL, RESPECTED. LATER I HEARD HE GOT A BULLET IN THE EYE, SITTING IN HIS CAR AT A RED LIGHT.
WHO IS QO SHIN LEE?
HE IS BUSINESS-MAN-GANGSTER. HEAD OF CHINESE MAFIA. ONE OF THE RICHEST MEN IN THE WHOLE WORLD.
THERE ARE SOME WHO THINK HE IS A DRAGON IN THE SHAPE OF MAN. MAYBE HE IS ALL OF THESE THINGS.
WHERE CAN I FIND HIM?
I DON'T KNOW WHO YOU ARE AND WHY YOU BRING UP THE PAST, BUT IF YOU THINK QO SHIN LEE HAD SOMETHING TO DO WITH IT, MY ADVICE WOULD BE TO FORGET IT AND MOVE ON WITH YOUR LIFE.
IT'S NOT THAT SIMPLE. WHERE CAN I FIND THIS QO SHIN LEE?
WELL, I THINK THAT IF YOU KEEP ASKING QUESTIONS ABOUT HIM, EITHER YOU'LL FIND HIM, OR HE'LL FIND YOU. IN ANY CASE IT WILL NOT END WELL. NOW PLEASE, I HAVE WORK.

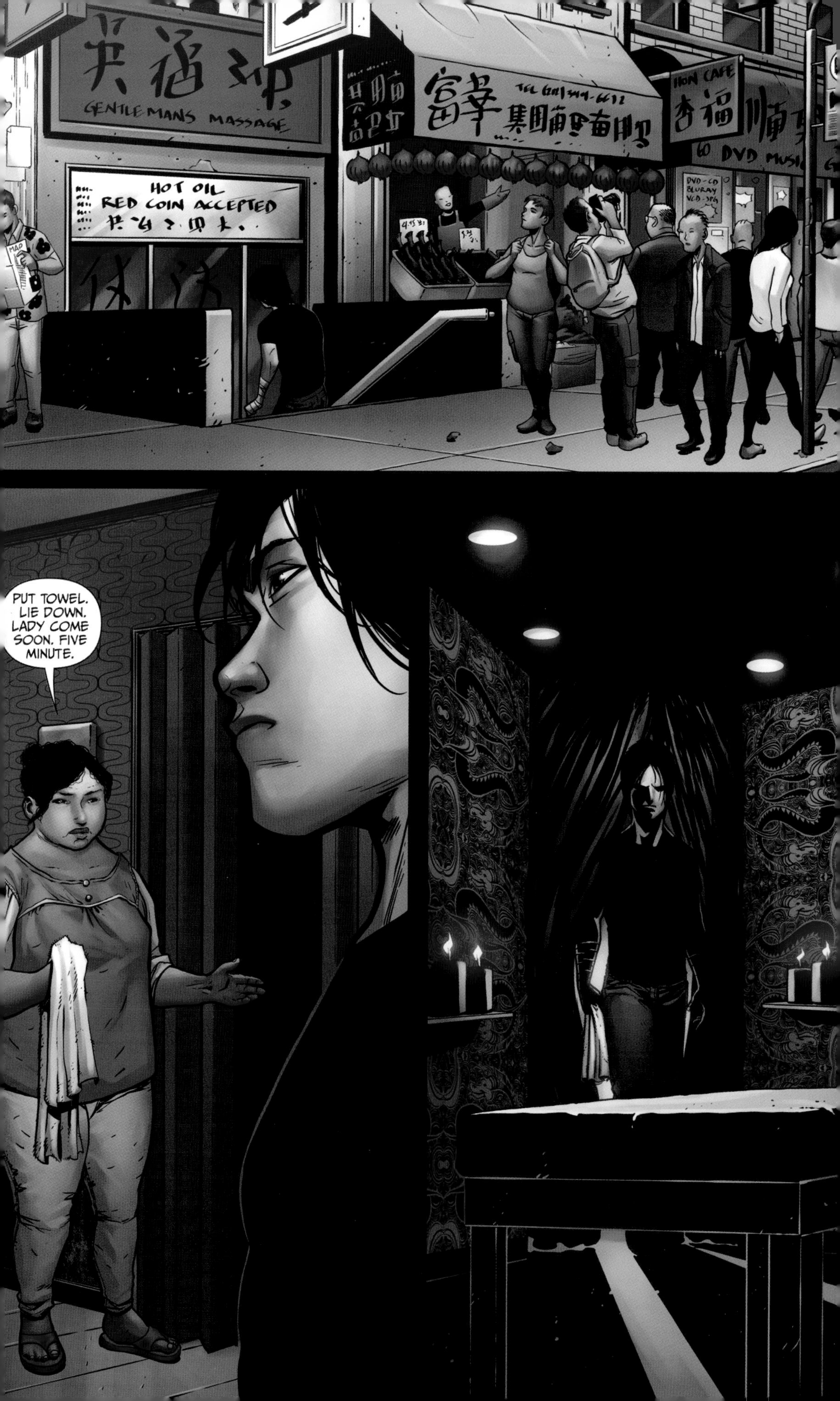
GENTLEMANS MASSAGE
HOT OIL
RED COIN ACCEPTED
HON CAFE
DVD MUSIC
MAP
PUT TOWEL. LIE DOWN. LADY COME SOON. FIVE MINUTE.

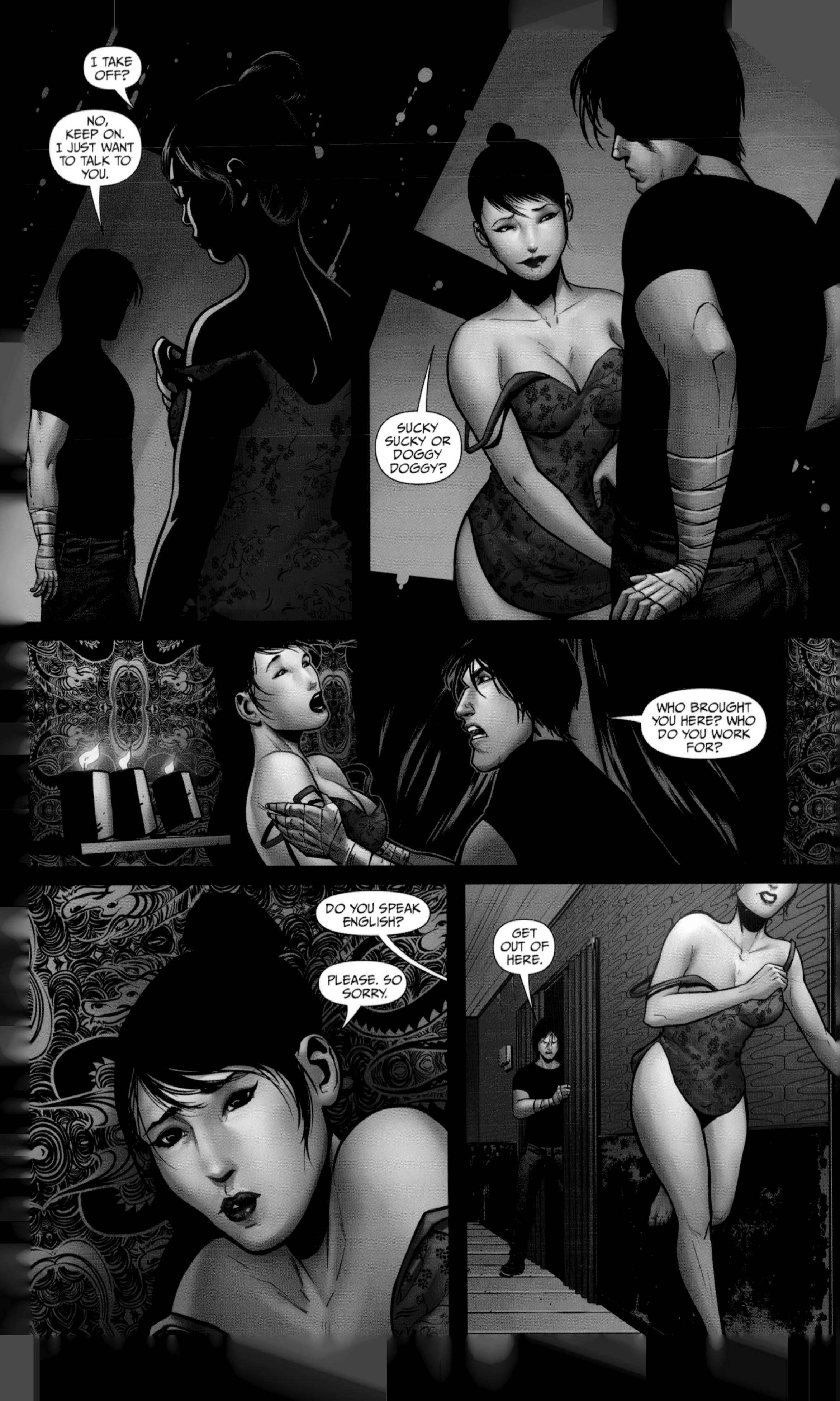
I TAKE OFF?
NO, KEEP ON. I JUST WANT TO TALK TO YOU.
SUCKY SUCKY OR DOGGY DOGGY?
WHO BROUGHT YOU HERE? WHO DO YOU WORK FOR?
DO YOU SPEAK ENGLISH?
PLEASE. SO SORRY.
GET OUT OF HERE.

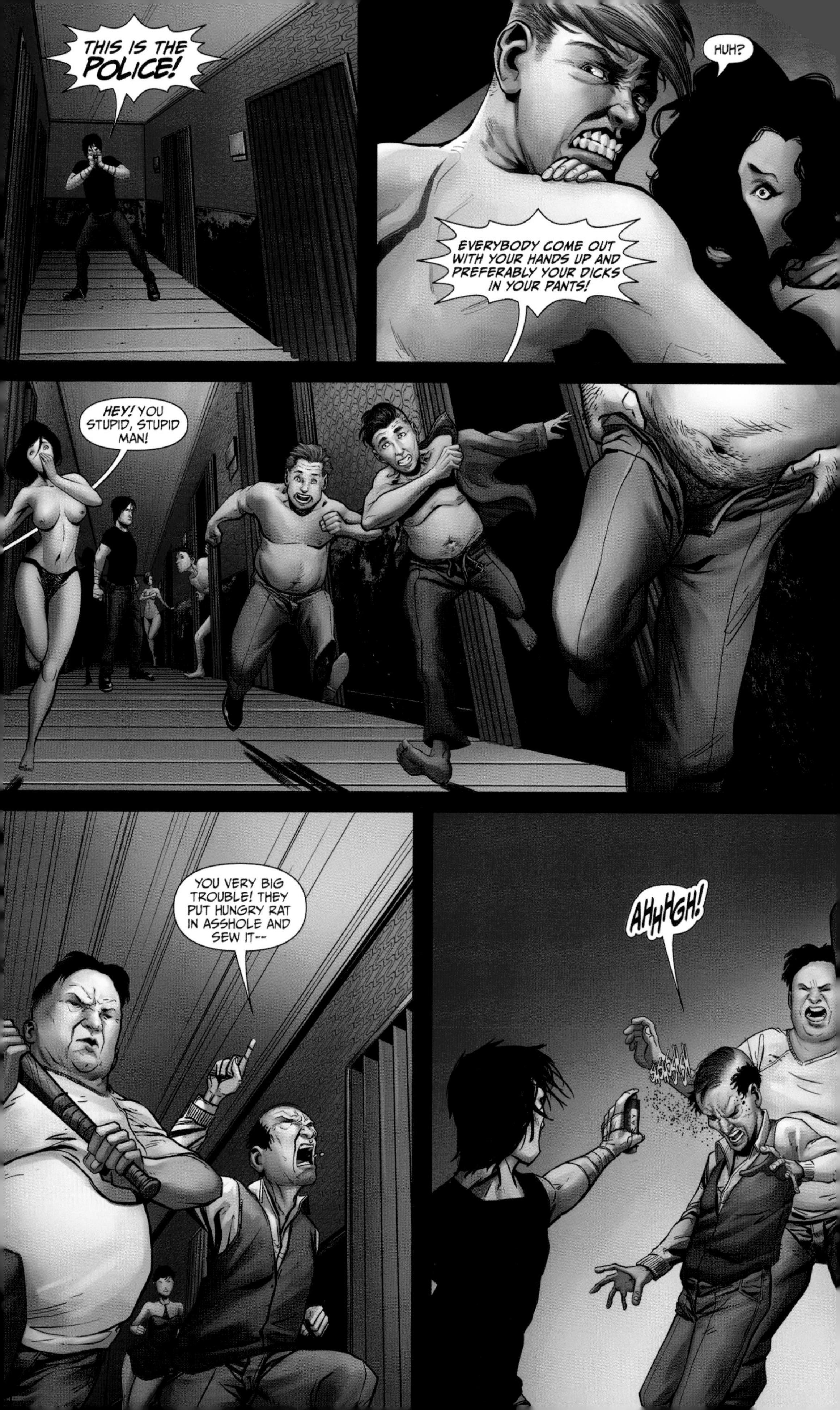
THIS IS THE POLICE!
HUH?
EVERYBODY COME OUT WITH YOUR HANDS UP AND PREFERABLY YOUR DICKS IN YOUR PANTS!
HEY! YOU STUPID, STUPID MAN!
YOU VERY BIG TROUBLE! THEY PUT HUNGRY RAT IN ASSHOLE AND SEW IT--
AHHHGH!

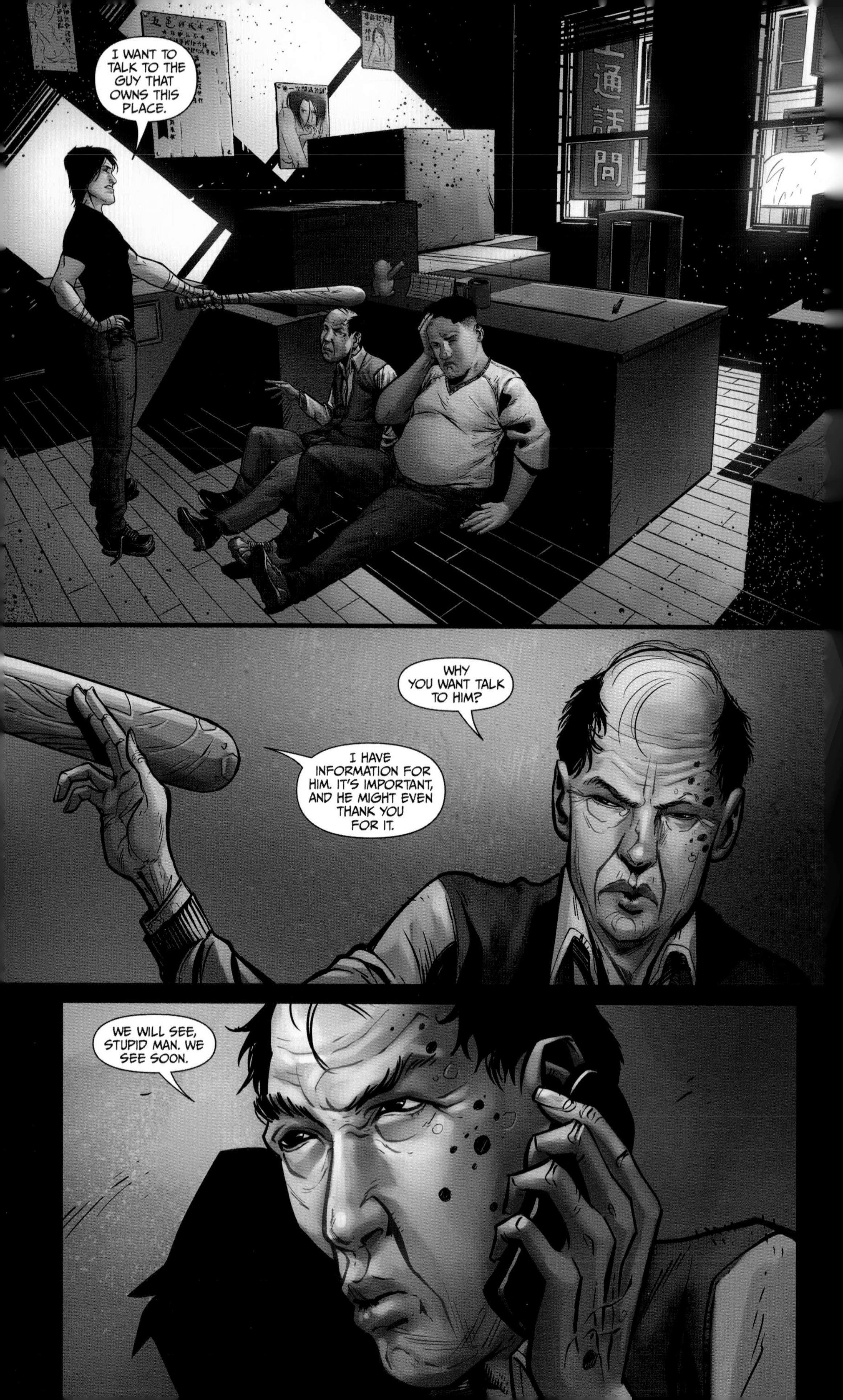
I WANT TO TALK TO THE GUY THAT OWNS THIS PLACE.
通話問
WHY YOU WANT TALK TO HIM?
I HAVE INFORMATION FOR HIM. IT'S IMPORTANT, AND HE MIGHT EVEN THANK YOU FOR IT.
WE WILL SEE, STUPID MAN. WE SEE SOON.

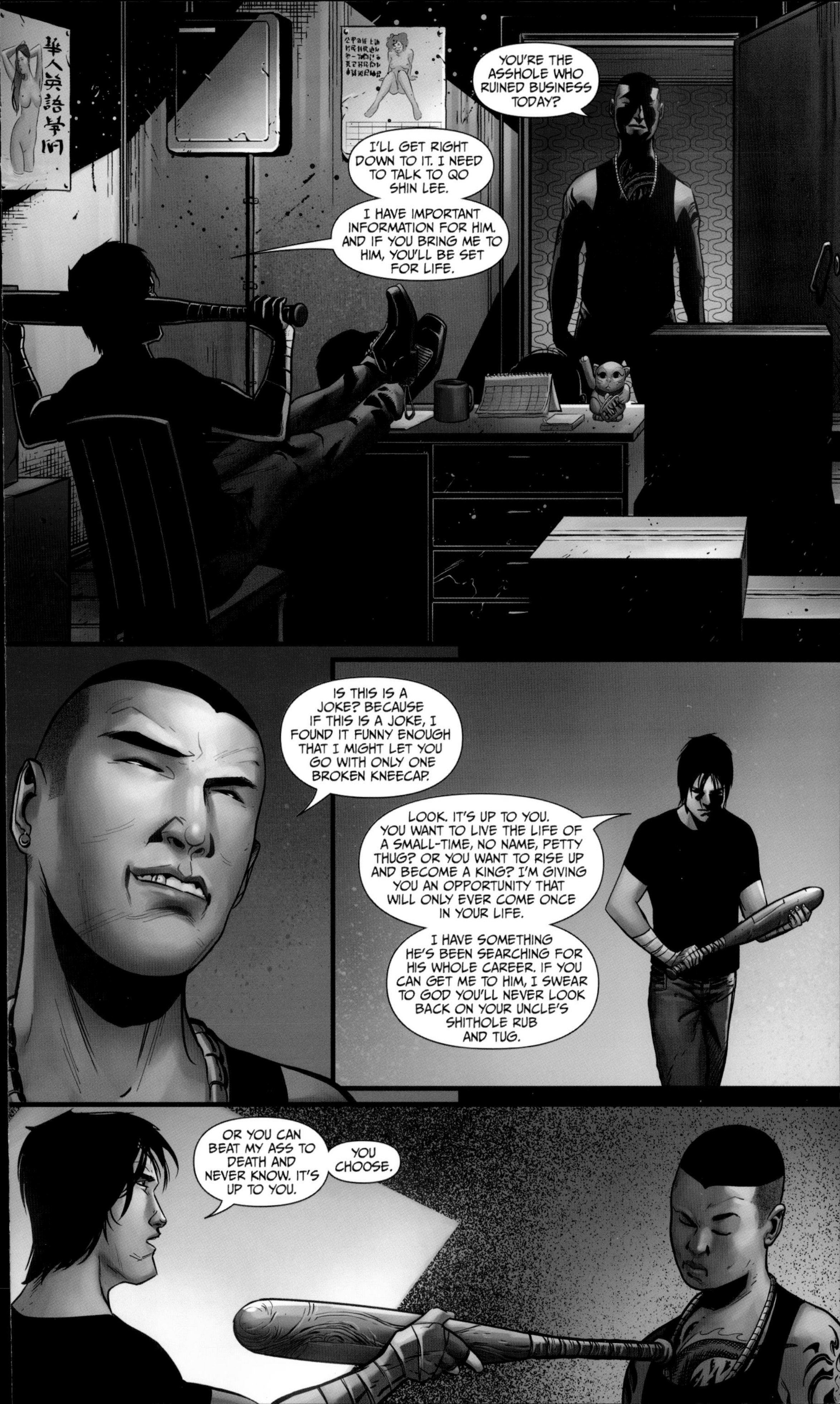
YOU'RE THE ASSHOLE WHO RUINED BUSINESS TODAY?
I'LL GET RIGHT DOWN TO IT. I NEED TO TALK TO QO SHIN LEE.
I HAVE IMPORTANT INFORMATION FOR HIM. AND IF YOU BRING ME TO HIM, YOU'LL BE SET FOR LIFE.
IS THIS IS A JOKE? BECAUSE IF THIS IS A JOKE, I FOUND IT FUNNY ENOUGH THAT I MIGHT LET YOU GO WITH ONLY ONE BROKEN KNEECAP.
LOOK. IT'S UP TO YOU. YOU WANT TO LIVE THE LIFE OF A SMALL-TIME, NO NAME, PETTY THUG? OR YOU WANT TO RISE UP AND BECOME A KING? I'M GIVING YOU AN OPPORTUNITY THAT WILL ONLY EVER COME ONCE IN YOUR LIFE.
I HAVE SOMETHING HE'S BEEN SEARCHING FOR HIS WHOLE CAREER. IF YOU CAN GET ME TO HIM, I SWEAR TO GOD YOU'LL NEVER LOOK BACK ON YOUR UNCLE'S SHITHOLE RUB AND TUG.
OR YOU CAN BEAT MY ASS TO DEATH AND NEVER KNOW. IT'S UP TO YOU.
YOU CHOOSE.

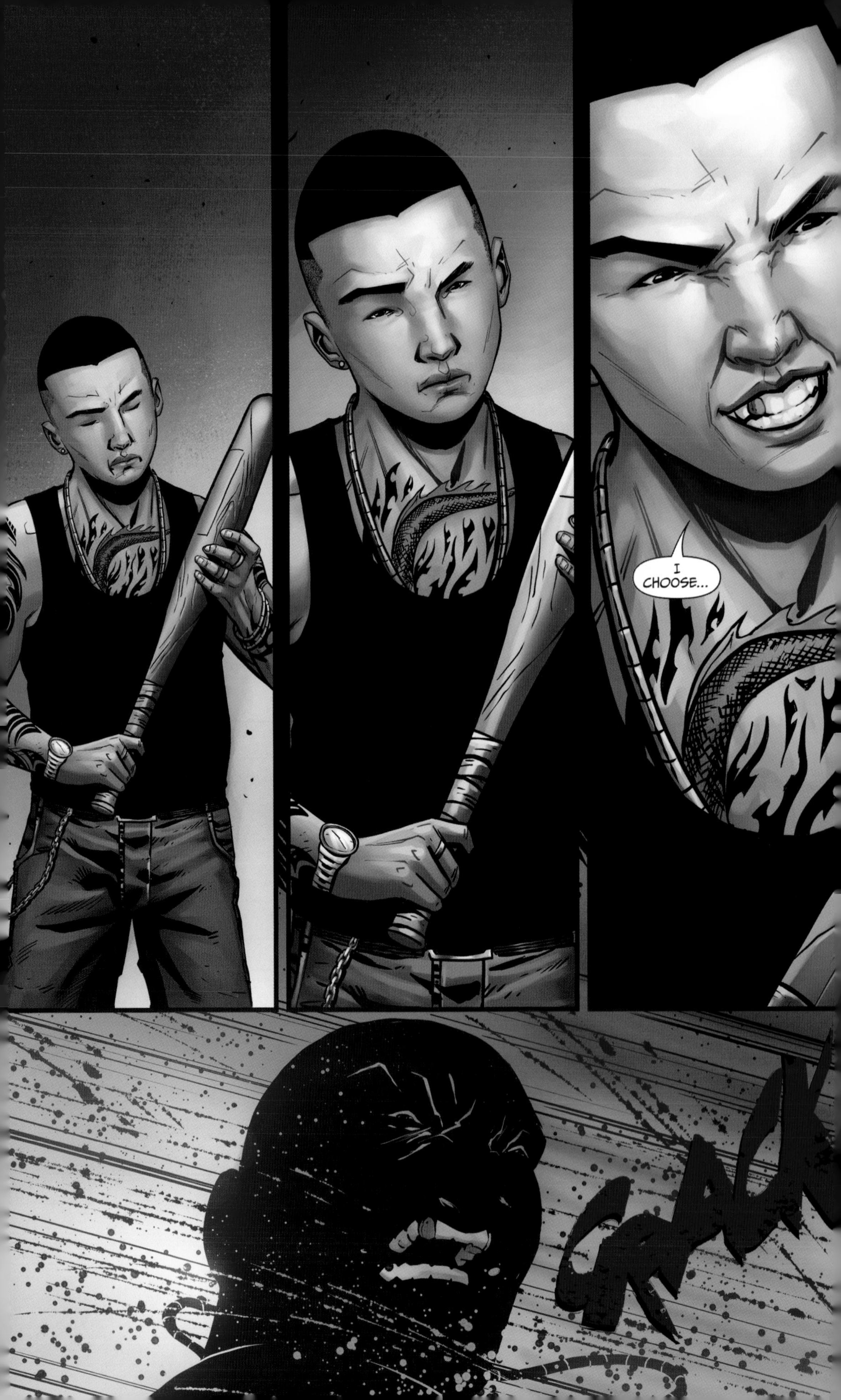
I CHOOSE...

BANG BANG BANG

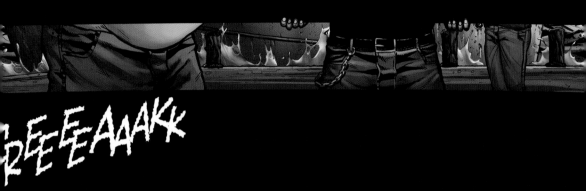

GREEEEAAAKK

MMMMM!

THE ASTROS? ARE YOU CRAZY?

WAIT! MORE ROCK IN POCKET. PUT MORE ROCK!

I CARE ABOUT METRICS, NOT STREAKS. NOT HUNCHES. NOT WISHES.

ENOUGH, ENOUGH! THROW!

MMFFF!

I SWEAR TO GOD, JONNY, YOU ARE DUMBER THAN YOU LOOK.

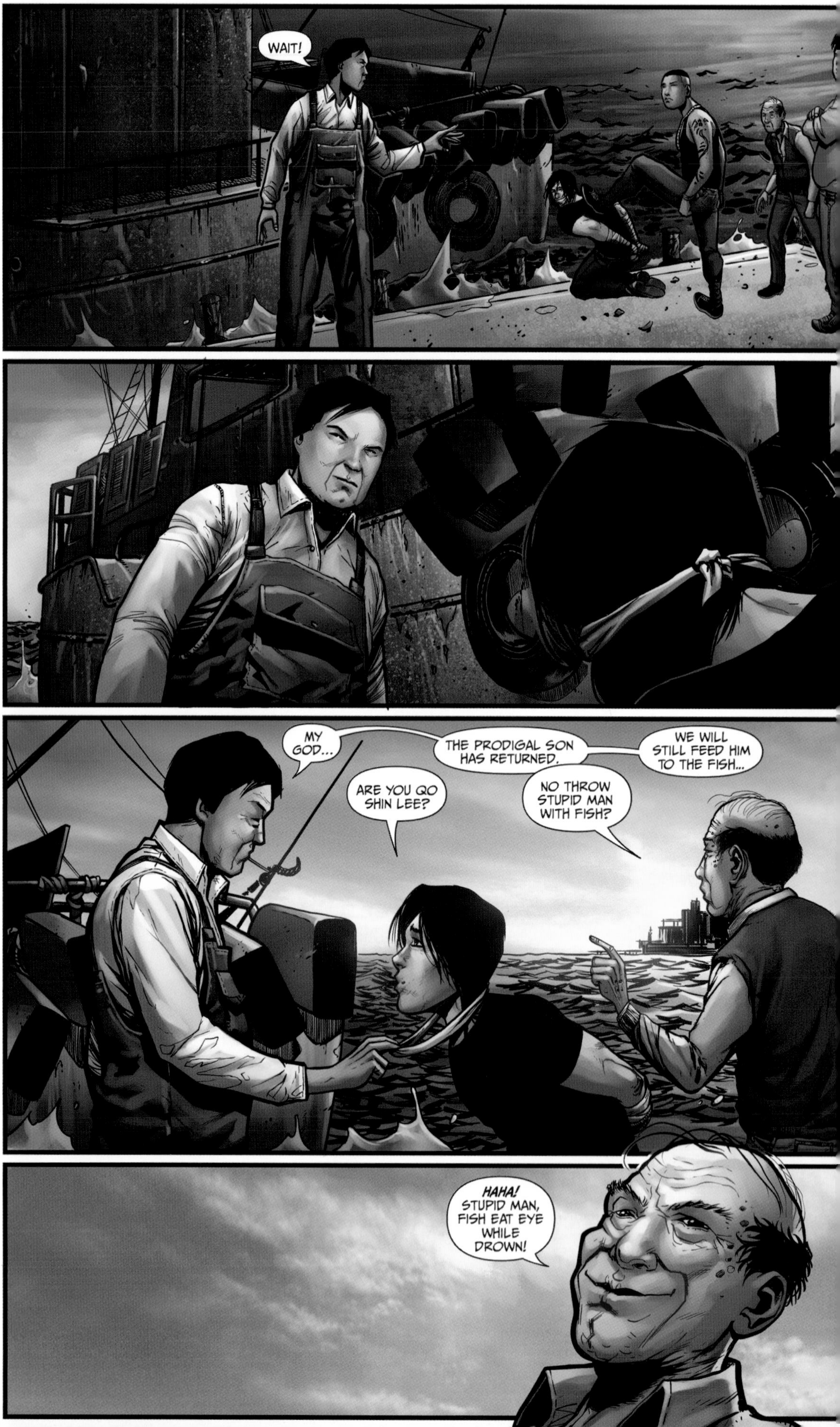
WAIT!
MY GOD...
THE PRODIGAL SON HAS RETURNED.
WE WILL STILL FEED HIM TO THE FISH...
ARE YOU QO SHIN LEE?
NO THROW STUPID MAN WITH FISH?
HAHA! STUPID MAN, FISH EAT EYE WHILE DROWN!

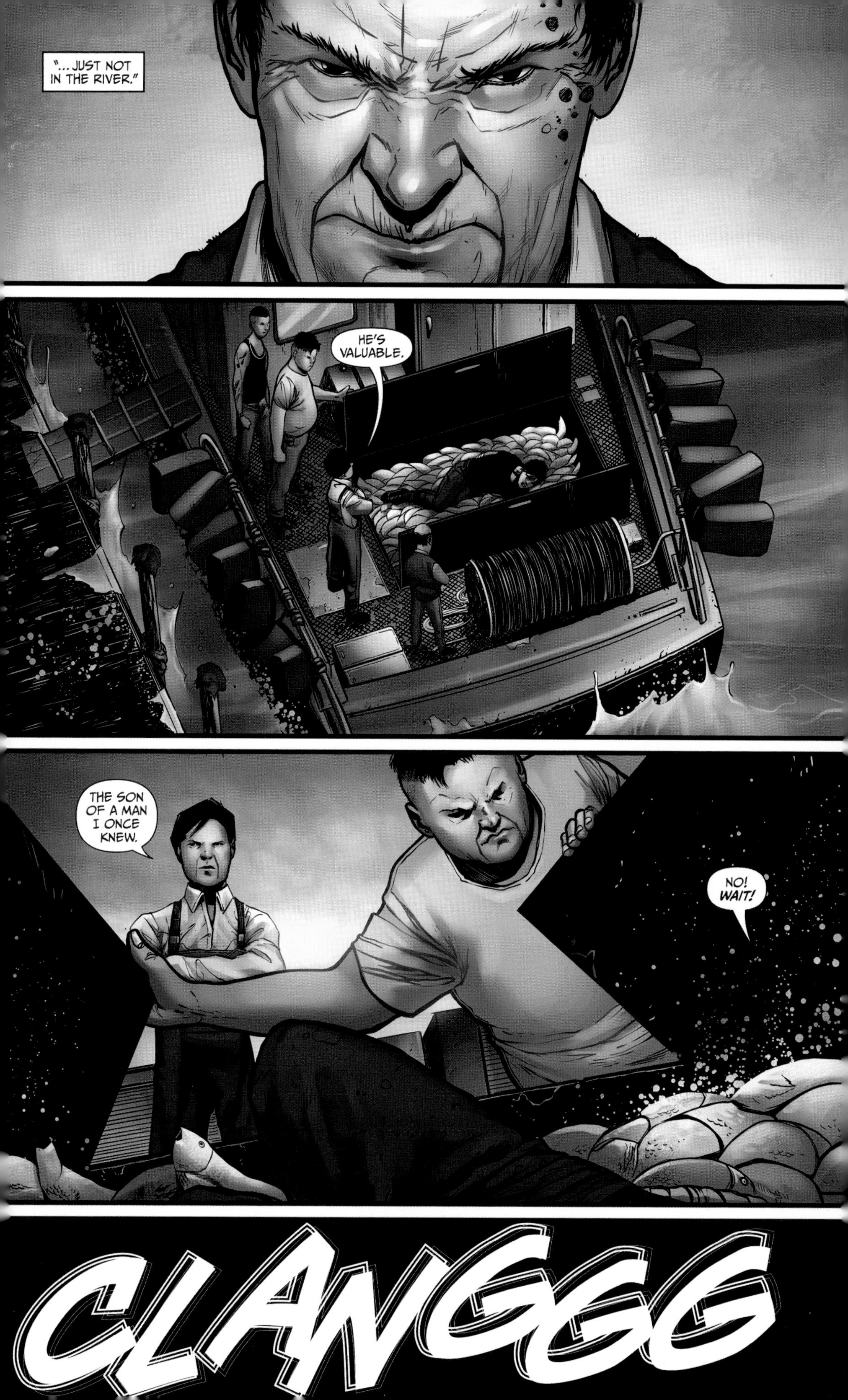
"... JUST NOT IN THE RIVER."
HE'S VALUABLE.
THE SON OF A MAN I ONCE KNEW.
NO! WAIT!
CLANGGG

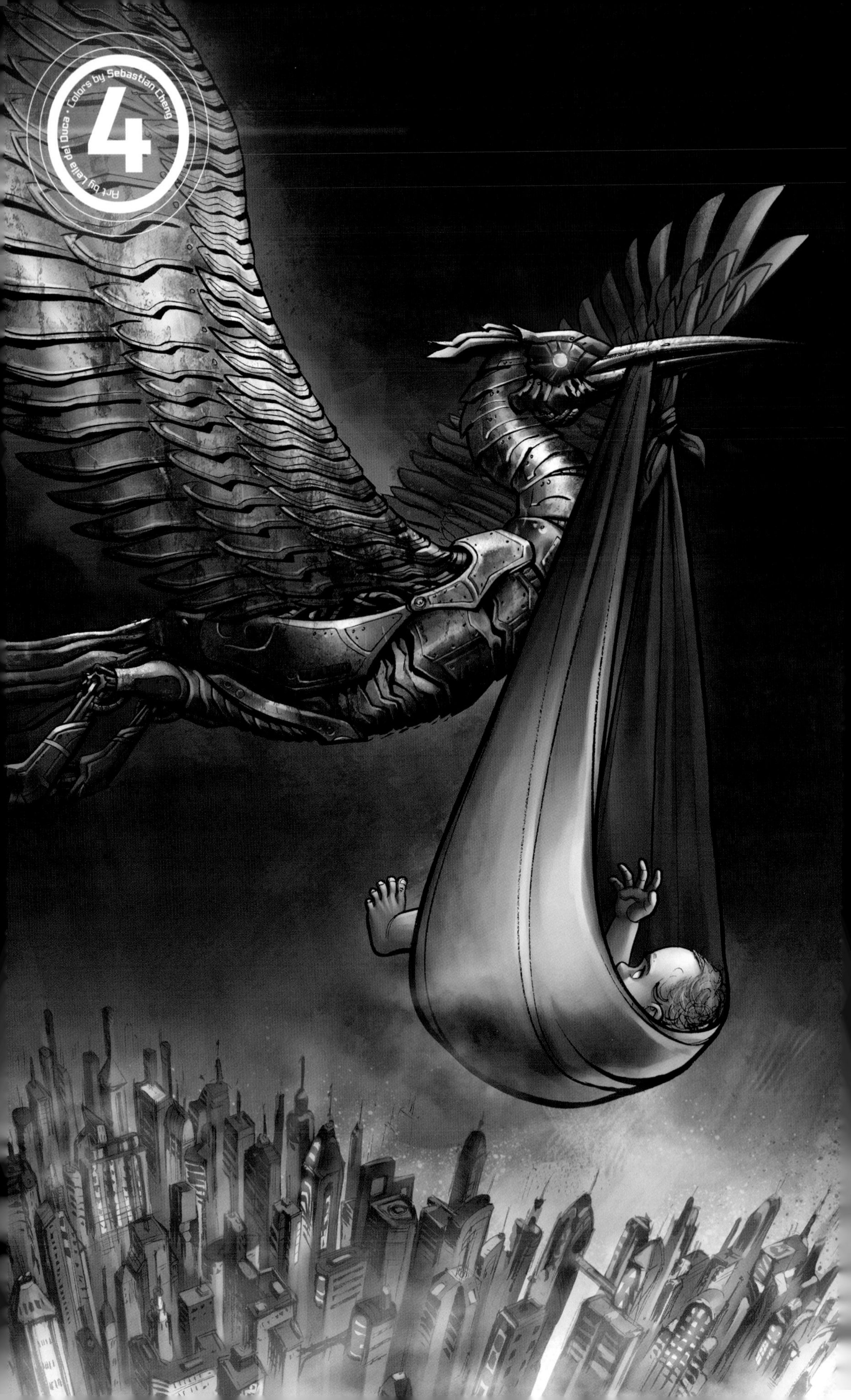
4
Art by Leila del Duca • Colors by Sebastian Cheng

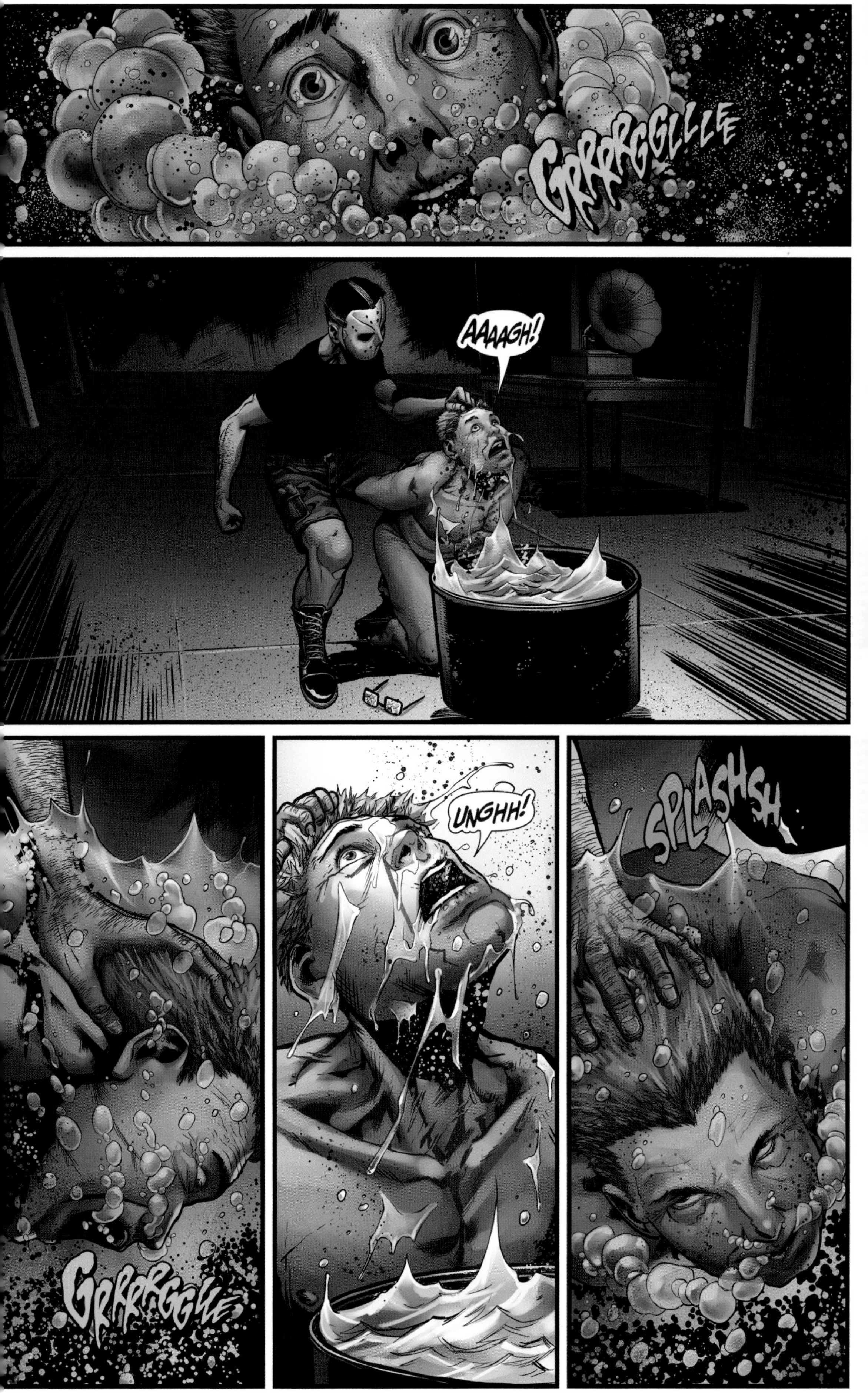
GRRRGGLLLEE
AAAAGH!
UNGHH!
SPLASHSH
GRRRGGLLE

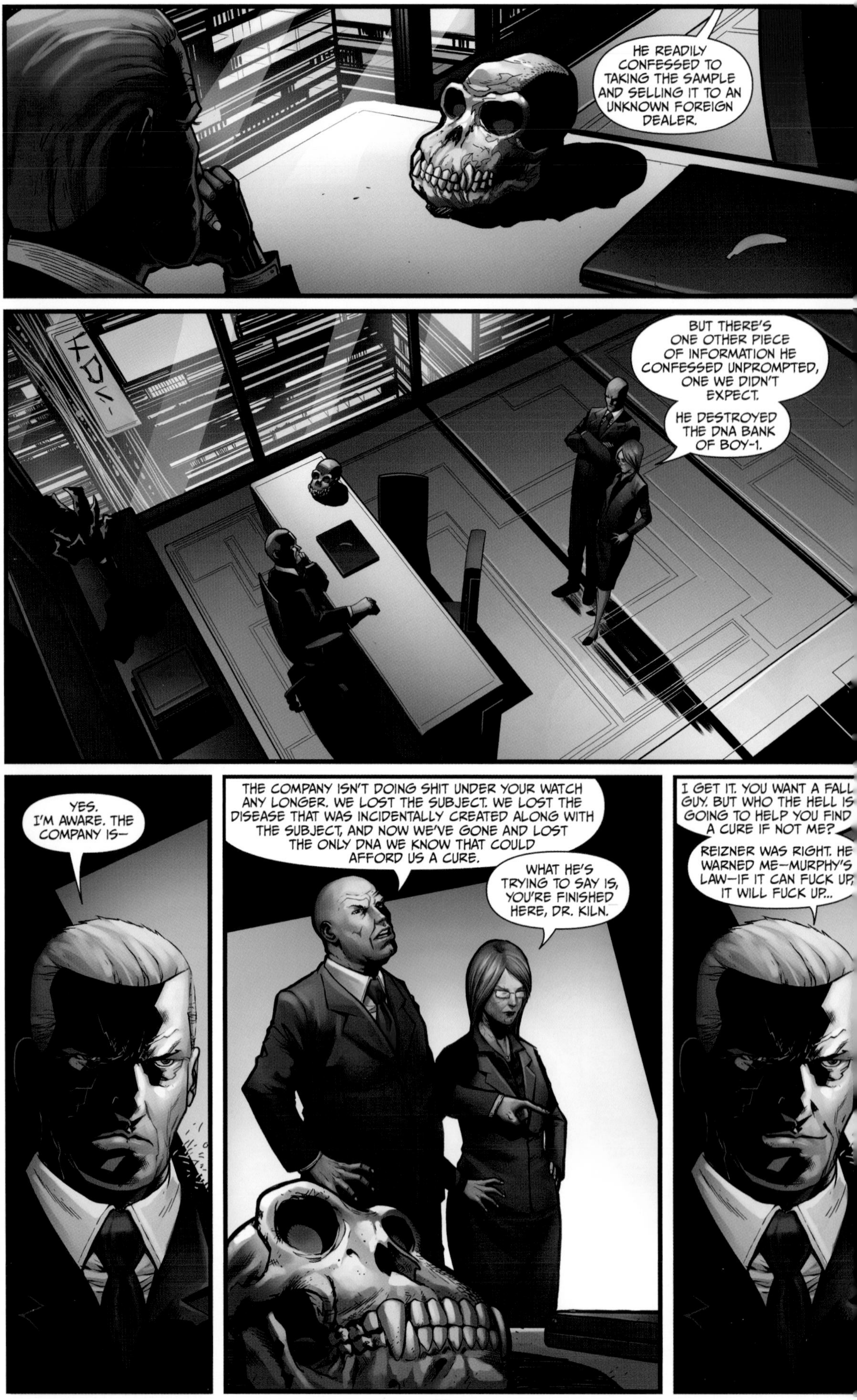
HE READILY CONFESSED TO TAKING THE SAMPLE AND SELLING IT TO AN UNKNOWN FOREIGN DEALER.
BUT THERE'S ONE OTHER PIECE OF INFORMATION HE CONFESSED UNPROMPTED, ONE WE DIDN'T EXPECT.
HE DESTROYED THE DNA BANK OF BOY-1.
YES. I'M AWARE. THE COMPANY IS—
THE COMPANY ISN'T DOING SHIT UNDER YOUR WATCH ANY LONGER. WE LOST THE SUBJECT. WE LOST THE DISEASE THAT WAS INCIDENTALLY CREATED ALONG WITH THE SUBJECT, AND NOW WE'VE GONE AND LOST THE ONLY DNA WE KNOW THAT COULD AFFORD US A CURE.
WHAT HE'S TRYING TO SAY IS, YOU'RE FINISHED HERE, DR. KILN.
I GET IT. YOU WANT A FALL GUY. BUT WHO THE HELL IS GOING TO HELP YOU FIND A CURE IF NOT ME?
REIZNER WAS RIGHT. HE WARNED ME—MURPHY'S LAW—IF IT CAN FUCK UP, IT WILL FUCK UP...

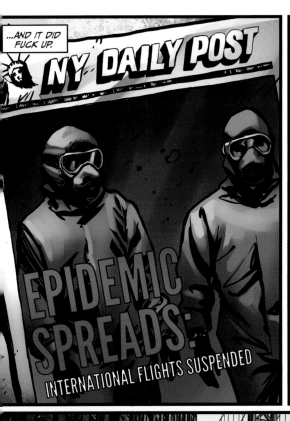

...AND IT DID FUCK UP.

NY DAILY POST

EPIDEMIC SPREADS: INTERNATIONAL FLIGHTS SUSPENDED

NY DAILY

EPIDEMIC SPREADS: INTERNATIONAL FLIGHTS SUSPENDED

PS 47 - Madam Walker School

EXCUSE ME, MS. ESTRADA?

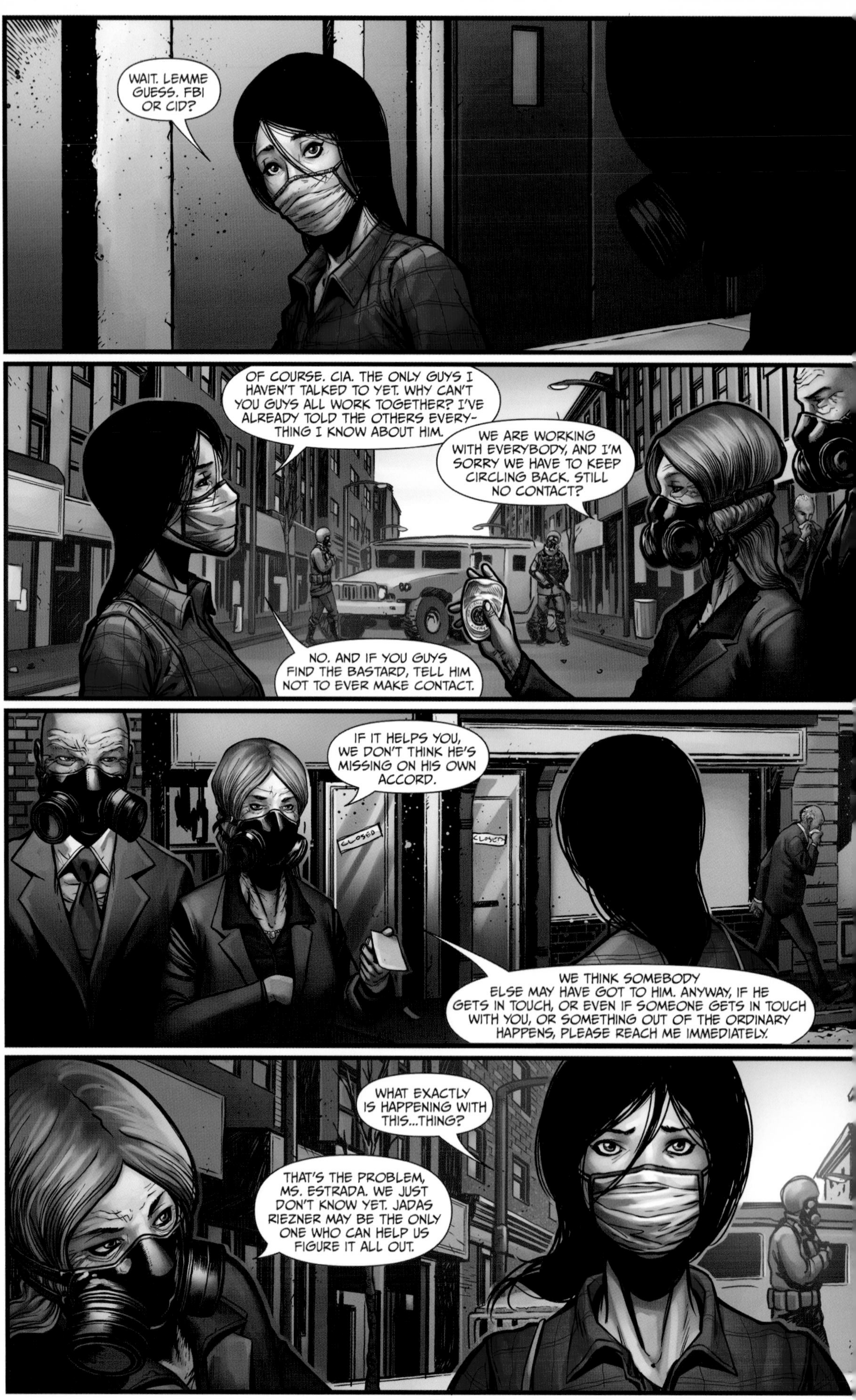

WAIT. LEMME GUESS. FBI OR CID?
OF COURSE. CIA. THE ONLY GUYS I HAVEN'T TALKED TO YET. WHY CAN'T YOU GUYS ALL WORK TOGETHER? I'VE ALREADY TOLD THE OTHERS EVERYTHING I KNOW ABOUT HIM.
WE ARE WORKING WITH EVERYBODY, AND I'M SORRY WE HAVE TO KEEP CIRCLING BACK. STILL NO CONTACT?
NO. AND IF YOU GUYS FIND THE BASTARD, TELL HIM NOT TO EVER MAKE CONTACT.
IF IT HELPS YOU, WE DON'T THINK HE'S MISSING ON HIS OWN ACCORD.
CLOSED
CLOSED
WE THINK SOMEBODY ELSE MAY HAVE GOT TO HIM. ANYWAY, IF HE GETS IN TOUCH, OR EVEN IF SOMEONE GETS IN TOUCH WITH YOU, OR SOMETHING OUT OF THE ORDINARY HAPPENS, PLEASE REACH ME IMMEDIATELY.
WHAT EXACTLY IS HAPPENING WITH THIS...THING?
THAT'S THE PROBLEM, MS. ESTRADA. WE JUST DON'T KNOW YET. JADAS RIEZNER MAY BE THE ONLY ONE WHO CAN HELP US FIGURE IT ALL OUT.

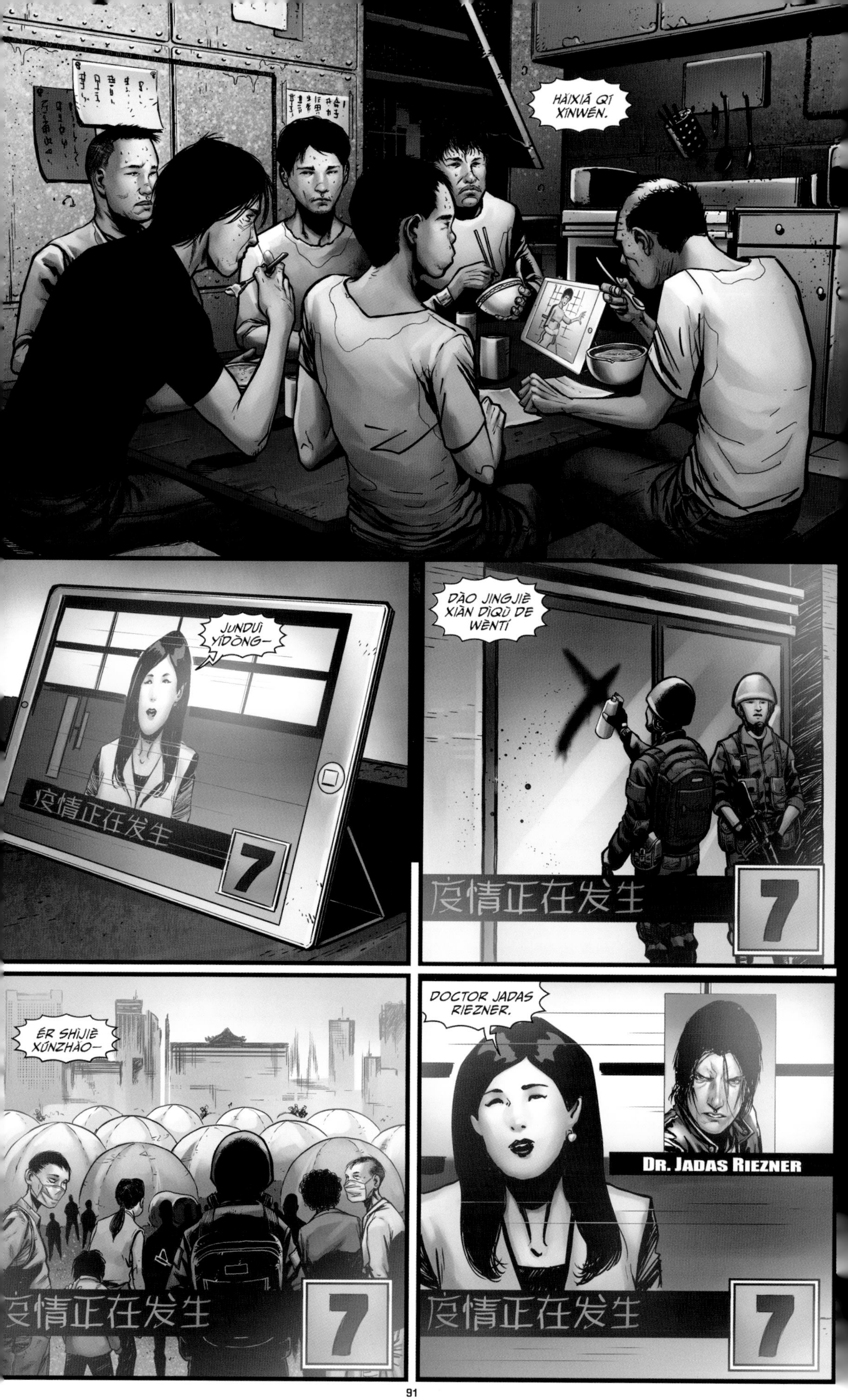
HǍIXIÁ QÍ XĪNWÉN.
JUNDUÌ YÍDÒNG—
疫情正在发生
7
DÀO JINGJIÈ XIÀN DÌQÙ DE WÈNTÍ
疫情正在发生
7
ÉR SHÌJIÈ XÚNZHǍO—
疫情正在发生
7
DOCTOR JADAS RIEZNER.
DR. JADAS RIEZNER
疫情正在发生
7

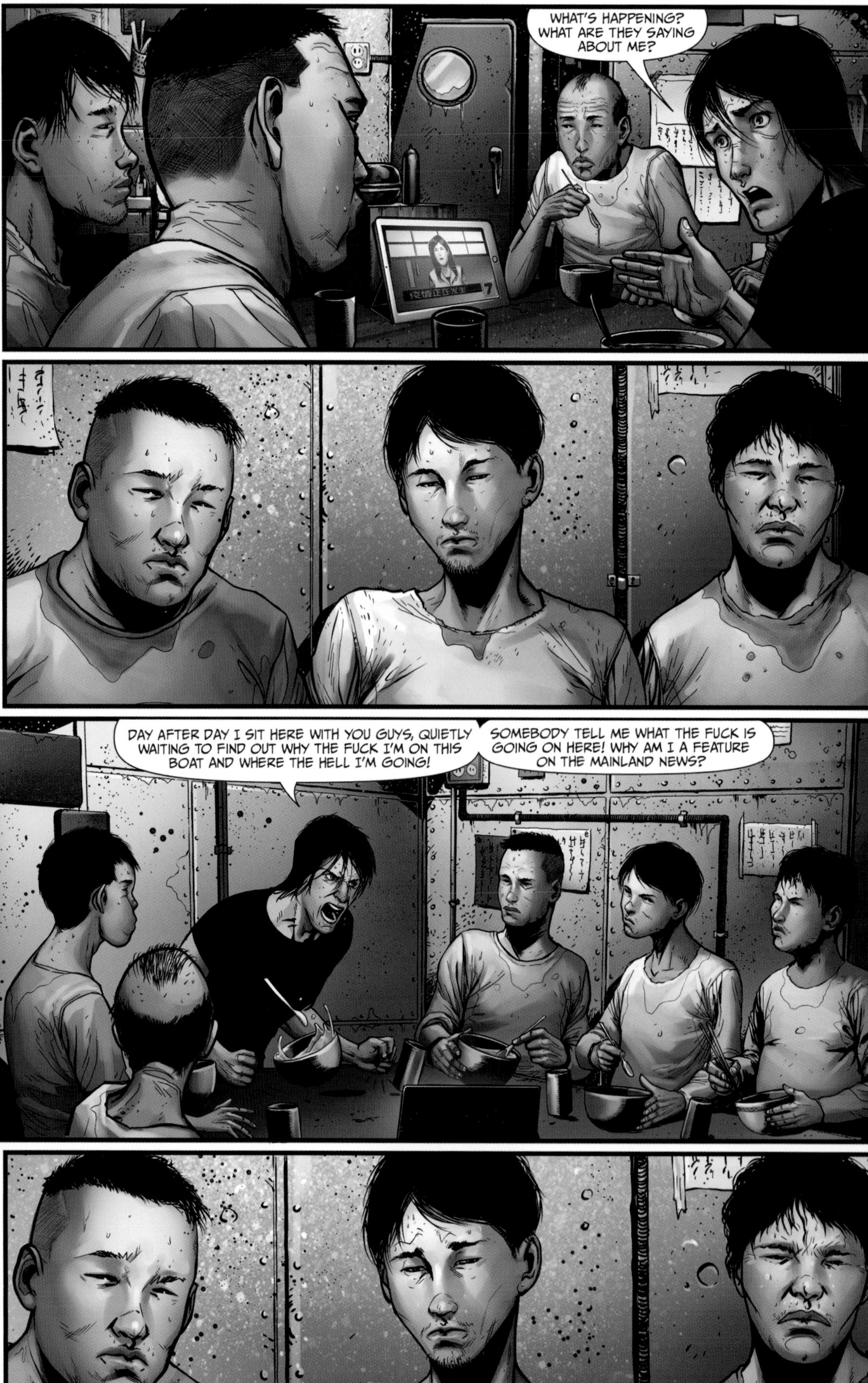
WHAT'S HAPPENING? WHAT ARE THEY SAYING ABOUT ME?
DAY AFTER DAY I SIT HERE WITH YOU GUYS, QUIETLY WAITING TO FIND OUT WHY THE FUCK I'M ON THIS BOAT AND WHERE THE HELL I'M GOING!
SOMEBODY TELL ME WHAT THE FUCK IS GOING ON HERE! WHY AM I A FEATURE ON THE MAINLAND NEWS?

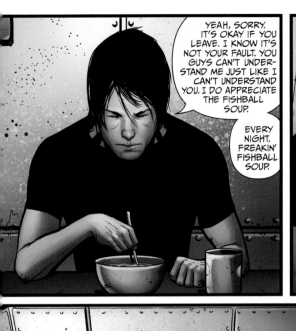

YEAH, SORRY. IT'S OKAY IF YOU LEAVE. I KNOW IT'S NOT YOUR FAULT. YOU GUYS CAN'T UNDERSTAND ME JUST LIKE I CAN'T UNDERSTAND YOU. I DO APPRECIATE THE FISHBALL SOUP.

EVERY NIGHT. FREAKIN' FISHBALL SOUP.

100 MILLION IN REDCOIN.

THE INTERNATIONAL PRICE ON YOUR HEAD.

WHY?

WHATEVER IS HAPPENING AROUND THE WORLD, PEOPLE SEEM TO THINK YOU'RE THE ANSWER.

AM I?

I'M NOT SMART ENOUGH TO FIGURE THAT OUT.

SO WHERE ARE YOU TAKING ME?

I'M ONLY TAKING YOU WHERE YOU WANTED TO GO.

"I'M TAKING YOU TO YOUR MAKER."

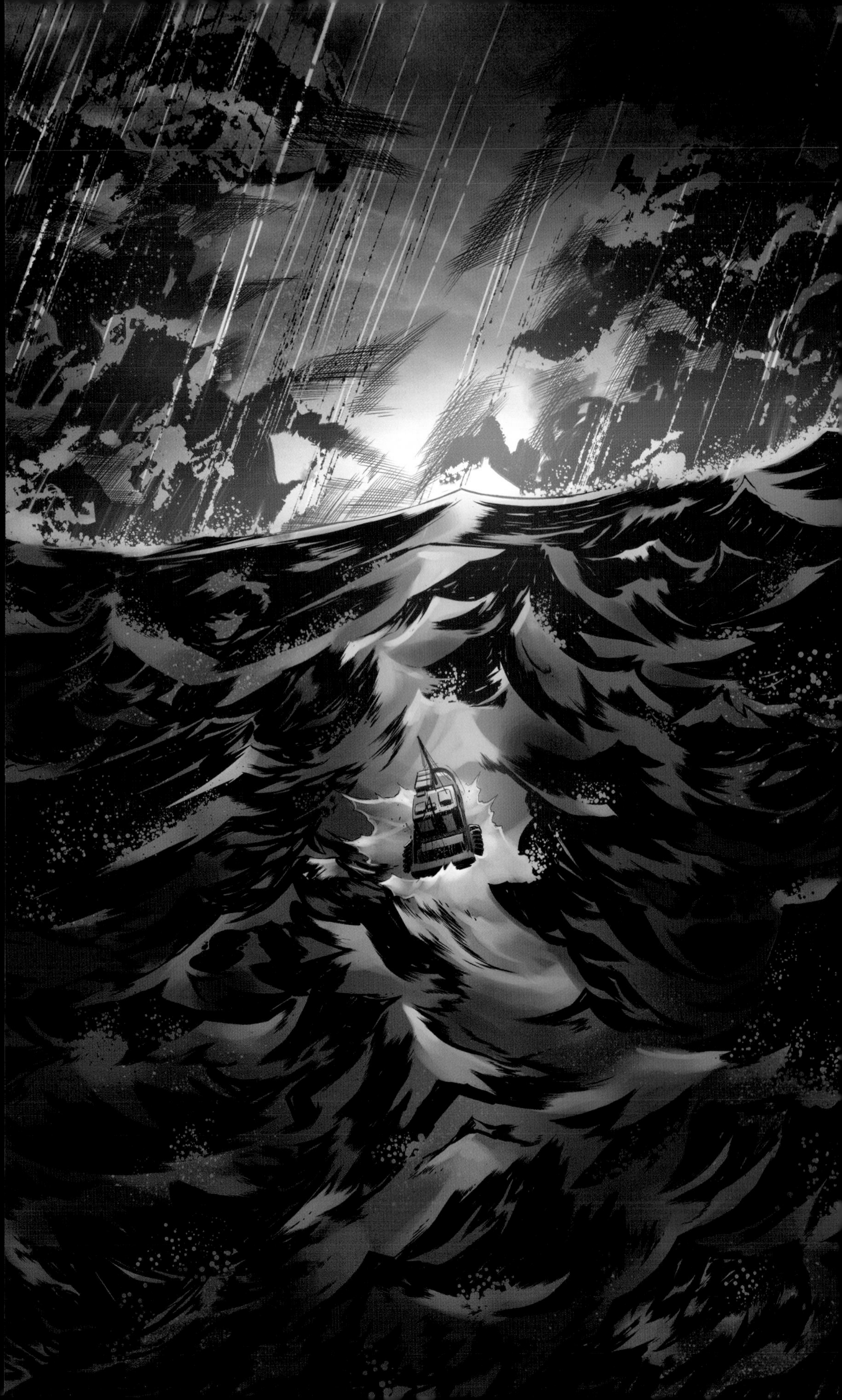

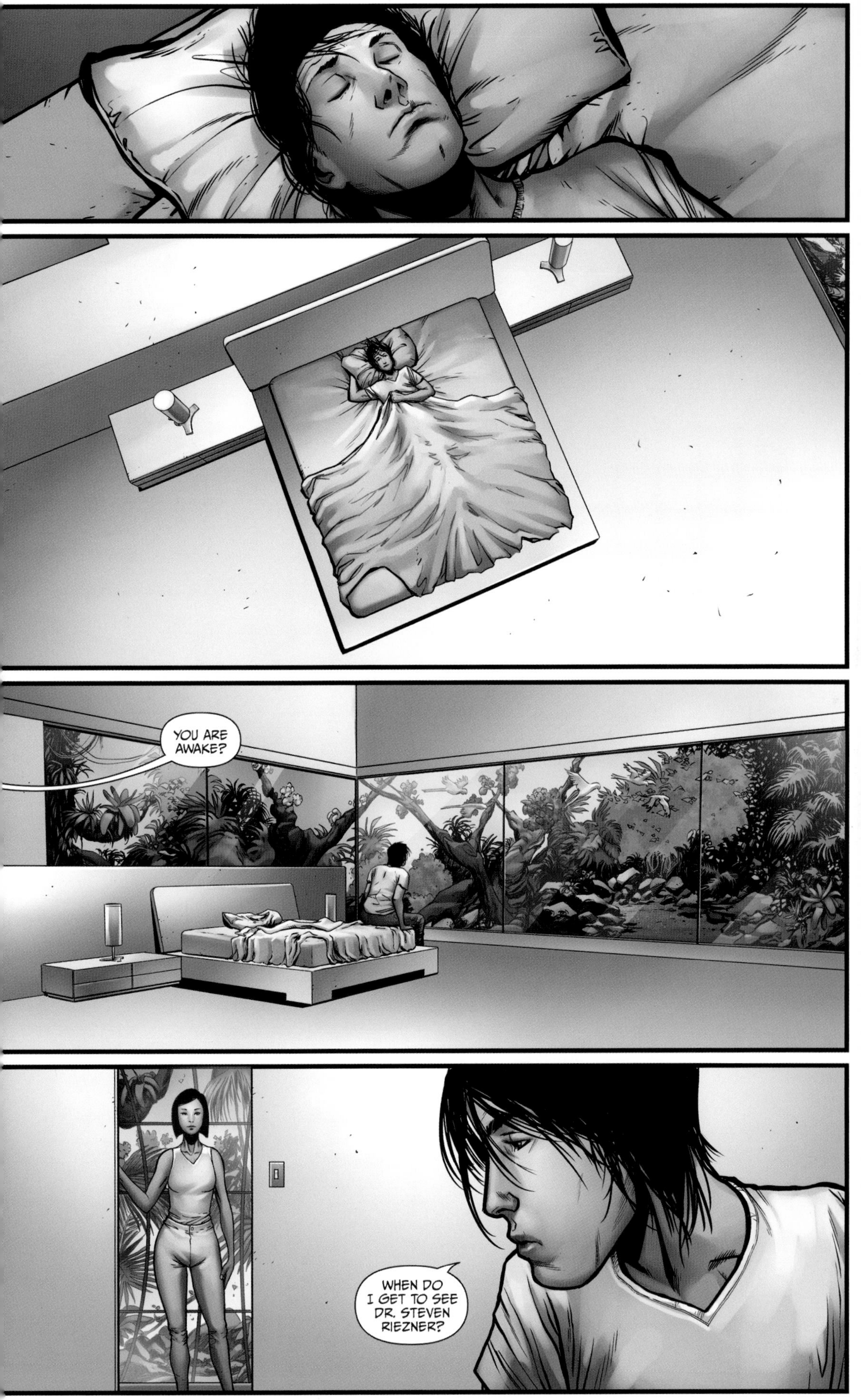
YOU ARE AWAKE?
WHEN DO I GET TO SEE DR. STEVEN RIEZNER?

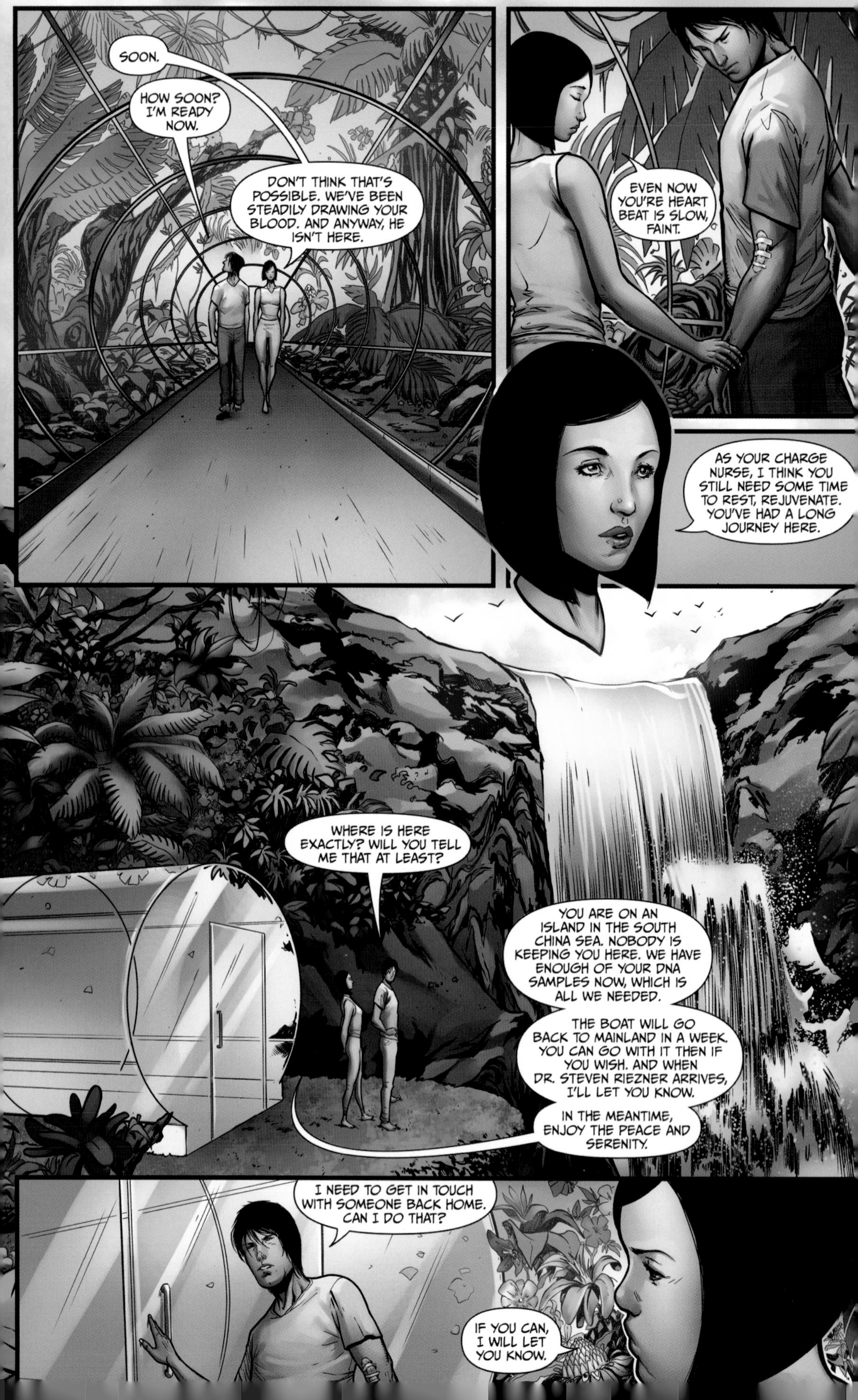
SOON.
HOW SOON? I'M READY NOW.
DON'T THINK THAT'S POSSIBLE. WE'VE BEEN STEADILY DRAWING YOUR BLOOD. AND ANYWAY, HE ISN'T HERE.
EVEN NOW YOU'RE HEART BEAT IS SLOW, FAINT.
AS YOUR CHARGE NURSE, I THINK YOU STILL NEED SOME TIME TO REST, REJUVENATE. YOU'VE HAD A LONG JOURNEY HERE.
WHERE IS HERE EXACTLY? WILL YOU TELL ME THAT AT LEAST?
YOU ARE ON AN ISLAND IN THE SOUTH CHINA SEA. NOBODY IS KEEPING YOU HERE. WE HAVE ENOUGH OF YOUR DNA SAMPLES NOW, WHICH IS ALL WE NEEDED.
THE BOAT WILL GO BACK TO MAINLAND IN A WEEK. YOU CAN GO WITH IT THEN IF YOU WISH. AND WHEN DR. STEVEN RIEZNER ARRIVES, I'LL LET YOU KNOW.
IN THE MEANTIME, ENJOY THE PEACE AND SERENITY.
I NEED TO GET IN TOUCH WITH SOMEONE BACK HOME. CAN I DO THAT?
IF YOU CAN, I WILL LET YOU KNOW.

YOU ARE SATELLITE-LINKED AND CAN REACH WHOEVER YOU WANT, BUT EACH COMMUNICATION SESSION CAN ONLY LAST TWO MINUTES, THIRTY SECONDS. THIS WAY EVERYTHING IS COMPLETELY SECURE AND UNTRACEABLE.

PLEASE DON'T MAKE ANY MENTION OF WHERE YOU ARE, OR YOUR SURROUNDINGS. AS MUCH AS WE WANT TO ACCOMMODATE YOU, WE ALSO NEED TO PROTECT OURSELVES.

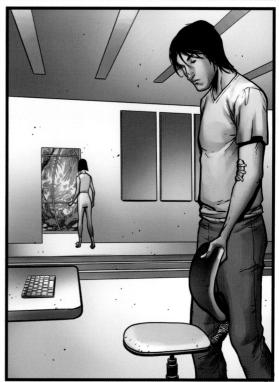

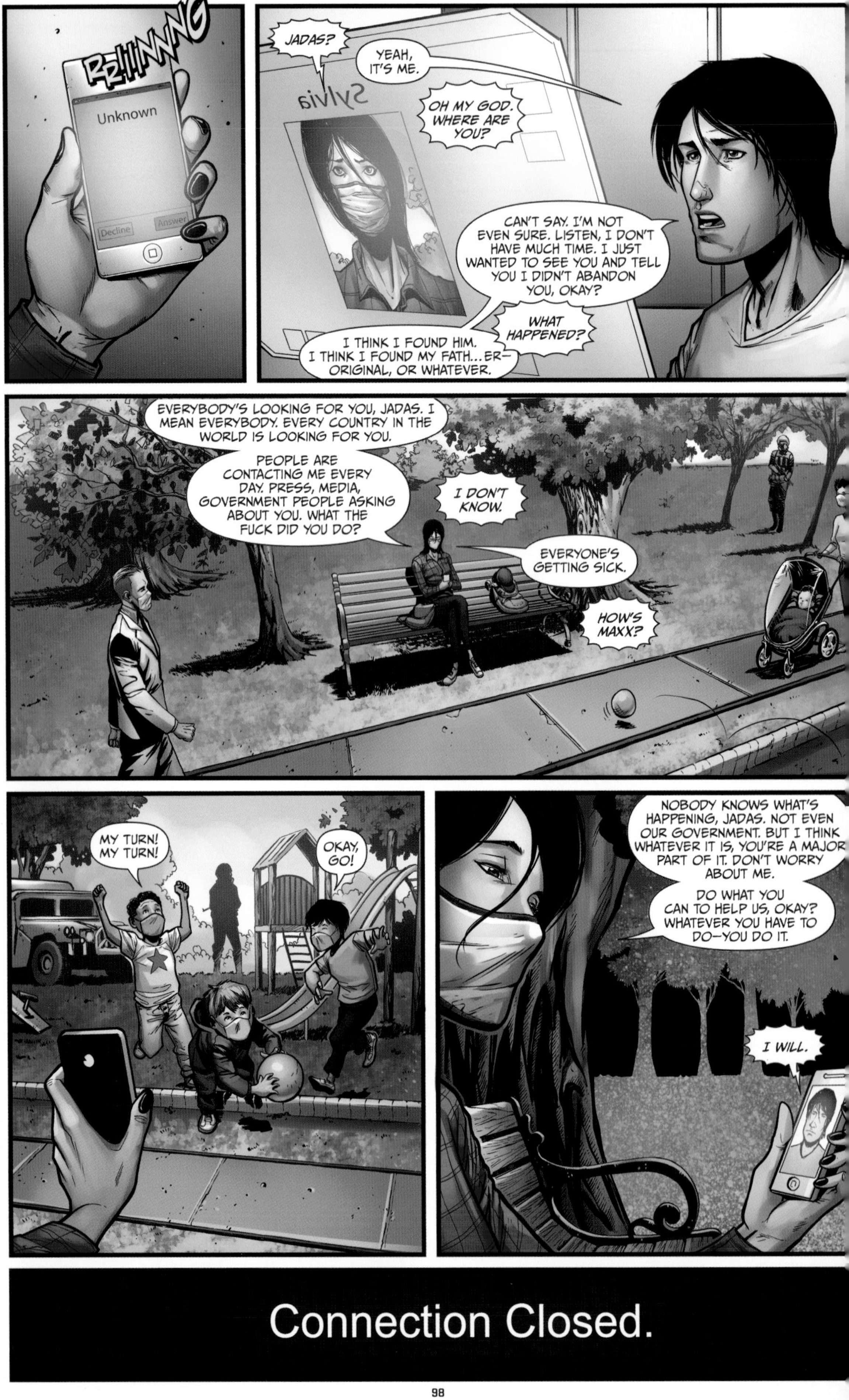
RRIIINNNG
Unknown
Decline
Answer
JADAS?
YEAH, IT'S ME.
OH MY GOD. WHERE ARE YOU?
CAN'T SAY. I'M NOT EVEN SURE. LISTEN, I DON'T HAVE MUCH TIME. I JUST WANTED TO SEE YOU AND TELL YOU I DIDN'T ABANDON YOU, OKAY?
WHAT HAPPENED?
I THINK I FOUND HIM. I THINK I FOUND MY FATH... ER—ORIGINAL, OR WHATEVER.
EVERYBODY'S LOOKING FOR YOU, JADAS. I MEAN EVERYBODY. EVERY COUNTRY IN THE WORLD IS LOOKING FOR YOU.
PEOPLE ARE CONTACTING ME EVERY DAY. PRESS, MEDIA, GOVERNMENT PEOPLE ASKING ABOUT YOU. WHAT THE FUCK DID YOU DO?
I DON'T KNOW.
EVERYONE'S GETTING SICK.
HOW'S MAXX?
MY TURN! MY TURN!
OKAY, GO!
NOBODY KNOWS WHAT'S HAPPENING, JADAS. NOT EVEN OUR GOVERNMENT. BUT I THINK WHATEVER IT IS, YOU'RE A MAJOR PART OF IT. DON'T WORRY ABOUT ME.
DO WHAT YOU CAN TO HELP US, OKAY? WHATEVER YOU HAVE TO DO—YOU DO IT.
I WILL.
Connection Closed.

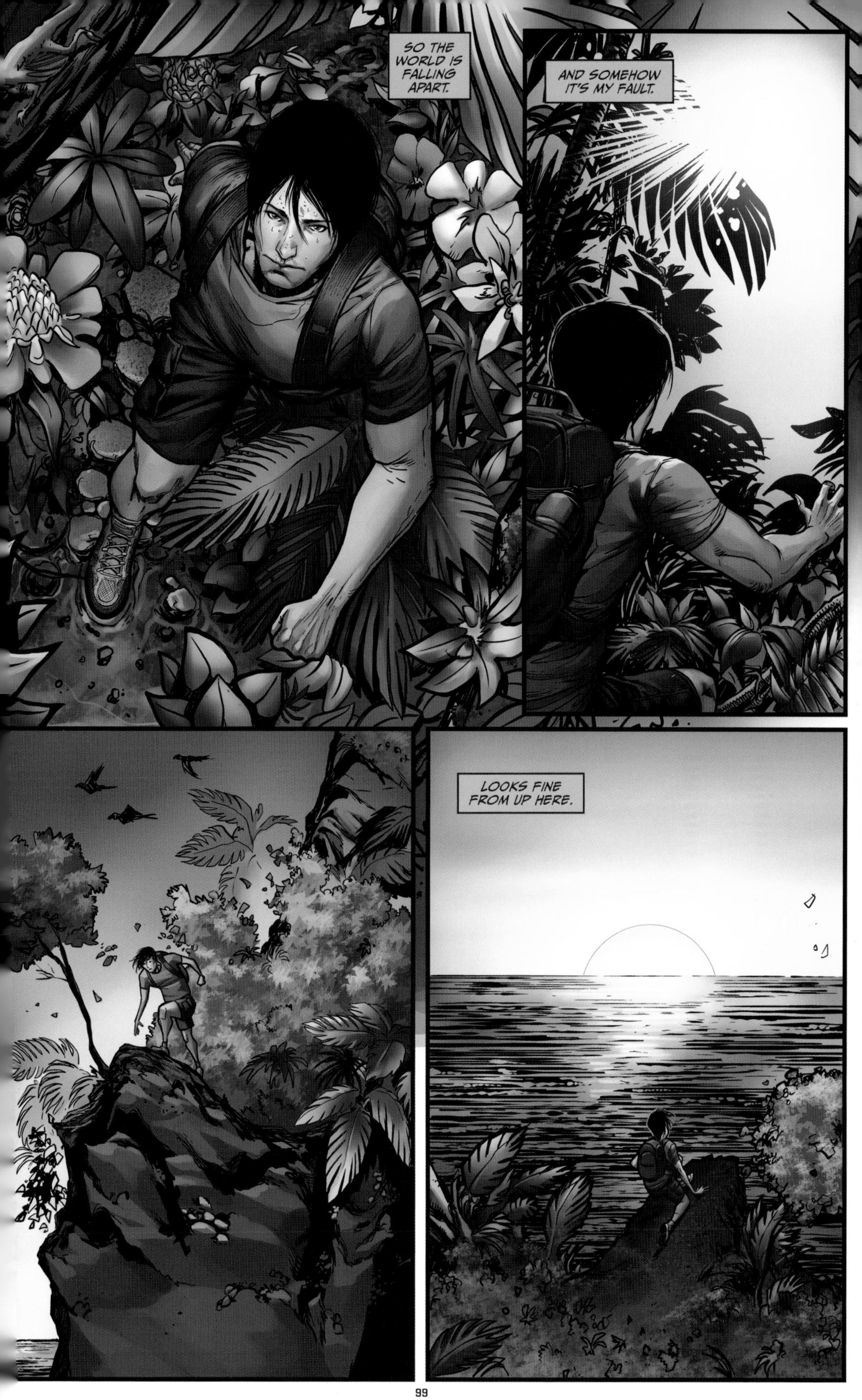
SO THE WORLD IS FALLING APART.
AND SOMEHOW IT'S MY FAULT.
LOOKS FINE FROM UP HERE.

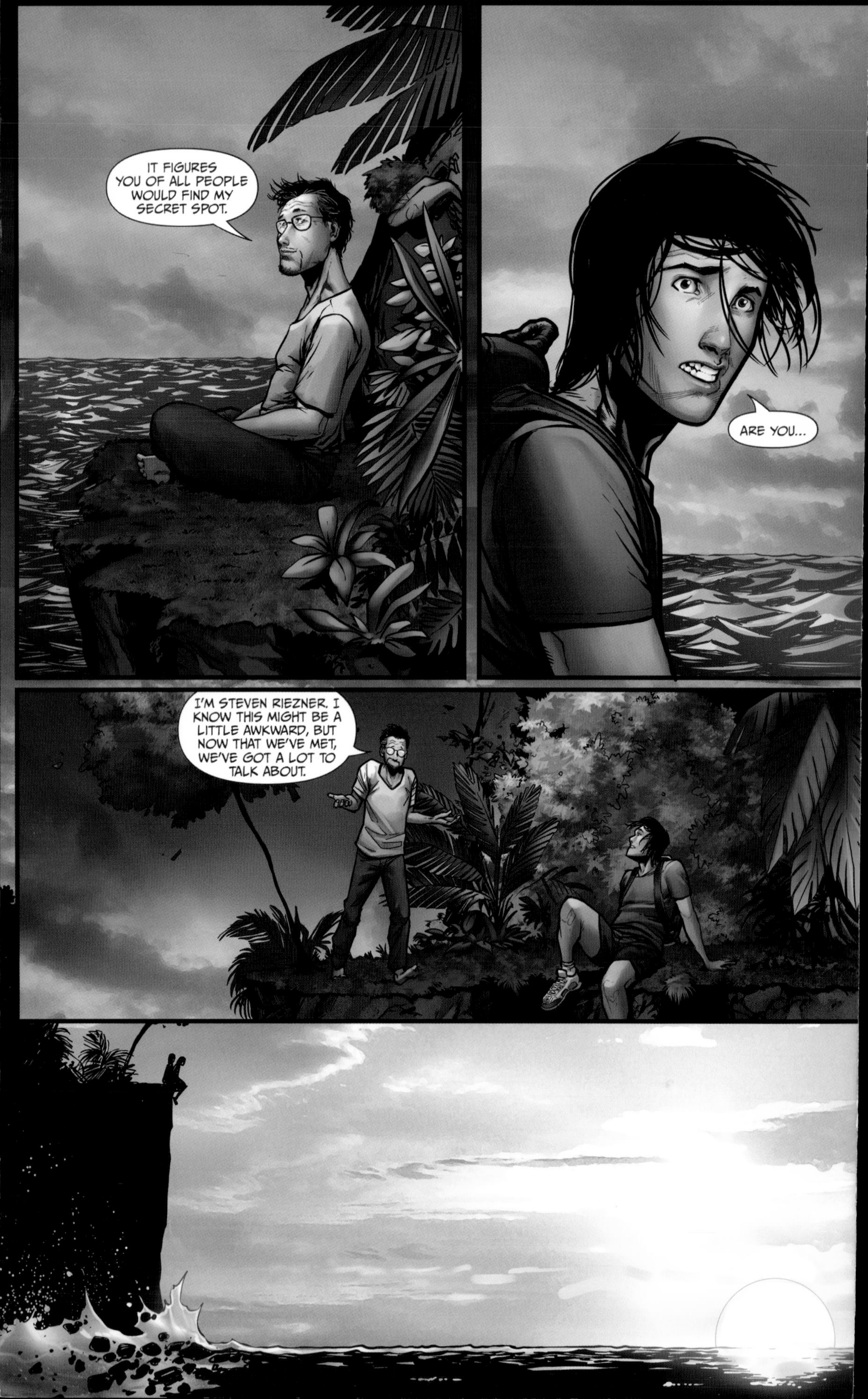
IT FIGURES YOU OF ALL PEOPLE WOULD FIND MY SECRET SPOT.
ARE YOU...
I'M STEVEN RIEZNER. I KNOW THIS MIGHT BE A LITTLE AWKWARD, BUT NOW THAT WE'VE MET, WE'VE GOT A LOT TO TALK ABOUT.

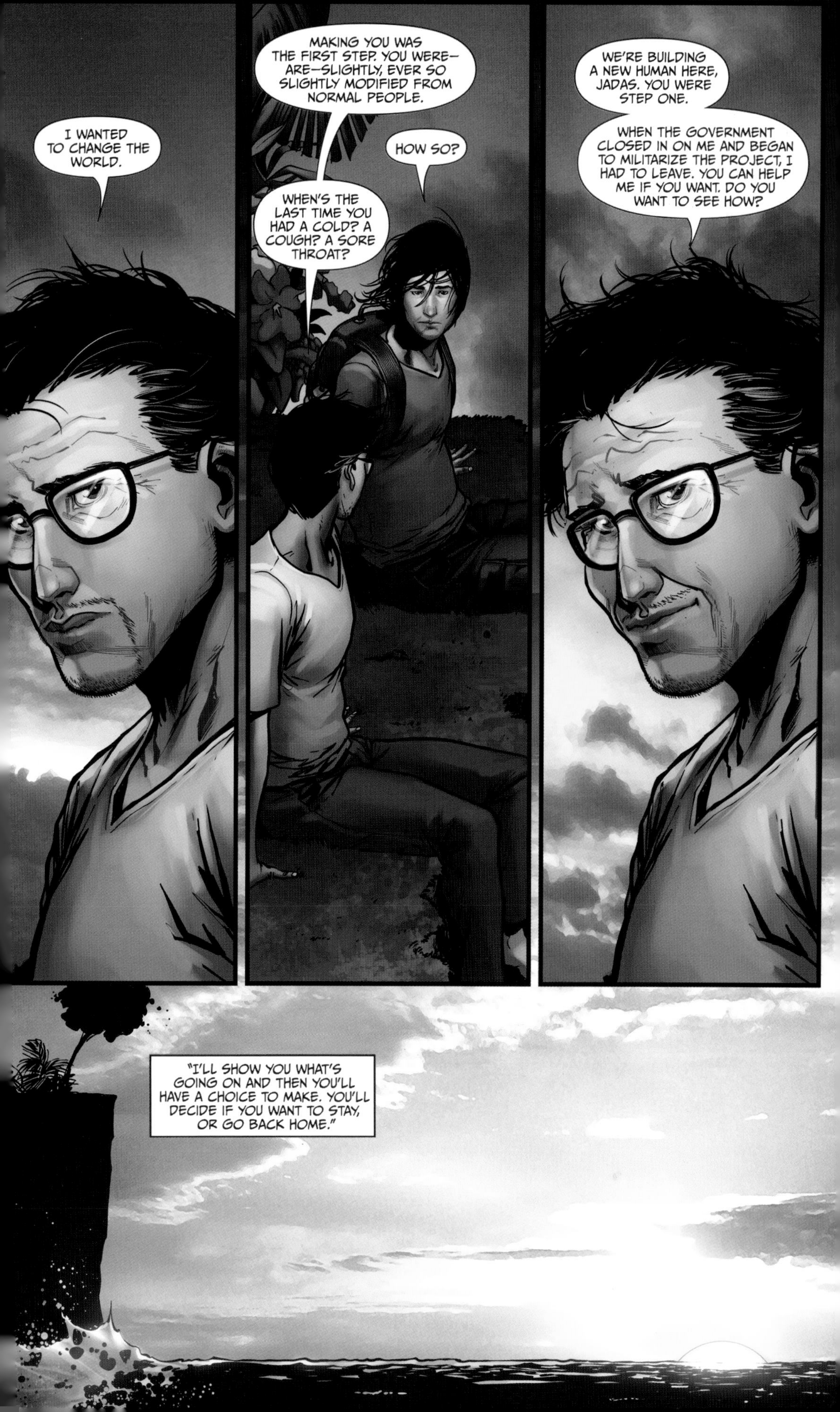
I WANTED TO CHANGE THE WORLD.
MAKING YOU WAS THE FIRST STEP. YOU WERE—ARE—SLIGHTLY, EVER SO SLIGHTLY MODIFIED FROM NORMAL PEOPLE.
HOW SO?
WHEN'S THE LAST TIME YOU HAD A COLD? A COUGH? A SORE THROAT?
WE'RE BUILDING A NEW HUMAN HERE, JADAS. YOU WERE STEP ONE.
WHEN THE GOVERNMENT CLOSED IN ON ME AND BEGAN TO MILITARIZE THE PROJECT, I HAD TO LEAVE. YOU CAN HELP ME IF YOU WANT. DO YOU WANT TO SEE HOW?
"I'LL SHOW YOU WHAT'S GOING ON AND THEN YOU'LL HAVE A CHOICE TO MAKE. YOU'LL DECIDE IF YOU WANT TO STAY, OR GO BACK HOME."

I'M HONESTLY NOT SURE HOW THE DISEASE GOT OUT. THE P.L.A., WHO HAS BEEN FUNDING MY RESEARCH HERE, PROMISED ME IT WASN'T THEM. I'M NOT SURE IF IT MAKES A DIFFERENCE.

EITHER WAY, EK3 WAS KEPT SECURE BY THE U.S. CHEMICAL CORPS TO COME OUT AT SOME POINT IN TIME. WHY ELSE WOULD THEY WANT TO KEEP IT AROUND?

NOW THAT EK3 IS OUT OF THE BAG AND BEGINNING TO DECIMATE POPULATIONS IN DIFFERENT PARTS OF THE WORLD, IT WAS A GODSEND WE FOUND YOU. YOUR GENES HAVE A NATURAL, BUILT-IN IMMUNITY.

HOW MANY PEOPLE HAVE DIED SO FAR?

BY CHINA'S INTELLIGENCE, FIFTY-FIVE TO SIXTY SO FAR.

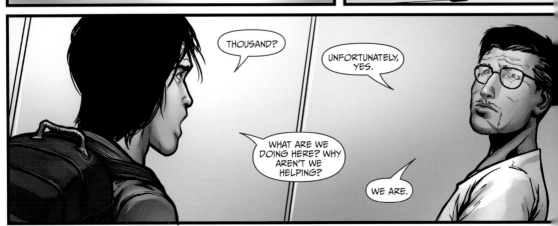

THOUSAND?

UNFORTUNATELY, YES.

WHAT ARE WE DOING HERE? WHY AREN'T WE HELPING?

WE ARE.

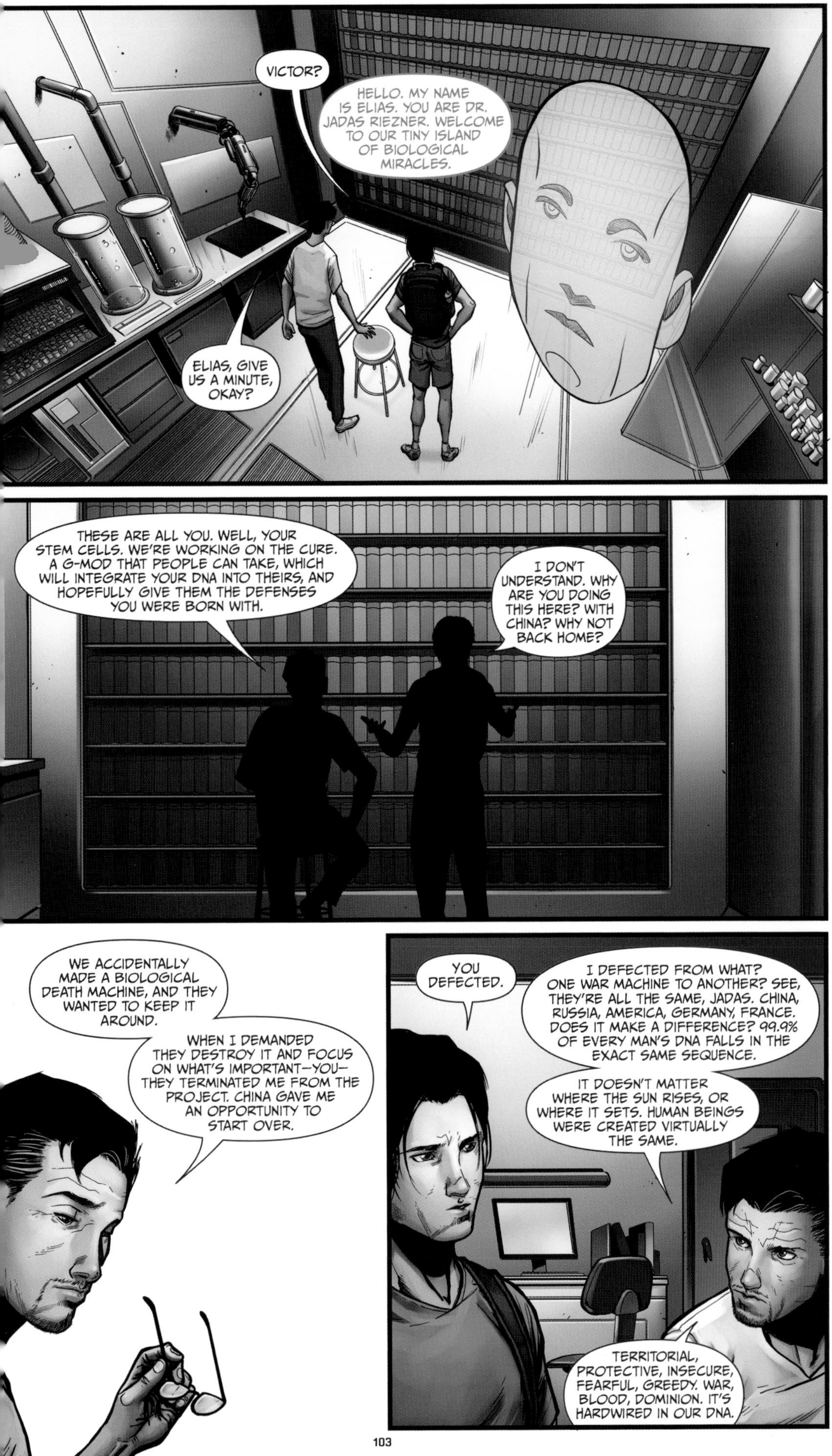
VICTOR?
HELLO. MY NAME IS ELIAS. YOU ARE DR. JADAS RIEZNER. WELCOME TO OUR TINY ISLAND OF BIOLOGICAL MIRACLES.
ELIAS, GIVE US A MINUTE, OKAY?
THESE ARE ALL YOU. WELL, YOUR STEM CELLS. WE'RE WORKING ON THE CURE. A G-MOD THAT PEOPLE CAN TAKE, WHICH WILL INTEGRATE YOUR DNA INTO THEIRS, AND HOPEFULLY GIVE THEM THE DEFENSES YOU WERE BORN WITH.
I DON'T UNDERSTAND. WHY ARE YOU DOING THIS HERE? WITH CHINA? WHY NOT BACK HOME?
WE ACCIDENTALLY MADE A BIOLOGICAL DEATH MACHINE, AND THEY WANTED TO KEEP IT AROUND.
WHEN I DEMANDED THEY DESTROY IT AND FOCUS ON WHAT'S IMPORTANT—YOU—THEY TERMINATED ME FROM THE PROJECT. CHINA GAVE ME AN OPPORTUNITY TO START OVER.
YOU DEFECTED.
I DEFECTED FROM WHAT? ONE WAR MACHINE TO ANOTHER? SEE, THEY'RE ALL THE SAME, JADAS. CHINA, RUSSIA, AMERICA, GERMANY, FRANCE. DOES IT MAKE A DIFFERENCE? 99.9% OF EVERY MAN'S DNA FALLS IN THE EXACT SAME SEQUENCE.
IT DOESN'T MATTER WHERE THE SUN RISES, OR WHERE IT SETS. HUMAN BEINGS WERE CREATED VIRTUALLY THE SAME.
TERRITORIAL, PROTECTIVE, INSECURE, FEARFUL, GREEDY. WAR, BLOOD, DOMINION. IT'S HARDWIRED IN OUR DNA.

THE WORLD IS AT A TIPPING POINT RIGHT NOW. WITH THE ONSET OF THIS DISEASE THREATENING MASS HUMAN EXTINCTION, WE HAVE THE ABILITY TO NUDGE HUMANITY, OR WHATEVER IS LEFT OF IT, INTO ANOTHER DIRECTION.

WHAT DO YOU MEAN EXACTLY?

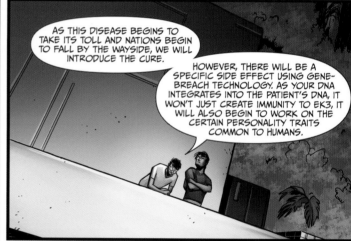

AS THIS DISEASE BEGINS TO TAKE ITS TOLL AND NATIONS BEGIN TO FALL BY THE WAYSIDE, WE WILL INTRODUCE THE CURE.

HOWEVER, THERE WILL BE A SPECIFIC SIDE EFFECT USING GENE-BREACH TECHNOLOGY. AS YOUR DNA INTEGRATES INTO THE PATIENT'S DNA, IT WON'T JUST CREATE IMMUNITY TO EK3, IT WILL ALSO BEGIN TO WORK ON THE CERTAIN PERSONALITY TRAITS COMMON TO HUMANS.

YOU'RE GOING TO FUNDAMENTALLY CHANGE HUMAN BEHAVIOR?

YES. AT THEIR CORE. AT THEIR DNA. GREED, SELF-PRESERVATION, FEAR. MOST OF IT ALL COMES FROM FEAR. WE'VE IDENTIFIED THE GENES EXPRESSING THESE TRAITS, AND WE'RE GOING TO ERADICATE THEM.

HOW DO YOU KNOW IT WILL WORK? I MEAN, YOU'RE TAKING A HUGE FUCKING RISK WITH CONSEQUENCES YOU CAN'T POSSIBLY SEE.

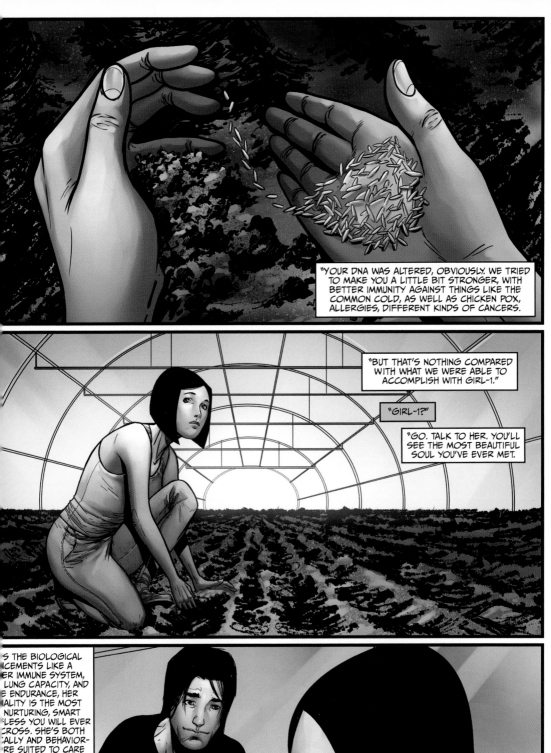

"YOUR DNA WAS ALTERED, OBVIOUSLY. WE TRIED TO MAKE YOU A LITTLE BIT STRONGER, WITH BETTER IMMUNITY AGAINST THINGS LIKE THE COMMON COLD, AS WELL AS CHICKEN POX, ALLERGIES, DIFFERENT KINDS OF CANCERS.

"BUT THAT'S NOTHING COMPARED WITH WHAT WE WERE ABLE TO ACCOMPLISH WITH GIRL-1."

"GIRL-1?"

"GO. TALK TO HER. YOU'LL SEE THE MOST BEAUTIFUL SOUL YOU'VE EVER MET.

S THE BIOLOGICAL
NCEMENTS LIKE A
ER IMMUNE SYSTEM,
LUNG CAPACITY, AND
E ENDURANCE, HER
ALITY IS THE MOST
NURTURING, SMART
LESS YOU WILL EVER
CROSS. SHE'S BOTH
ALLY AND BEHAVIOR-
RE SUITED TO CARE
HIS EARTH AND THE
E WHO LIVE ON IT."

YOU HAVE A BIG DECISION TO MAKE. STAY HERE, COURT ME, AND TRY TO START A NEW RACE OF UBER-HUMANS. OR GO BACK HOME AND HELP YOUR COUNTRY.

WHAT WOULD YOU DO?

I HAVE NO IDEA. YOU LIVED YOUR OWN LIFE. HAD YOUR OWN EXPERIENCES, WHICH SHAPED YOU AND SHAPED THE WAY YOU VIEW THINGS. MY CHOICES ARE EASY.

IT'S IN MY NATURE TO DO WHAT'S BEST FOR THOSE AROUND ME. IF THAT MEANS TAKING SOME CONFUSED AMERICAN BOY AND MAKING A FAMILY WITH HIM, I'LL DO MY DUTY.

I'M COOL LIKE THAT. THE WORLD IS FUCKED UP, YOU KNOW. IF WE CAN MAKE IT BETTER TOGETHER...

...WHY NOT?

HAVE YOU EVER LEFT THIS ISLAND, JU-WEN?

THAT'S NOT A FAIR QUESTION. IF I ANSWER YOU WILL JUDGE ME NA INNOCENT, LIMITED. I ANSWER YES, YOU WILL ME PRIVILEGED, ELI SPOILED.

I KNOW THE THINGS I KNOW. I KNOW MY IQ IS 161.

YOURS IS 129.

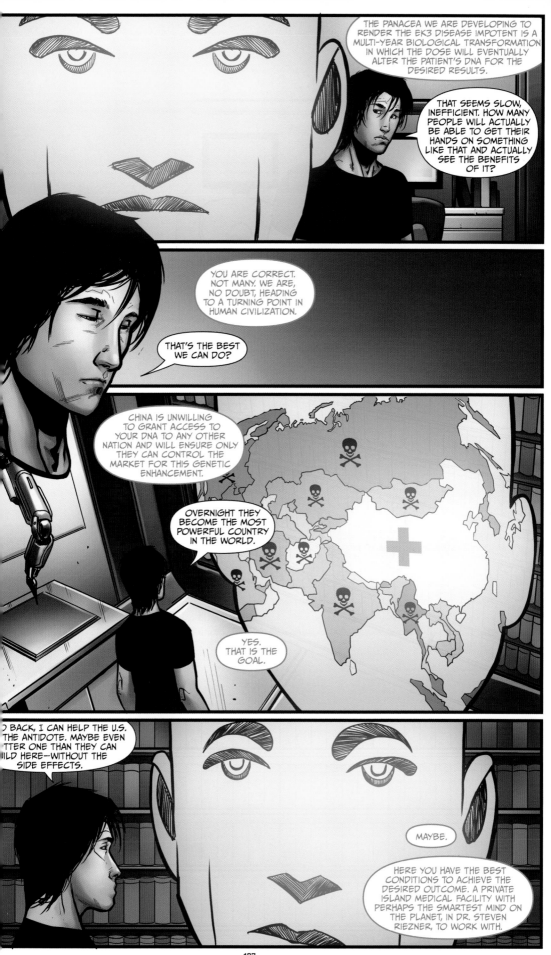

THE PANACEA WE ARE DEVELOPING TO RENDER THE EK3 DISEASE IMPOTENT IS A MULTI-YEAR BIOLOGICAL TRANSFORMATION IN WHICH THE DOSE WILL EVENTUALLY ALTER THE PATIENT'S DNA FOR THE DESIRED RESULTS.

THAT SEEMS SLOW, INEFFICIENT. HOW MANY PEOPLE WILL ACTUALLY BE ABLE TO GET THEIR HANDS ON SOMETHING LIKE THAT AND ACTUALLY SEE THE BENEFITS OF IT?

YOU ARE CORRECT. NOT MANY. WE ARE, NO DOUBT, HEADING TO A TURNING POINT IN HUMAN CIVILIZATION.

THAT'S THE BEST WE CAN DO?

CHINA IS UNWILLING TO GRANT ACCESS TO YOUR DNA TO ANY OTHER NATION AND WILL ENSURE ONLY THEY CAN CONTROL THE MARKET FOR THIS GENETIC ENHANCEMENT.

OVERNIGHT THEY BECOME THE MOST POWERFUL COUNTRY IN THE WORLD.

YES. THAT IS THE GOAL.

GO BACK, I CAN HELP THE U.S. THE ANTIDOTE. MAYBE EVEN BETTER ONE THAN THEY CAN BUILD HERE—WITHOUT THE SIDE EFFECTS.

MAYBE.

HERE YOU HAVE THE BEST CONDITIONS TO ACHIEVE THE DESIRED OUTCOME. A PRIVATE ISLAND MEDICAL FACILITY WITH PERHAPS THE SMARTEST MIND ON THE PLANET, IN DR. STEVEN RIEZNER, TO WORK WITH.

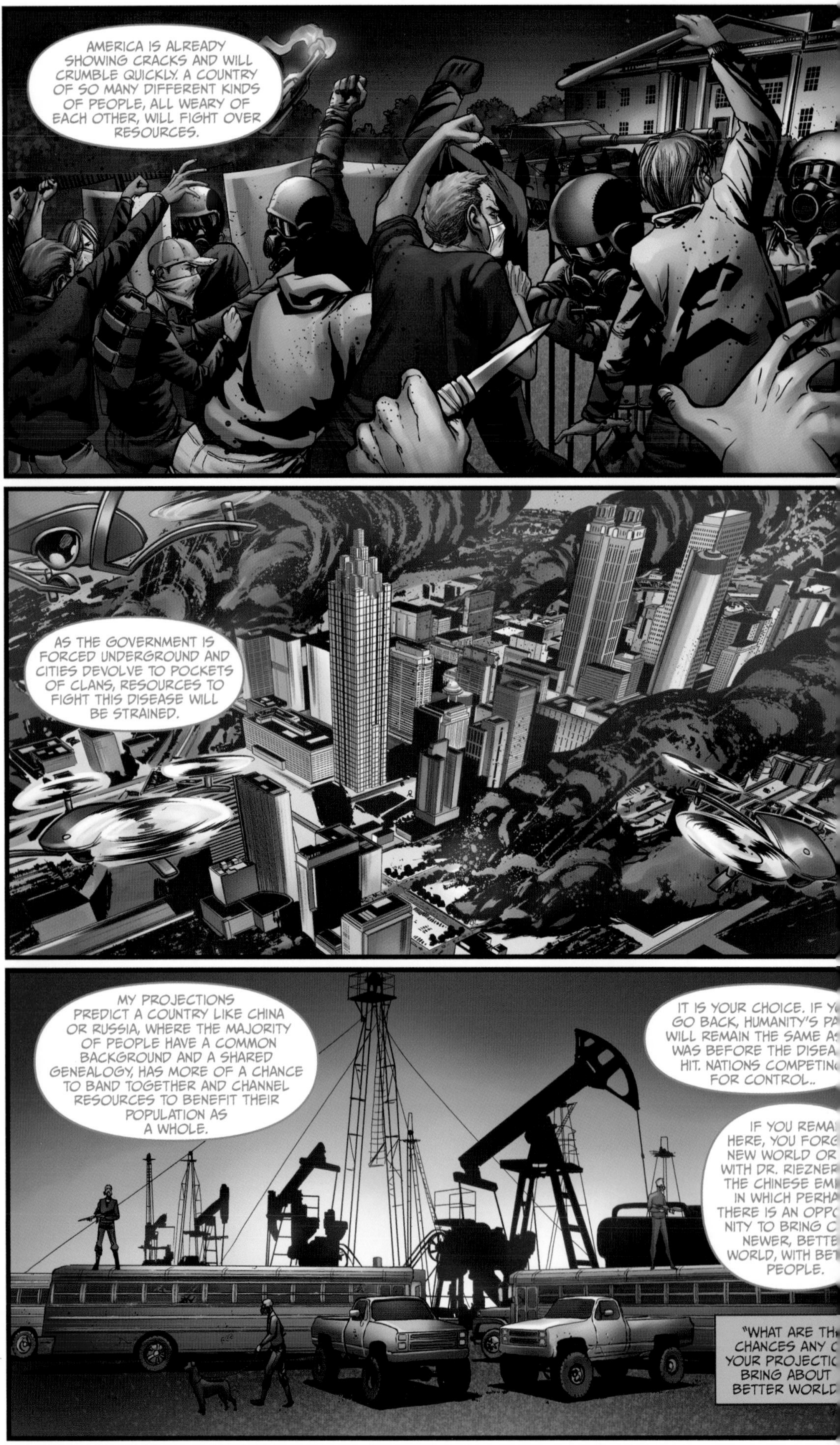
AMERICA IS ALREADY SHOWING CRACKS AND WILL CRUMBLE QUICKLY. A COUNTRY OF SO MANY DIFFERENT KINDS OF PEOPLE, ALL WEARY OF EACH OTHER, WILL FIGHT OVER RESOURCES.
AS THE GOVERNMENT IS FORCED UNDERGROUND AND CITIES DEVOLVE TO POCKETS OF CLANS, RESOURCES TO FIGHT THIS DISEASE WILL BE STRAINED.
MY PROJECTIONS PREDICT A COUNTRY LIKE CHINA OR RUSSIA, WHERE THE MAJORITY OF PEOPLE HAVE A COMMON BACKGROUND AND A SHARED GENEALOGY, HAS MORE OF A CHANCE TO BAND TOGETHER AND CHANNEL RESOURCES TO BENEFIT THEIR POPULATION AS A WHOLE.
IT IS YOUR CHOICE. IF Y GO BACK, HUMANITY'S PA WILL REMAIN THE SAME A WAS BEFORE THE DISEA HIT. NATIONS COMPETIN FOR CONTROL..
IF YOU REMA HERE, YOU FORG NEW WORLD OR WITH DR. RIEZNER THE CHINESE EM IN WHICH PERHA THERE IS AN OPPO NITY TO BRING C NEWER, BETTE WORLD, WITH BE PEOPLE.
"WHAT ARE TH CHANCES ANY YOUR PROJECTI BRING ABOUT BETTER WORLD

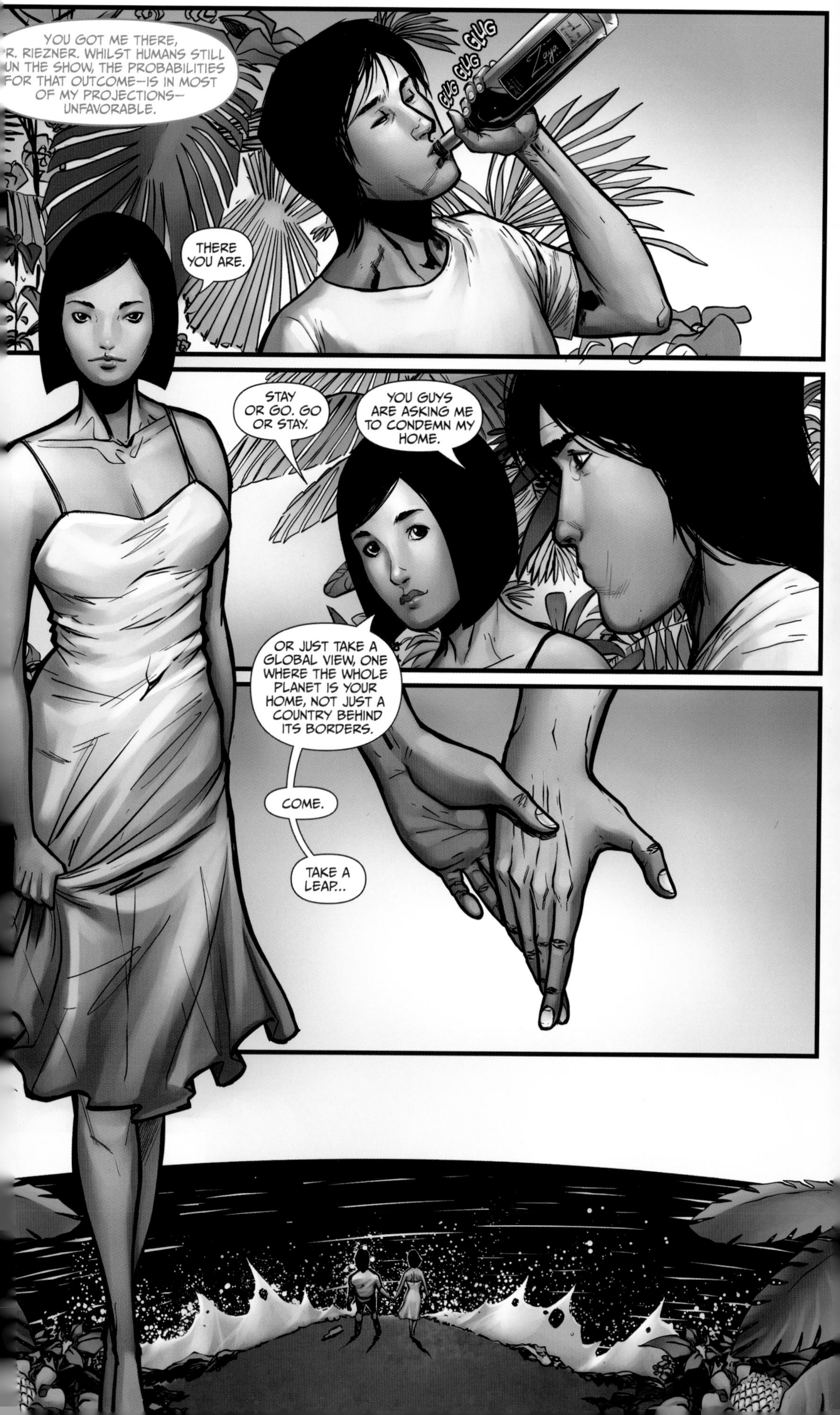
YOU GOT ME THERE, R. RIEZNER. WHILST HUMANS STILL UN THE SHOW, THE PROBABILITIES FOR THAT OUTCOME—IS IN MOST OF MY PROJECTIONS—UNFAVORABLE.
GLUG GLUG GLUG
THERE YOU ARE.
STAY OR GO. GO OR STAY.
YOU GUYS ARE ASKING ME TO CONDEMN MY HOME.
OR JUST TAKE A GLOBAL VIEW, ONE WHERE THE WHOLE PLANET IS YOUR HOME, NOT JUST A COUNTRY BEHIND ITS BORDERS.
COME.
TAKE A LEAP...

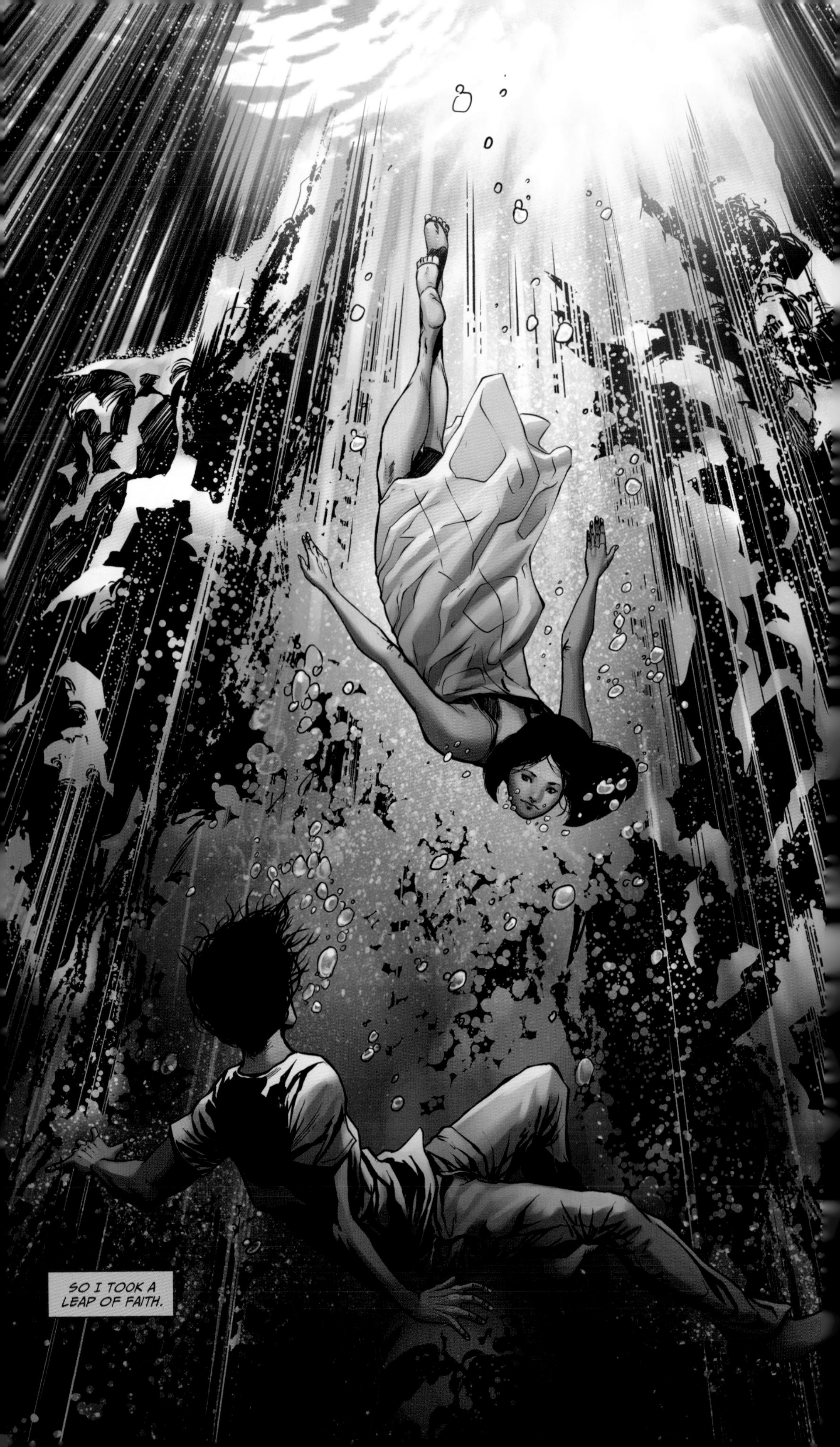
SO I TOOK A
LEAP OF FAITH.

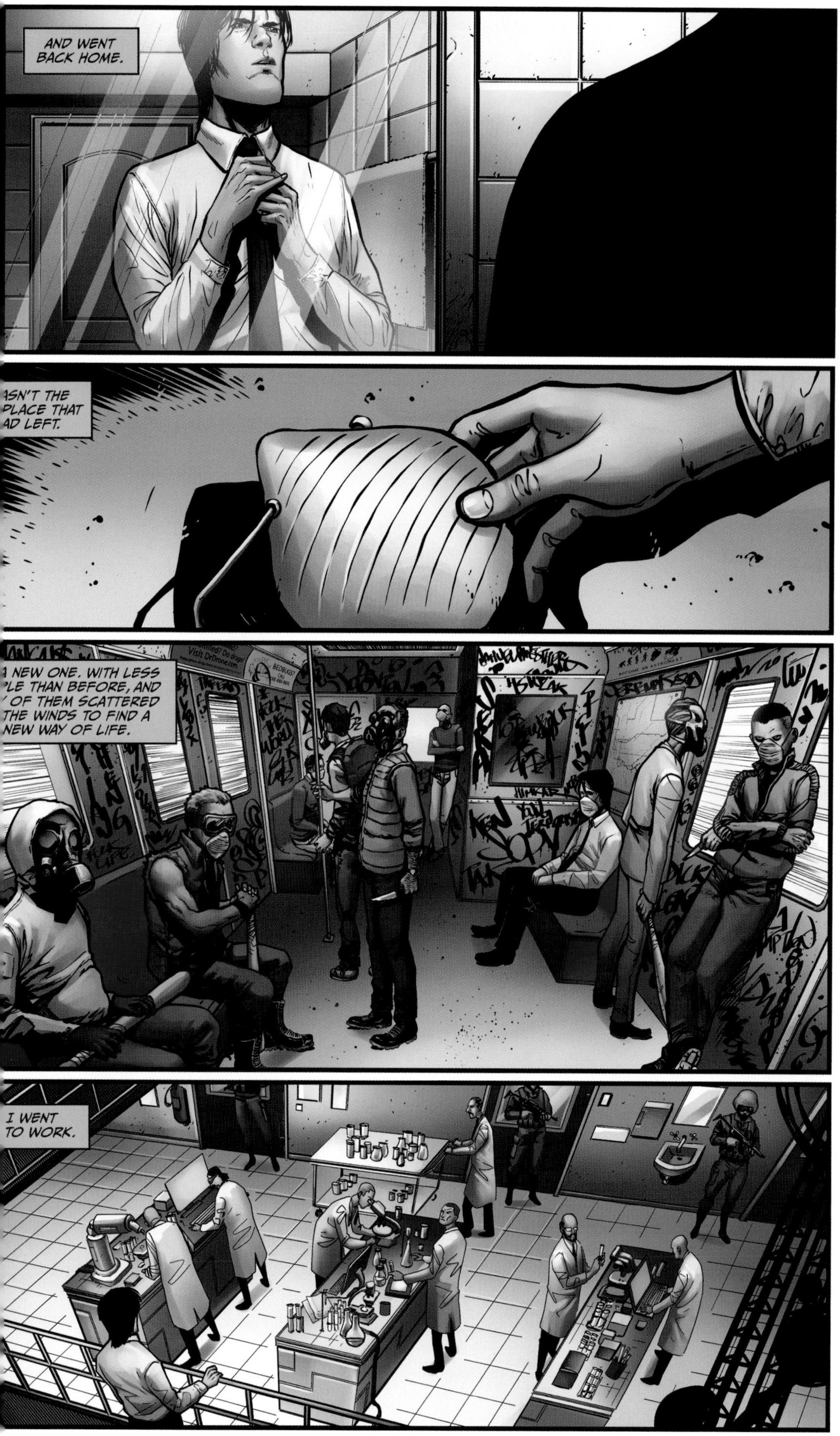
AND WENT
BACK HOME.
ASN'T THE
PLACE THAT
AD LEFT.
A NEW ONE. WITH LESS
PLE THAN BEFORE, AND
OF THEM SCATTERED
THE WINDS TO FIND A
NEW WAY OF LIFE.
I WENT
TO WORK.

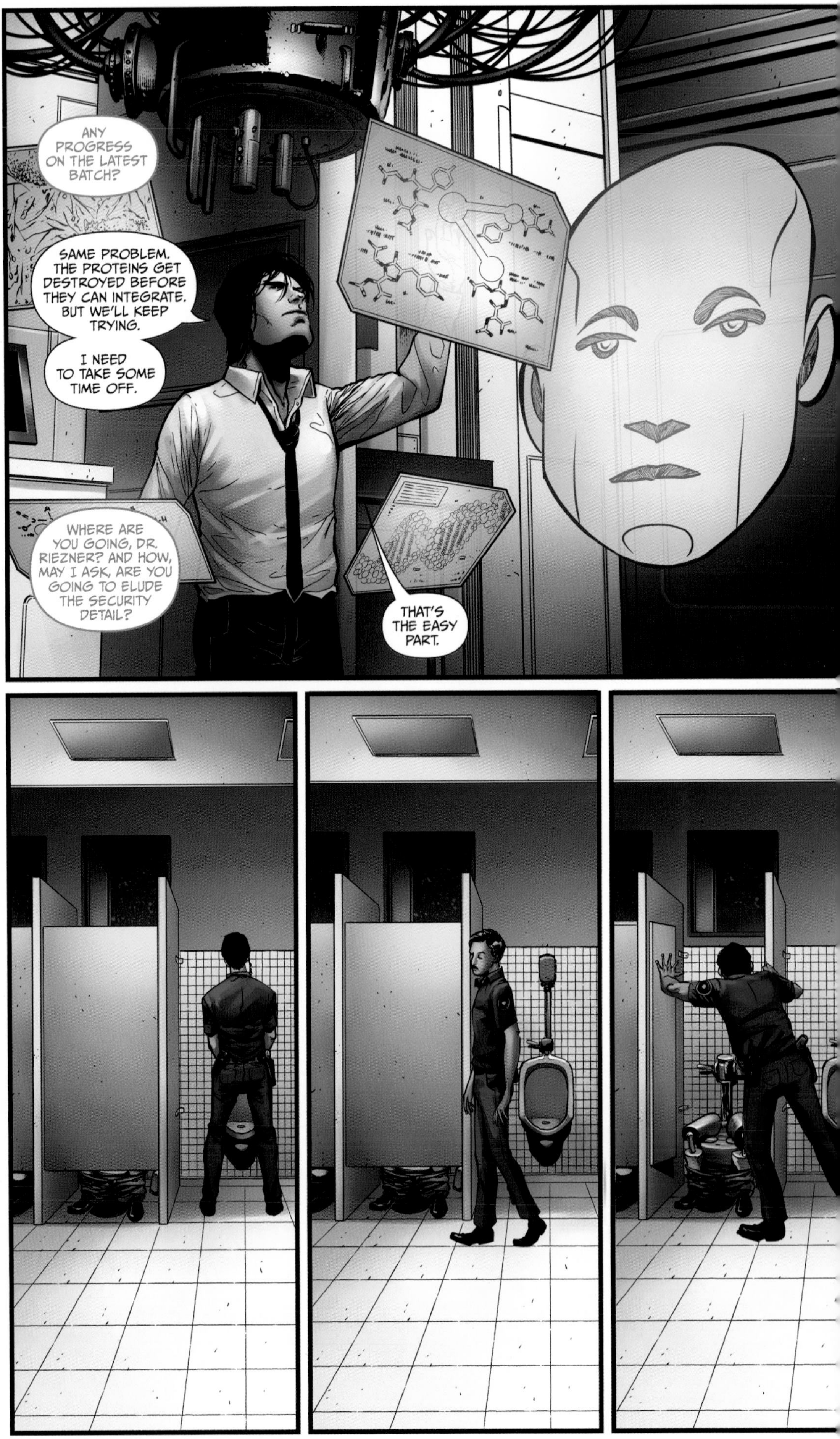
ANY PROGRESS ON THE LATEST BATCH?
SAME PROBLEM. THE PROTEINS GET DESTROYED BEFORE THEY CAN INTEGRATE. BUT WE'LL KEEP TRYING.
I NEED TO TAKE SOME TIME OFF.
WHERE ARE YOU GOING, DR. RIEZNER? AND HOW, MAY I ASK, ARE YOU GOING TO ELUDE THE SECURITY DETAIL?
THAT'S THE EASY PART.

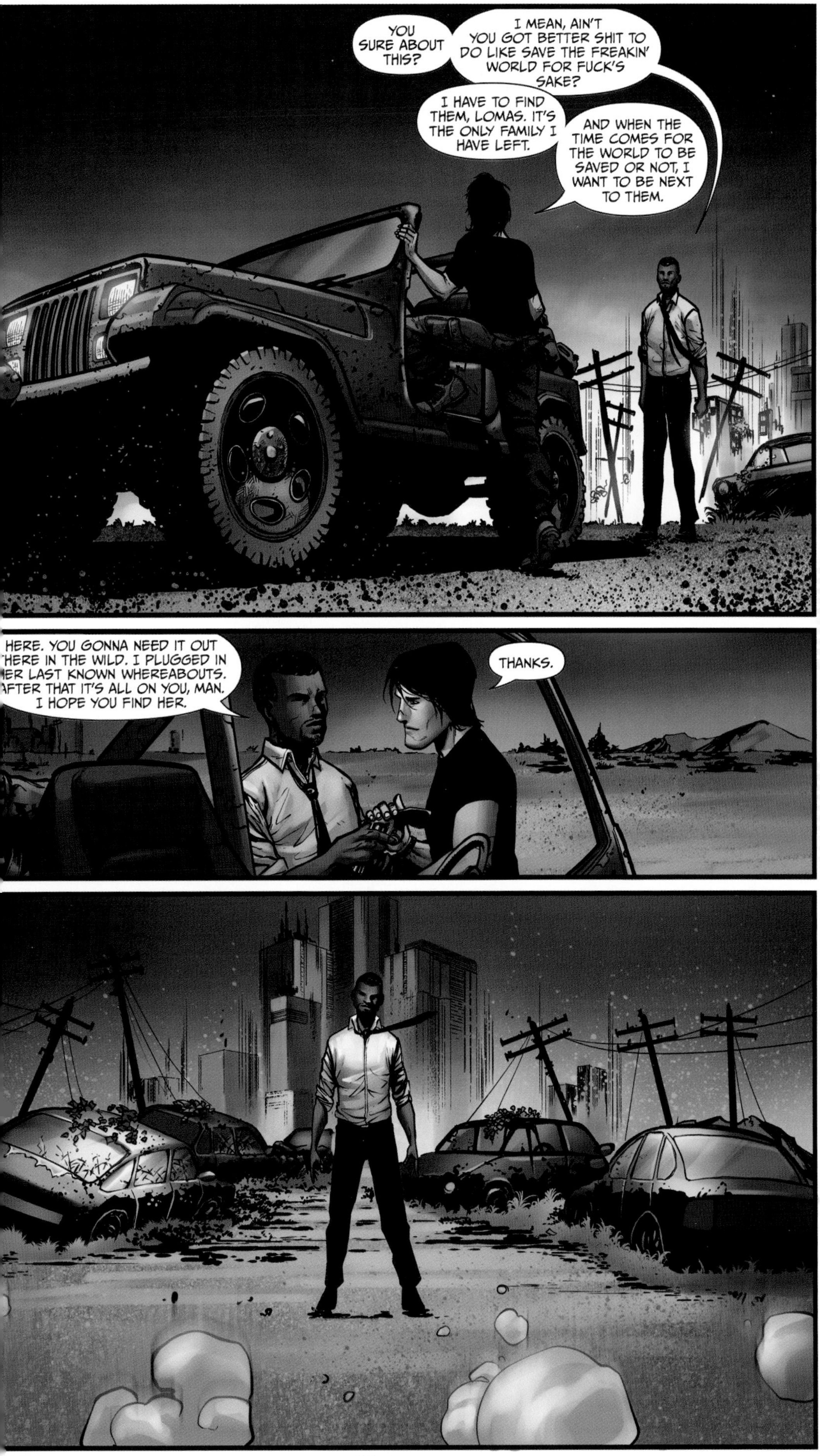
YOU SURE ABOUT THIS?
I MEAN, AIN'T YOU GOT BETTER SHIT TO DO LIKE SAVE THE FREAKIN' WORLD FOR FUCK'S SAKE?
I HAVE TO FIND THEM, LOMAS. IT'S THE ONLY FAMILY I HAVE LEFT.
AND WHEN THE TIME COMES FOR THE WORLD TO BE SAVED OR NOT, I WANT TO BE NEXT TO THEM.
HERE. YOU GONNA NEED IT OUT THERE IN THE WILD. I PLUGGED IN ER LAST KNOWN WHEREABOUTS. AFTER THAT IT'S ALL ON YOU, MAN. I HOPE YOU FIND HER.
THANKS.

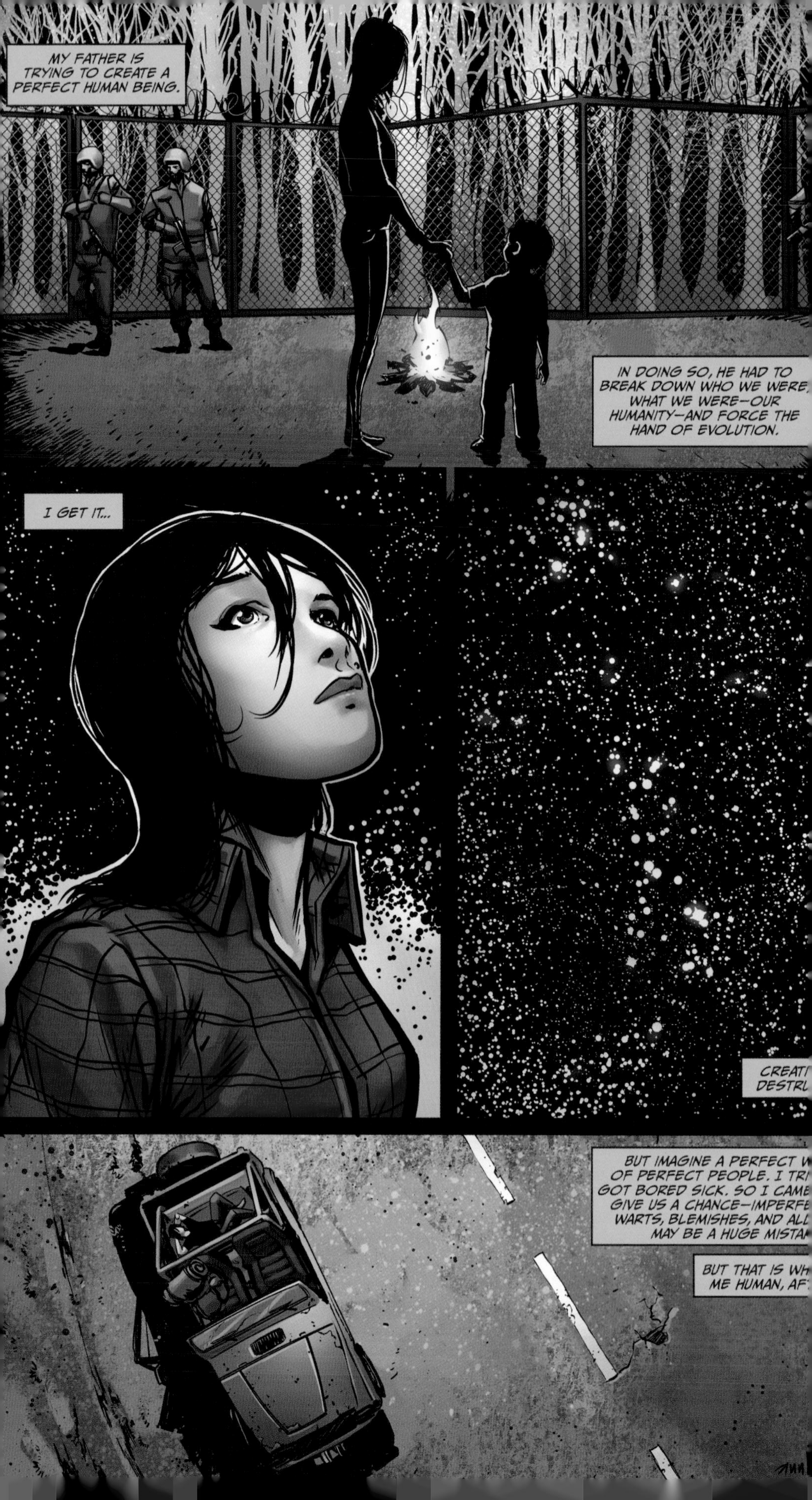
MY FATHER IS TRYING TO CREATE A PERFECT HUMAN BEING.
IN DOING SO, HE HAD TO BREAK DOWN WHO WE WERE, WHAT WE WERE—OUR HUMANITY—AND FORCE THE HAND OF EVOLUTION.
I GET IT...
CREATI
DESTRU
BUT IMAGINE A PERFECT W
OF PERFECT PEOPLE. I TRI
GOT BORED SICK. SO I CAME
GIVE US A CHANCE—IMPERFE
WARTS, BLEMISHES, AND ALL
MAY BE A HUGE MISTAK
BUT THAT IS WH
ME HUMAN, AF

— 1322-Arab chieftains first used artificial insemination to produce superior horses.

— 1663-Robert Hooke discovered the existence of the cell.

— 1863-Gregor Mendel discovered that traits are transmitted from parents to progeny by discrete, independent units, later called genes.

— 1944-Oswald Avery found that a cell's genetic information was carried in DNA.

— 1953-Francis Crick and James Watson discovered the structure of DNA.

— 1964-F.C. Steward grew a complete carrot plant from a fully differentiated carrot root cell.

— 1973-Stanley Cohen and Herbert Boyer created the first recombinant DNA organism using recombinant DNA techniques. Also known as gene splicing, this technique allows scientists to manipulate the DNA of an organism - the basis of genetic engineering.

— 1977-Karl Illmensee and Peter Hoppe created mice with only a single parent.

— 1990-The National Institutes of Health officially launched the Human Genome Project to locate the 50,000 to 100,000 genes and sequence the estimated 3 billion nucleotides of the human genome.

— 1995-Physical map of human genome completed.

— 1996-Dolly, the first organism ever to be cloned from adult cells, was born.

— 1997-President Clinton proposed a five-year moratorium on federal and privately funded human cloning research.

— 1998-Nineteen European nations signed a ban on human cloning.

— 2005-The United Nations passed the Declaration on Human Cloning, by which Member States are called on to prohibit all forms of human cloning as they are incompatible with human dignity and the protection of human life.

— 2012- Genomyne Bioworks Inc. is established by Dr. Steven Riezner to further advance genetic testing and it's benefits on fighting the biological calamities of mankind like ALS, Alzheimer's, Cancer and HIV.

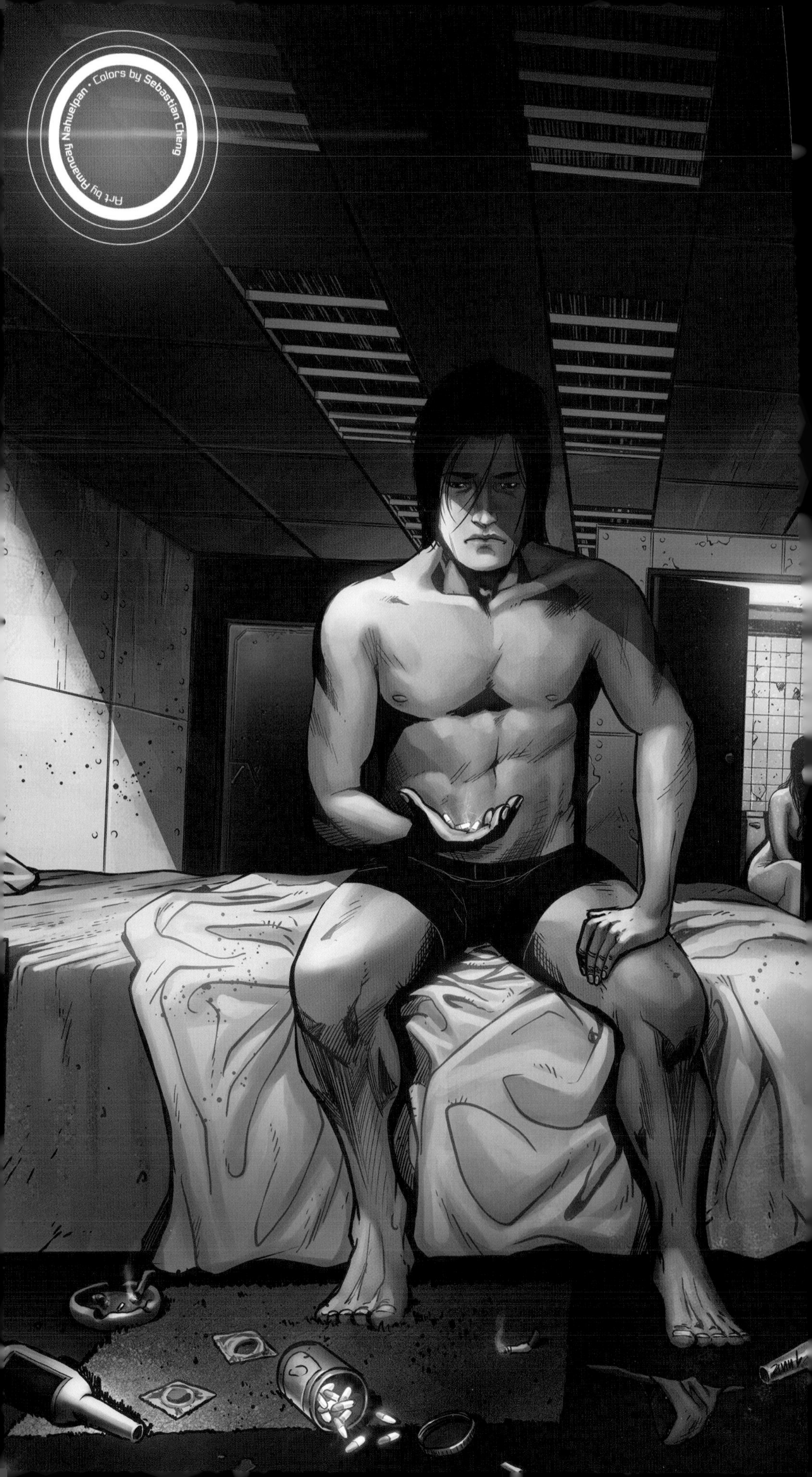
Art by Amancay Nahuelpan • Colors by Sebastian Cheng

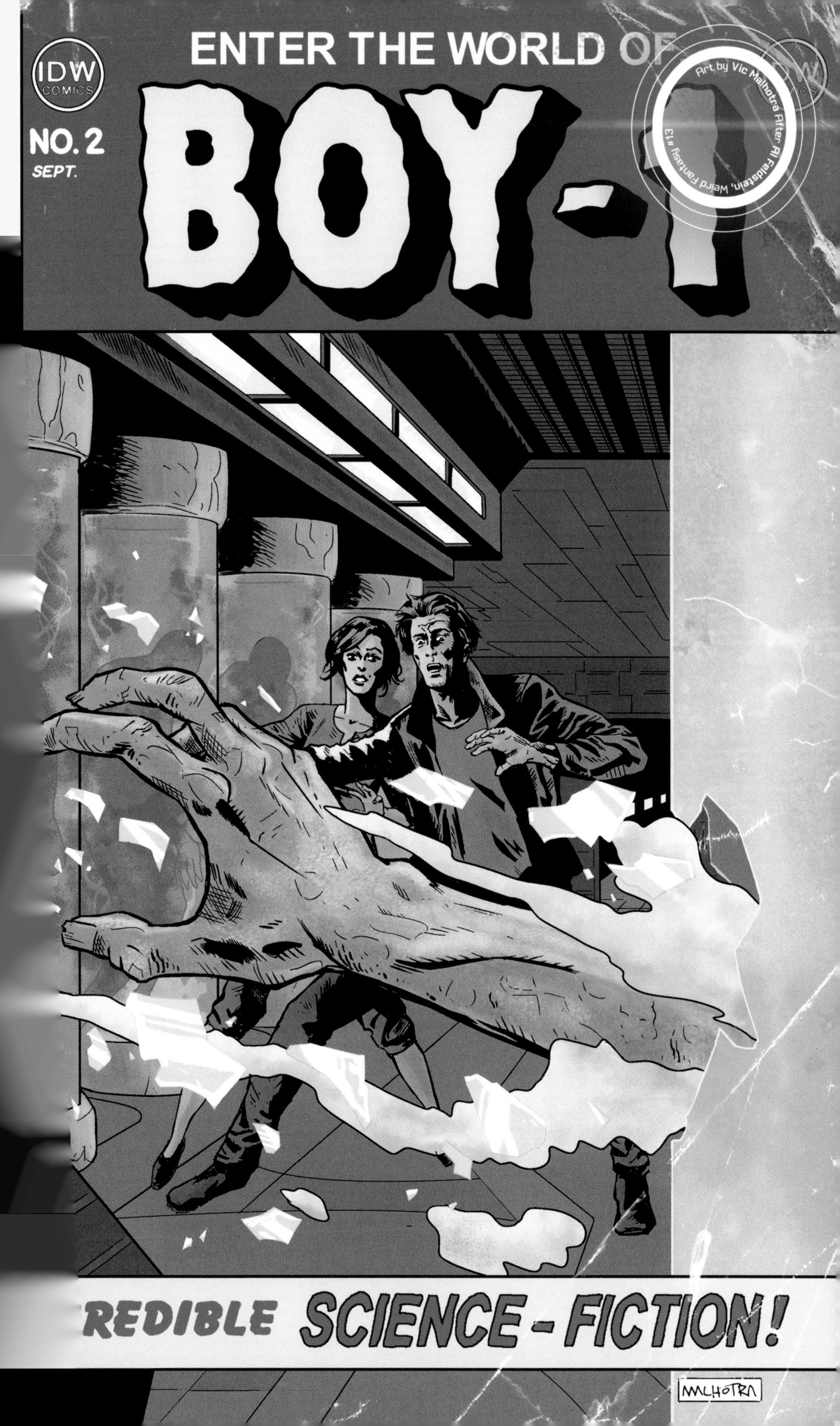
ENTER THE WORLD OF
IDW COMICS
NO. 2
SEPT.
BOY-1
Art by Vic Malhotra After Al Feldstein, Weird Fantasy #13
REDIBLE SCIENCE-FICTION!
MALHOTRA

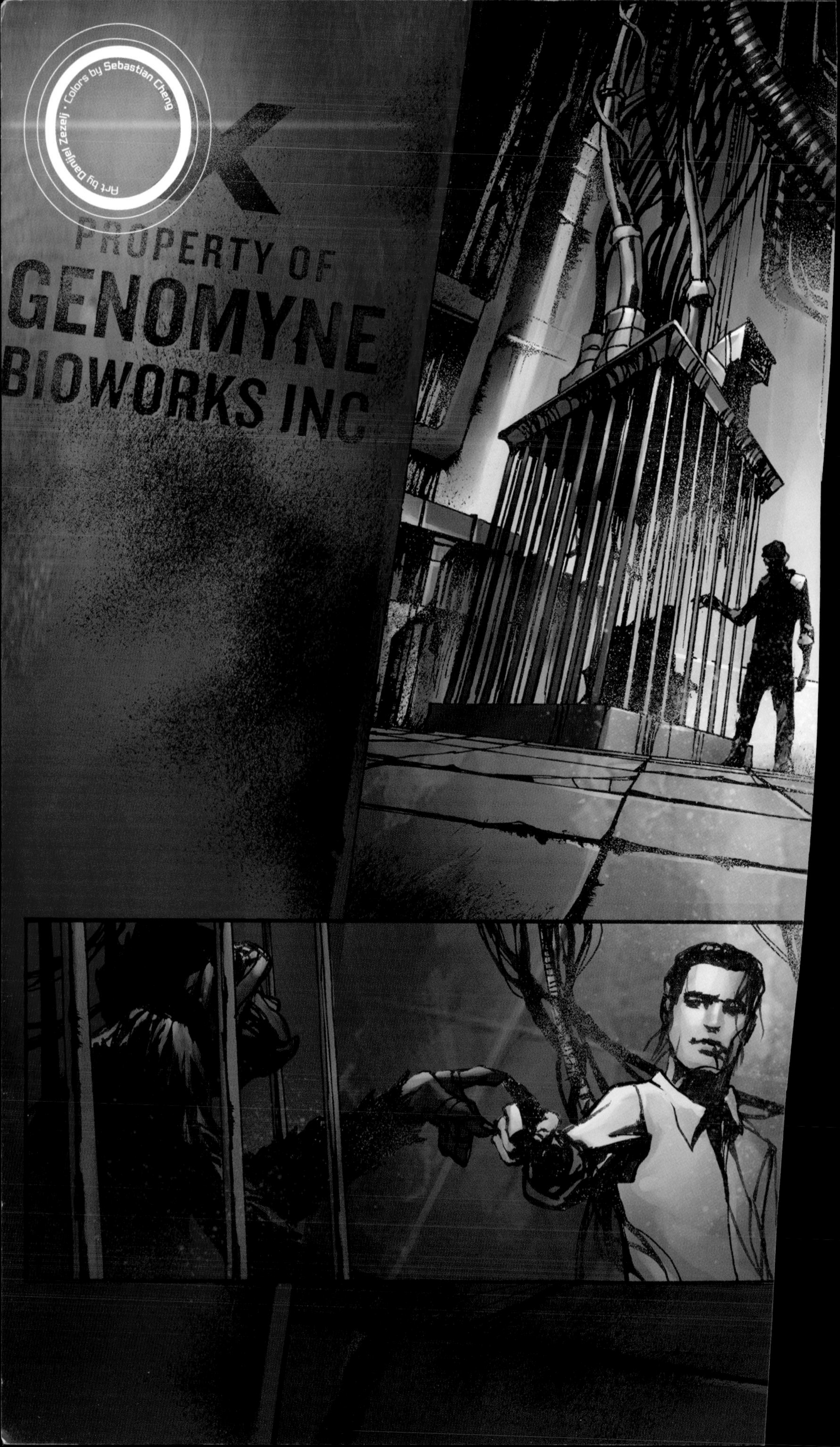
Art by Danijel Zezelj • Colors by Sebastian Cheng
PROPERTY OF
GENOMYNE
BIOWORKS INC

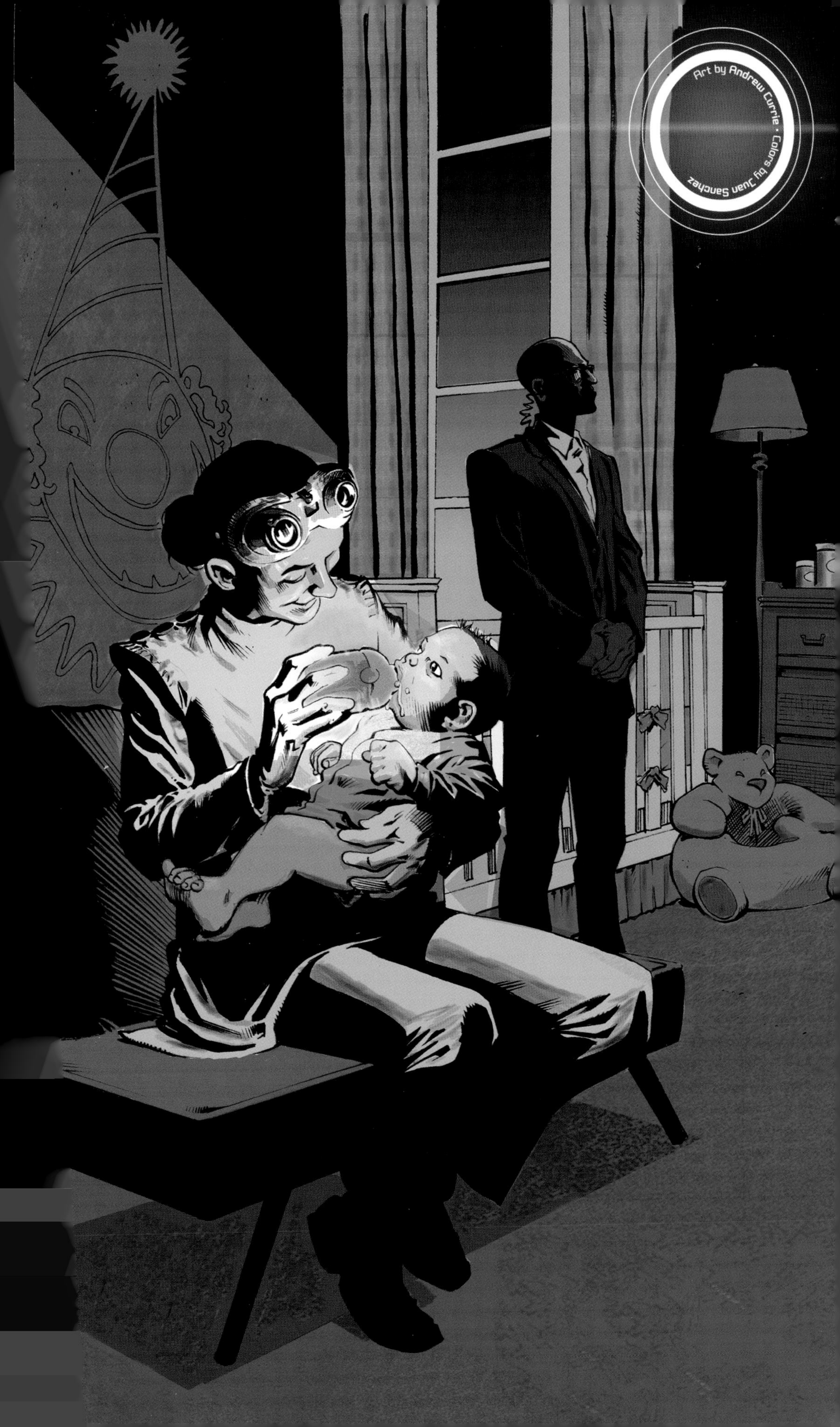
Art by Andrew Currie • Colors by Juan Sanchez

BEFORE BOY-1

First off, thanks for buying our humble little sci-fi tale. When our editor, Denton Tipton, asked me to look over the TPB and see what was missing, I realized there is a whole part of this process that you guys didn't get to see. But you know what? You do now.

This book, like most, was a culmination of many things falling into place and a lot of grind.

It took a few years and a few false starts.

Artists came and went. Publishers came and went. Luckily I had a core group of people like my producer Jeremy, letterer Dezi, and the unwavering support of Chri Ryall at IDW.

The whole time the story was changing, because the science and technology that inspired us is moving forward at rocket speed, and I was left having to catch up a each turn. It was a good thing though. It kept me banging away at the script, tryir to make it reasonable. If you ever try to reason with a story you're trying to get down, good luck.

In the end we did the best we could and we hope you enjoy what we made. If you want to see the beginning of this journey and the prototype we used to wheel an deal, go here: spacewaysindustries.com/boy1. Now you have both the beginning a the end.

You can follow me @hstronic, Amancay @annbonnonline, and the exclusive lab where we experiment all things BOY-1 at https://www.facebook.com/boy1projec

Salutations, Satellites and Supernovas